In the Open

TIMOTHY E. DONOHUE

In the Open

Diary of a Homeless Alcoholic

The University of Chicago Press

Chicago and London

The University of Chicago Press, Chicago 60637
The University of Chicago Press, Ltd., London
© 1996 by The University of Chicago
All rights reserved. Published 1996
Printed in the United States of America
05 04 03 02 01 00 99 98 97 96   1 2 3 4 5

ISBN: 0-226-15767-9 (cloth)

Library of Congress Cataloging-in-Publication Data

Donohue, Timothy E.
    In the open : diary of a homeless alcoholic / Timothy E. Donohue.
        p.   cm.
    ISBN 0-226-15767-9 (cloth : acid-free paper)
    1. Donohue, Timothy . E.—Diaries. 2. Alcoholics—United
States—Diaries. 3. Alcoholics—United States—Biography.
I. Title.
HV5293.D65A3   1996
362.29′2′092—dc20
[B]   96-8513
                                                                     CIP

The photographic collage on page iii is © 1996 by Kevin Riordan.

⊗ The paper used in this publication meets the minimum requirements
of the American National Standard for Information Sciences—Perma-
nence of Paper for Printed Library Materials, ANSI Z39.48-1984.

Contents

PART ONE *February to July 1990* 1

PART TWO *July to September 1990* 83

PART THREE *December 1990 to February 1991* 129

PART FOUR *June 1991* 153

PART FIVE *January 1992 to December 1994* 161

Part One

THURSDAY FEBRUARY 15, 1990   I am hoping that, by writing down feelings and conclusions that consideration of alcohol evokes in me day by day or week by week as the case may be, I will be able to ameliorate what for me has come to be a very serious problem. For the last eleven years, at least, my drinking has been wildly excessive and has precipitated the whole range of troubles and difficulties that customarily follow in the wake of abuse of that substance.

I think that a large obstacle to introspection and self-scrutiny on this issue up to now has been the preconceived notion of how one ought to regard the problem as promulgated by Alcoholics Anonymous (AA). Because that organization associates abstinence so strongly with religion, its philosophy tends to steer someone like me away from the self-examination and the articulation of emotions that may be necessary to avoid taking comfort in the bottle. In other words, because intense consideration of one's inner feelings is such a key component of the AA program, and because this self-exploration is combined and woven together so inextricably with the religious belief that a "higher power" is the pivotal factor in recovery, a nonreligious person like myself recoils from the whole idea of even acknowledging that inner feelings need to be looked at and ruminated upon in order to establish some resistance to taking a drink. For my part, the only function a "higher power" has apparently played in relation to my use of alcohol has been to subject me to such intense retribution, dragging me through the mud nose down, so to speak, and generally inflicting such misery on me for these last eleven years that I cannot help but cite it as the prime cause of my alcoholism to begin with.

Perhaps a subtle form of self-deception is inherent in the AA conviction that a reliance on the intervention of a higher power is the only way to sobriety, in that what they are really relying on is that their higher power will leave them alone, suspend the hostilities, and allow them an interlude sufficiently long to sort through their thoughts on the matter and discover that, yes indeed, they ought to quit drinking. For me this poses a dilemma. If what certain people perceive as spiritual influences really are an active agent in triggering and sustaining alcoholism, does this mean that God is then condoning or encouraging the abuse of that intoxicant?

My reasoning in the past has gone something like this: Since I believe that I have been placed in a painful situation by a higher power, and since immersion in the stupor induced by alcohol effectively transforms that situation into one not only free from pain but suffused with pleasantness indeed, my higher power is virtually directing me to get drunk, isn't He? And since God is good, then the advertised ill effects of too much drinking can't really be all that bad, can they? This is a formidable argument for debauchery and prodigality of all kinds.

And there are certain other influences in society that, when compounded with the spiritual rationalization just described, constitute a powerful inducement to abandon all restraint with respect to alcohol. First, there are the pronouncements of the medical profession and the academics concerning the damage that alcohol can inflict on the human animal. In particular, their assertion that too much alcohol kills brain cells in vast quantities can act as an especially alluring motivation to drink. "What?" you ask. "How can the fact that excessive consumption destroys the most prized portion of the anatomy be a motivation to such consumption?" It is simply this: my own experience teaches me that their claims are not true. If I had killed millions of those cells in my own brain (which has only a fixed quantity to begin with, starting at around age eighteen, say the experts), then whatever it is inside my head would by now have been rotted out to the degree that I would be a mental cripple.

I have indeed imbibed extraordinarily. I would estimate that over eleven years I have consumed more alcohol than two typical moderate drinkers might both partake of in a lifetime. Yet I cannot believe that my brain has deteriorated to the incapacitating extent required by the formulas and the dicta of the doctors and the biologists. It is true that my memory and my powers of concentration have declined. I no longer have the mental stamina of a college student. And judging by the improved perspicacity I attain near the end of those two- or three-day periods that I sometimes allow myself for a temporary "drying out" and withdrawal from daily inebriation, these declines can be attributed directly to too much alcohol. So it can't be good for me. At the same time, the fact that my heavy drinking has not reduced me to utter imbecility would seem to imply that perhaps our doctors are exaggerating the deleterious nature of inordinate liquor intake, at least with respect to the brain.

Have they appointed themselves some kind of moral guardians for the masses? Have they stepped onto a didactic pedestal of some sort and lied to people for their own good? If so, then in my opinion those members of the medical establishment and others responsible for perpetrating the myth ought to be strung up, teased, tormented, and forced, at long last, for the benefit of that great audience of inferior, uninformed peons for whom their solicitude and compassion supposedly have been mustered, to confess exactly how the alcoholic component of their own brotherhood manages to dispense such professional advice while operating with brains that contain something less than a full complement of cells. Because in my case at least their undermined credibility has frequently spurred a swing to the exact opposite belief—that there is absolutely no harm whatsoever to

3

the brain due to excessive consumption of alcohol. Of course I know that this can't be true. But the good doctors' apparent lies give one cause to hold fast to whatever truth is convenient. Any attempt to mush through fallacy or negotiate an information landscape that is strewn with lies fosters only an abiding cynicism and prompts one to opt for whatever truth he thinks might serve his own short-term interests.

So this is what I meant when stating that the doctors' warnings concerning alcohol-induced deterioration of the brain have for me actually led to unscrupulous tippling. Because I don't believe their exaggerations, I embrace whatever scientific reality happens to cater to my immediate longings and in so doing very probably do inflict actual damage. Doctor, if you want to discourage my abuse of alcohol, then tell me the truth, please.

FRIDAY FEBRUARY 16, 1990   Yesterday, after writing the diary, I walked across the street from the library to a Circle K store, bought a quart of Pabst beer, and drank it in a nearby park as a prelude to a lunch of hot dogs and ice-cream sandwiches. In the evening I bought a half-pint of brandy but drank only about half of it before eating chicken and canned beets at my campsite out in the desert. These minor episodes of drinking were mostly intended to ease the discomfort of a hangover from drinking more than two liters of white wine the day before. It will be interesting to discover, as the days go by, whether erecting this "window into my soul" by chronicling my daily use and the feelings attendant on that use will mitigate the habit or perhaps eliminate it altogether.

Right now the urge to get drunk is very strong. During the last couple of months I have been in correspondence with two musician friends back in Minnesota. I sent each of them a tape of about twenty songs I had made up in the hope of persuading one or both of them to accompany me on their guitars for the purpose of ultimately making a three-song demo to send to record companies. In fact, the reason I came here to Apache Junction, Arizona, from Santa Barbara last December was the offer from a friend to live in his home for a month while he vacationed in Australia. While here I would have the use of his tape recorder to make the tape. Well, after two months now of letters, phone calls, refashioning of lyrics, and a lot of foolish correspondence, it turns out that neither of my Minnesota friends is able to help me with the demo. One of them had been debilitated for the previous six months by some kind of vaguely defined "nervous disorder" and has just completed selling off his equipment to pay medical bills. Just this morning I talked to my other friend long distance, and although he intends to compose a bluegrass-folk accompaniment to a song called "Pancake Man" for me,* he is too busy teaching guitar and is too chary of reentering the "business side" of music to assist me with a demo. So the last two months have seemingly washed down the drain, and I have a powerful inclination right now to get deliriously tanked.

Music and alcohol do seem to have an intriguing interaction. Of course, because there are similar symbioses between alcohol and coffee, alcohol and tobacco, alcohol and "self-love," alcohol and marijuana, alcohol and sex, alcohol and loneliness, alcohol and social confidence, and alcohol and artistic creativity in general, music cannot exactly claim a monogamous relationship. But it is not irrelevant perhaps that during this last year when my drinking has gathered momentum and culminated in a crescendo of abuse, my songwriting has exploded in tandem so that twenty-eight of the fifty-eight melodies I have now have been created in the last twelve months. Has the alcohol somehow prompted a higher creativity? It seems possible—although I tender this thought very circumspectly and with strong reservations—that the liquor has at least put me in a frame of mind at times where composition of melodies and lyrics seems more appropriate than when sober, at which time those endeavors sometimes seem frivolous or contemptibly futile. Sometimes the myopia of intoxication works like blinders, making one oblivious to the exceedingly slim chance of succeeding in a highly competitive field. Aside from this myopia there is also the question of whether the general effect of alcohol might contribute to a more musically creative sensibility. In order to answer this question, it might be useful to describe how I go about making up a melody.

First, all of the songs have in common this element: the majority of their notes were selected in an arduous, deliberate process of trial and error or else by following an emotional sense of

*This was an intention that subsequently went unfulfilled.

the propriety of the next musical phrase in the sequence. It is hardly credible that this part of composing could be enhanced much by alcohol, and inebriation may even be detrimental, but anything is possible. The first part of the process, however, might admit of an influence from drink. What this first part entails is obtaining or discovering or somehow concocting a musical phrase of as little as four or five notes that defines the mood or tone of the song (and the rhythm, of course) and so determines in a broad, flexible way what the remainder of the song will be like. This initially fabricated component of the song might end up being a part of the chorus or a segment in the main body of the song, but usually it simply turns out to be the very first part of the song. It comes about in several ways. The first and most satisfying way, of course, occurs when I decide very consciously to compose a song and then in a very calculated manner go about sifting through various possible melodies by summoning up unattached musical phrases from recent memory or by deliberately creating a new one or by transmuting an old one or by combining an old with a new in some satisfying way or generally just boiling up a swirl of tunes in my mind whereby it is possible to cull an appealing one from the overall seethe and turmoil thus generated inside my skull.

Now the second way that this first component comes about is actually a range of methods that start at the exact opposite terminal of the spectrum, where a short piece of melody bursts out spontaneously from somewhere inside and turns out to be good enough to base an entire song on. The latter has happened to me more times than I care to admit, but let me temper any rebuke it might call forth by adding that many of the songs that I somewhat carelessly relegate to "inspired" status are in all likelihood somewhere in the range that moves toward the more consciously composed. Moreover, those that do seem to spring out so automatically all come from the heart. This is not a cerebral process in the least, but rather a very complex phenomenon in which cues from the environment, one's mood, especially if it is dejected or "blue," and possibly some kind of mysterious algorithm of the soul all take part. For me, many of these types of melodic snippets come ready-outfitted with words, although not normally the words in which they are ultimately clothed. Some of the songs that come about in this more spontaneous manner can easily be traced in style or affinity to

quantity of alcohol, for example, I tell them "because it's there." So far today I have drunk one quart of beer and am currently working on the second. Yesterday, after abruptly abandoning work on the diary, I headed up toward the long foot of Superstition Mountain, where I stayed with a friend until a few weeks ago. We talked in the presence of his big-screen TV for a couple of hours while I waited for my very last unemployment check ($130) from California to arrive by mail carrier at around 1:00 P.M. When I brought the check in from his roadside mailbox he offered me a bed for the night before I headed down to Tucson to look for work, an offer I gratefully accepted. Actually I could have stayed much longer, but I didn't feel right about sponging off him again.

After I stowed my belongings in the unused bedroom I walked back to town and bought a pint of brandy at Osco Drug and drank half of it in the park down the road from the library. Then I walked to the grocery store in the wooden-pillar shopping center and bought two very thick pork loin chops on special, a jar of apple sauce, and a can of "new potatoes" for dinner later on. On the walk back I got a hankering to continue with the brandy, but I knew I would need at least the rest of the pint to appease me while I cooked the food and watched TV at my friend's house, so I took a short detour to a Circle K to get more booze. On the way I happened to meet a friend I'd worked with at the swap meet (a large flea market) here when I resided in this area about six years earlier.

It was gratifying to see him. I had thought about him on occasion over the years, and one time when I was just passing through here a few years ago I searched him out at his sister's house in a trailer court in Mesa. To my surprise he had joined the Marine Corps. That seemed out of character for him, because while I knew him he would at times display such contempt for duty, so to speak, at the swap meet where we helped supply the concession stands that he was fired before the end of the season.

He was younger than me and had grown up in New Jersey. He would tag along with me after work in a way reminiscent of an affectionate younger brother or sister you can't quite shake. I tried to avoid him mainly because he was always trying to get me to smoke joints with him, an indulgence I had come to realize was not worth the aftereffects. However, he was aggressive in his solicitations, and despite my warnings to the contrary, he discovered my campsite out in the desert, and on a couple of occasions while we sat already entranced by the blazing tongues of a paloverde fire, he managed to render me even more spellbound or addled, depending on your point of view, by succeeding in his mission.

One evening when we were out in a relatively densely wooded sector of the desert, we had a fire going and his cassette player was broadcasting rock and roll, and in a kind of a frisky way, it seemed to me, he climbed up onto the long horizontal branch of an unusually large mesquite tree. Maybe partly to suppress his undue enthusiasm, but mostly just out of sport, I walked over and shoved him off the branch. To my horror, I found I had pushed him directly onto a bed of low-growing cactus of the type that grows paddle-shaped lobes thickly covered with long, very sharp needles. For two hours, while he winced and grunted, I plucked the rigid shafts from his legs, buttocks, and torso. Finally, after we had succeeded in extracting only a third of the excruciating thorns from his hide, he got up and hobbled away, saying he'd get his sister to pull out the rest in a more medically acceptable way. I barked out a litany of apologetic remarks, but he waved aside any continued solicitude and retreated morosely through the cactus on that moonlit desert night. That pretty much adjourned any further socializing with my friend, and it was good to finally talk to him yesterday for a few minutes, meet his sister again, and find that life does indeed go on despite its accumulation of small tragedies and disappointments.

At the Circle K I bought a half-pint of cheap blended whiskey and mixed it with water in the large paper cup I had saved from the brandy earlier and drank it as I walked the mile and a half or so back to my other friend's house. This was an extremely pleasant amble as the sun was lowering toward the horizon to my back and imparting an orange and shadowed configuration to the sheer, rocky monolith known as Superstition Mountain to my fore, which marks the end of the Phoenix Valley and the beginning of some of the most rugged and challenging mountainous terrain on the continent. My other friend was asleep when I returned, preparing his psyche for the night shift at an electronics company in Phoenix. I consumed the rest of the brandy while gazing at "Hee Haw," "A Half Hour Live at the Grand Old Opry," and a special on Australian toads, and, of course, while cooking dinner, which turned out excellent, although in truth I think I would have a more comprehensive memory of the whole dining experience if I had not polished off that three-quarters of a quart of liquor in the five or six hours just preceding it.

THURSDAY FEBRUARY 22, 1990   I attribute the four-day diary lapse to the distractions of moving from Apache Junction to Tucson, even though in essence it was only a transfer from one vacant desert lot to another. I probably have enough money in savings now to rent a room for a couple of weeks, but I would hate to risk my scant capital on that only to find that I could not gain employment during the interval or, if I did, discover that my financial resources were now demanding that I move back out to the desert and assume all of the burdens of that lifestyle that so complicates or even precludes working for a living.

The trip down has also distracted me somewhat from alcohol. When I made the last entry (February 18) it was late afternoon, and I had just completed a ten-mile walk from Apache Junction in toward the more populous suburb of Mesa and to a place where I could catch a city bus to the Greyhound depot. That night I lacked still a few miles toward that goal, and after completing the diary entry and the quart of beer that accompanied it I walked to an nearby Osco and purchased a half-pint of flavored rum and a Pepsi Cola and drank those combined in   //
an expansive desert lot a little ways down the road. These vacant tracts were becoming rare by now, so after eating dinner at a nearby Wendy's I bedded down in that lot for the night. Rain came later, and I ended up accomplishing the remainder of sleep underneath the broad eaves of a savings and loan building adjacent to the main road. Fortunately, if any one of the numerous police officers who passed by happened to detect me, they decided to forbear enforcement as I dozed in fits and starts on a bed of rocks between the wall of the bank and a row of sparsely planted shrubs.

The next day, Monday, I made it to the city bus stop ragged yet intact, and waited for more than two hours at the corner where I believed the stop was scheduled, only to find out from an elderly woman hauling a cartload of groceries that the bus does not run on Washington's birthday. She told me, however, of a subsidized taxicab called Dial-a-Ride that I called up and took to the Greyhound depot. I got into Tucson after dark and walked for a couple of miles to a park I knew of from previous sojourns in this town where I could camp for the night—just a ribbon of desert land that hugs the dry bed of the Santa Cruz River. You might have to take flight occasionally and hide under the boughs of a large tamarack when a helicopter happens by with its searchlight glaring and scours the area like a golfer raking through the rough for his ball. That night, though, I got as much sleep as possible under the freezing conditions and woke at dawn to find my sleeping bag coated with sheets of frosty white ice. If this is the warmest place in the United States for a homeless man to escape to in the winter, I am going to secede from the union.

That first day in Tucson I took care of minor business, like depositing my scant capital in a bank, doing laundry, and canvassing local charity agencies by phone to discover if the old resources were still in place. It is extremely depressing to experience second or third visits to a number of American towns and know exactly where you can go for help each time around. This time my plan is to simply live outside, avoiding the missions and free housing places, possibly pay a service to take telephone messages for me, find a place to store my belongings during the day, and go out and find a job. My main task is to find a place to store my gear, and my success in this town will hinge on a resolution of that apparently simple problem.

FRIDAY FEBRUARY 23, 1990   That first Tuesday in town was also the occasion of finding some very short-term employment. Later in the afternoon I was walking to a liquor store to buy a quart of beer when I stopped and sat on a brick wall to take my shoes off and rub my feet with some antifungal ointment. This was in a part of town with a lot of abandoned businesses and houses, where weeds and yellow grasses define the cracks in empty, long-baked parking lots, and where swatches of plaster have fallen off the old adobe-style buildings to crumble and scatter on the adjacent swaths of buckling concrete. It seems to be only a pocket of dilapidation, however, for the road bisecting the area is a busy artery that connects two more beautified parts of the town. Across the side street from where I sat, long tables, erected along the perimeter of an abandoned corner lot, were covered with cheap new toys, tools, velvet paintings, and, on the end, a selection of surprisingly large saguaro and barrel cacti that looked to be freshly uprooted. The roots of even the ten-foot plants were exceedingly small, maybe around a foot or a foot and a half in length, testifying to the futility of sending tendrils any deeper in this desiccated soil and the need, if your object is to get water in the desert, to get it near the surface and get it pronto, before it's all absorbed or evaporated into thin air.

As I was passing by the display, I lingered over the merchandise, and the operator, a heavy-set man wearing a cowboy hat and a black leather vest and sporting a ragged, ginger-hued beard, started talking, asking me the basic questions. Where was I going? Just passing through? and so on. Then, out of the blue, he asked me if I'd like a job watching his merchandise for eight hours. It turned out that he had had some of his goods stolen the previous night and was now offering to pay me twenty-five dollars to stay up that night and guard the store, so to speak, while he slept in his motor home in the lot behind the tables. The suddenness of his proposition caused me to hesitate momentarily, but twenty-five dollars was enough to overcome my reluctance, and that night I stayed up in the frigid air, shivering and jumping around to arouse the blood flow while conducting the surveillance, and the next morning I was the happy recipient of twenty-five bona fide American bucks. In his trailer, over a cup of vaporizing coffee, he surprised me even further by offering to take me with him when he left town the next Sunday to work his merchandise in Douglas, Arizona, a small town near the Mexican border. He said he would pay me two hundred dollars a week to act as his assistant cashier—this time during days. I told him I'd have to think about it but that I'd let him know when I came back to guard his stuff that upcoming night. Well, that day I slept most fitfully in the warm sun on a patch of grass in the riverside park after drinking two quarts of beer and eating at a free-meal program in the vicinity, and I awoke to the realization that I could not work for the guy. The reason, I now knew, was simple: that guy had something hidden. At the rate he was doing business it seemed to me that twenty-five dollars was more profit than he might take in during a whole twelve-hour shift of daylight. So why was he so willing to turn it over to a stranger rather than pick up stakes and relo-

13

cate in a safer area? Why was he so eager to hire someone right off the street?

Of course I had worked for people before who had something hidden, and the course of the relationship is now most predictable. During close and ceaseless contact with those people the person who has nothing to hide feels an ever stronger urge to confront the deceiving person with his duplicity. "Hey," you feel like shouting, "I know goddamn well there's something amiss going on here." And then, staring him down nose to nose in your scenario, you would add, "and I know goddamn well that you know exactly what I'm talking about, too." But of course such a confrontation is impossible since it would not only cast doubt on your sanity, but likely get you fired in the bargain. So the guileless person is forced to go about his business sullenly and in constant discomfort over a growing indignation.

He watches the disingenuous person go about his business nonchalantly as if there were no dark secrets, as if there were no reason whatsoever to act out of the ordinary. "Hey, you son of a bitch," the honest person feels like barking, "how the hell can you operate like this knowing what you do?" And as a further goad in the side and burr in the ear, the blameless person now discerns a faint smugness in the culpable party, a hint of gloating almost, as if the malefactor was now expressing himself in some mysteriously assured yet voiceless manner: "Yes, heh, heh, I know that you know that I have something hidden. But guess what? It doesn't bother me in the least. Can't you see how smoothly and insouciantly I go about my business? Why, if you were to attempt to breach this veneer of normalcy here by some outrageous accusation, don't you know how foolish you would appear?" So the innocent party is compelled to withstand a seething contempt that cannot be explicitly acknowledged. But then, as time goes on, he starts to question his own validity as a human being. "Why am I always so angry at this other person?" he asks himself. By now his indignation has boiled over into disdain for the other person, but protocol and the instinct to preserve one's own sanity and one's sense of self-worth have converged to suppress his hatred and turn it, alas, in on himself. It's not normal, he tells himself, to feel such strong resentment against someone for a hidden condition that cannot be proved to exist and might not even be there to begin with! So the per-

history of how I arrived at that plateau of abuse from which I am now endeavoring to descend.

A little over a year ago I was back in Minnesota living at the Gospel Mission and trying to stay afloat economically by working through a daily labor office in nearby downtown St. Paul. However, my lungs were severely inflamed and congested, and my throat and left ear were extremely sore and sensitive. I did not have the money to solicit a doctor's advice, and besides I judged I knew why I was so afflicted. During the previous fall and early winter months I had been sleeping outside on the shores of Lake Michigan on the Milwaukee waterfront while partaking of meals at the charity agencies there and writing in the downtown libraries at a furious pace for about eight or ten hours each day. Unfortunately, I found the mission there so depressing and disheartening that I frequently would sleep in freezing or rainy conditions by the lake, and a few times I had to spread out my bedroll on a layer of hard snow. So I attributed my illness in St. Paul to this earlier, imprudent exposure to the nocturnal elements, and fancied that a cure might be forthcoming by escape to a more benevolent climate.

So I tried to hitchhike out of town. The first time I had only twenty dollars in my pocket, and the temperature had plunged due to a stinging cold front that had just blustered in from the Arctic regions of the far north. That time I got only as far as Burnsville, just south of the Twin Cities. I was fortunate that I was able to plod across a snow-packed parking lot that night through the sharp subzero air and find a heated vestibule to a small shopping complex that just happened to be left unlocked. If that was an oversight on the part of the maintenance man, I can only thank the stars that such men are not endowed with flawless memories, diligent habits, or excessive concern for their employer's property. I slept very well that night, thank you, and promptly hitchhiked back the next day to the Gospel Mission near downtown St. Paul, Minnesota.*

SUNDAY FEBRUARY 18, 1990   In philosophy at least, I like to think that I am in accord with the great sportsmen and adventurers. When people ask me why I drink such a mountainous

*This story line will be continued in the entry for February 26. For now I return to Apache Junction, Arizona.

antecedent songs one may have been putting words to a little earlier or to melodies heard in the environment or even to the environment itself. I have a song called "Old Established Pattern," whose chorus came about while I was bedding down for the night in a meadow in southern Minnesota and which I am convinced resulted from a subconscious rendering of the songs of the chickadee which I had heard so many times before in similar pastoral surroundings.

So this is one area of songwriting, then, that might very well be affected by alcohol. It's not something I can prove, but I have made up songs when at least slightly subdued by drink that I think might not have "come around the horn" without the disinhibiting influence of the liquor, without its creation of a certain buoyant mood, or without its dissolving that natural barricade between one's conscious mind and the muse or those cues in the surroundings which might interact with our emotions. So, in the right setting, when one is walking along the seashore, for example, exposed to the slow rolling rhythms of clear aquamarine waves and the brilliance of the blue sky or when one is stepping alone along firm desert sands over the shadows of cactus in the receding winter sun, then it seems very possible that alcohol might breach a small aperture to the light of the muse that might not otherwise have appeared.

SATURDAY FEBRUARY 17, 1990   Yesterday after leaving the library I walked down the road to a large lot of vacant desert land where I sat down on my bedroll and finished the half-pint I had started the evening before. Then, feeling hungry and wanting more booze, I walked to a grocery store in an old western-style, wooden-post kind of shopping center nearby and purchased a container of sour cream, a bag of tortilla chips, and a pint of E&J brandy. These I consumed in the park down the road from the library, sitting at a picnic table hidden among the mesquite trees and the shrubs adjacent to a wash. By this time it was getting dark, so I walked to a restaurant on a highway leading out of town toward the mountains and spent about six dollars on pork chops, mashed potatoes, soup, and salad.

Perhaps it is a gauge of my recent history that the quantities imbibed yesterday appear tame and ordinary and even virtuous compared to what I might have poured down a couple of months ago. For any reader other than myself, I will give a short

son who originally had nothing to conceal is now the one who is the vessel of an unseen combination of checked anger and self-loathing. "Does he know," he asks himself, "that I feel this inner rage against him?" He starts to examine his own emotional condition as if *it* were the offending entity in the dance of the psyches. "Am I a psychopath?" he asks himself in a piercing moment of self-doubt, for by now his self-abhorrence has been transposed in some morbid way into an inner torch that ignites his heart and mind to a promiscuous incandescence of arousal. The strong rage one ultimately feels is repressed, shunted to the depths of the soul, and reshaped to emerge as a grotesque mixture of undirected resentment and aberrant emotional posturing.

So, then, suspecting that this course of events might be even remotely possible if I were to go to work for the man selling cacti, how could I possibly consent? Of course I couldn't—my working days would just have to be postponed for the time being. But then again this would not prevent my guarding his merchandise for a few more nights and picking up some easy cash. So the next night I returned to the lot for duty only to find it vacated, host solely to some scattered gravel and some hamburger wrappers skittering across the concrete. What did I believe this man was hiding? Well, I don't know, of course, but the longer I thought about it, the more sense it made that this entrepreneur was likely procuring his cacti in some illicit way, perhaps lifting them from the Saguaro National Monument nearby or maybe smuggling them from across the Mexican border. This would explain why he was so eager to protect them from theft at least: his profit margin was the whole price he got paid for the plant. This is all conjecture, however, and it's possible that what he had hidden was something else altogether.

SATURDAY FEBRUARY 24, 1990   I have a final thought on dealing with duplicitous people that ought to be committed to print if it might benefit others who find themselves in similar situations. Most people who hide some major fault in their makeup, like the cactus man, will transmogrify their secret into a desirable or exclusive possession. They will even embrace the belief that their secret makes them privy to some mystery not accessible to a less special person, going so far on occasion as to convince themselves that they are a conduit of some sort for dispensing a wisdom only they can partake of at firsthand.

Now the problem arises when, in response to their perceived superiority and privileged condition, they attempt to communicate to those around them what they believe is only theirs to know. The conflict between their human desire to confess, perhaps, and what they fancy as their more noble instinct to preserve their secret and maintain an aloof superiority, results in verbal expressions, physical representations, and body language that can only be described as the most tortured attempts at communication that the human animal is capable of achieving. Ambiguity is usually the hallmark of these communications because it reflects the equivocal attitude of the source. The innocent, however, who has never been exposed to these strange utterances is struck with a sort of wonderment at first beholding them and is somewhat ravished by the person who executes them. This hearer takes the mysterious nature of the communication as a reinforcement of the original impression conveyed by the transgressing party that he is the incarnation of some kind of sacred knowledge. But of course if the truth were ever to be unveiled, the communicating party's deep shame would be revealed, and he would be betrayed for the scoundrel he really is.

Presumably my experience with these kinds of self-protective people has qualified me to dispense some advice on how to defend against their monstrous attempts at communication. First, since it is impossible to know if they are really the repository of some kind of precious wisdom, pursuing that possibility is not a prudent tactic. Second, and what has worked most effectively for me, the outsider must realize that the offending party's very method of communication—via double meanings and vague allusions, for example—betrays his inferior abilities. If a truth can be communicated openly and free of confusing metaphors, symbols, facial tics, and spasmodic gestures, then our higher human nature—and reason—tells us that it ought to be so communicated. But if a person conveys a thought, whether true or false, in ambiguous language that can be taken in more than one way and so does not pinpoint his ideas or information, then that person deserves to be banished from consideration as a communicator altogether.

MONDAY FEBRUARY 26, 1990   The weekend saw me revert to the abusive levels of drinking that I sustained for a number of months while tramping along the seashore and collecting unemployment out in California. On Saturday afternoon I bought a 750-milliliter bottle of Canadian whiskey (approximately a fifth) and drank most of it under the shade of a paloverde on the abrupt edge of the Pantano Wash, which courses through the eastern section of Tucson. This is a more attractive part of town, with clean neighborhoods and fine shopping centers occupying the pocket of land formed by handsome mountains that tower to the near east and north. The mountains here, unlike those around Phoenix, are not just bald, stony upthrusts sparsely dotted by creosote and cacti. The desert terrain gives way near the high ridges to some kind of dark green chaparral, where patches of white snow lodge on occasion for days at a time during the winter months. I am camping on a large empty lot of desert land between a shopping center and the Pantano Wash. This wash is actually deeper and wider, it seems to me, than the similar topographical feature they call a river (Santa Cruz) closer to downtown. The walls are sheer and the floor a carpet of sand, shaped and contoured to the whims of the latest rainstorm. It's a very pleasant formation to contemplate while indulging in drink, which might explain why I finished the bottle of Canadian whiskey on Sunday morning and further tempered the residual hangover with most of a 375-milliliter bottle (approximately a pint) of Gordon's vodka, mixed with lemonade, as the day progressed. Today I am feeling slightly scorched and perhaps ought to quit for a while.

/7

I think that a lot of the finer arguments and more abstruse considerations that people often set forth as motivations to abuse can be pruned down to an essential cause: the alcoholic, for whatever reason, feels that life is too painful to continue in sobriety. He thinks that destiny has dealt him some kind of stacked hand, that his existence is likely just a joke for an audience on Olympus, that there is no hope of entering into fulfilling relationships with fellow human beings or of raising himself to his rightful place in society. If he has access to alcohol, then any damage he perceives as resulting from intoxication is overshadowed by the immediate escape from the pain of loneliness and by the temporary flight from the despair of alienation.

When I drink the quantities I did on Saturday, I feel as though some kind of anesthetizing milk is flowing through my soul. The mountains in the distance come into sharp focus and clear relief, and their ridges pulsate with a subdued gleam that seems to beckon my mind to those faraway lands that always shine from somewhere just beyond the horizon. Sure, I tell myself, everything will fall into place—sometime in the intermediate future, of course, because tomorrow I will be emotionally eviscerated and craving only further forays into stupor.

It takes a while to arrive at that cellar of despair, though, and perhaps now is an appropriate juncture to continue with the story line of causative elements that I suspended at the end of the entry for February 17, 1990. My memory of the period just after the aborted flight by hitchhiking is sketchy. I should mention that I had already traversed the south-bound freeways out of Minnesota a number of times by thumb. The most recent time was almost immediately after I had returned to Minnesota from Milwaukee, in December, when I hitchhiked down to Des Moines. I stayed in one of the missions there that was new and clean and fairly habitable as far as missions go. A novel feature of this one was its nightly charge of four or five dollars for lodging. However, this seemed to me more of a device to extract money from the local government, which issued a voucher for your rent payable as long as you complied with certain work-search requirements. Curiously, many of the missions, Salvation Armies, and free shelters that I have encountered around the country place a limit of three days or five that a person is allowed to stay for free, after which time he cannot return, in some cases even with money, for a month or six months or a year as the case may be. This always struck me as bizarre, since that length of time is hardly sufficient to climb into solvency or gain a foothold into a productive lifestyle. One of the most liberal shelters in this respect is the Union Gospel Mission in St. Paul, which lets you stay forever, if need be, on a nightly basis as long as you attend an evening service in the chapel. This includes dinner and breakfast, of course, and all the AA and Bible meetings you care to attend.*

In Des Moines I worked for a couple of weeks as a janitor

*This policy has been changed so that residents of the St. Paul mission must now register with the local welfare office after a specified number of free nights.

part-time and then got a full-time job as a houseman in a large hotel downtown. This did not work out for reasons . . . for reasons that I can only describe as having their issue in the more malevolent reaches of the universe. The people were okay here, but, as had happened before, the Devil of disease and affliction seemed to be particularly averse to anything touching a productive lifestyle for me. I returned to St. Paul, then, victim of the perception that my hometown is a never-ending source of rejuvenation and hope, only to find that it was the same old stale, depressing void that had prompted me to leave just a month or so earlier. This is the juncture in time, then, when my illness waxed severe and I failed in my attempt to flee.* Perhaps a measure of my desperation is that I was still waiting for a late check to arrive via general delivery from the janitorial service in Des Moines. I took the chance that I could intercept it at the agency there on my way to a balmier environment rather than wait for it even a few more days in the cold embrace of a Twin Cities winter. But as I've said I did not make it past Burnsville on that particular flight.

After the about-face I returned to live at the mission and worked sporadically through the daily labor agency while treating my infirmity with large doses of hard liquor. I couldn't drink at the mission, though, and to do so outside would only exacerbate the intense soreness in my throat and eustachian tube, so I devised a way to drink in warmth in a unique indoor park in a city development called Town Square. Fountains, walkways, and artificial streams are interspersed amidst a profusion of dark green plants on several terraced levels below a vast glass roof that looks up between the skyscrapers to the clouds above downtown St. Paul. Here I was able to slip into a restroom and mix some vodka or whiskey in a paper soda cup so as not to arouse the authoritarian instincts of the security guards or of those observers viewing through TV cameras hidden in black plastic globes on the ceiling.

One day, in an incident mysteriously reminiscent of something I had heard of happening earlier at the mission, I was in the restroom mixing a drink when two corpulent men in jeans, black boots, and heavy winter jackets came in and milled

19

---

*The strange chronology of this "disease" is due partially to my flawed memory at the time of writing this entry. But the events are clarified somewhat in the entry for March 3.

around momentarily without performing any of those functions normally associated with a bathroom. Then the larger one, with a very substantial belly, stationed himself at the door. When I tried to leave he would not move out of my way. After a moment or two of shuffling back and forth I said, "Oh yeah, two against one, huh?" I was pretty drunk, and when he wouldn't let me by I tried shoving his very resistant bulk to the side. Suddenly his partner rushed up, and together they swung me around back toward the stalls. Headlong I flew over the tiled floor; my forehead hit hard against the edge of a wall of one of the stalls, and blood started pouring into my eye from above the brow. I shouted something like "Yeah, you guys don't have to live with the results, do you?" as they retreated in haste from the restroom. I got up from the floor and slowly washed the wound while trying to assuage my deeply mortified soul. It was this incident and others there in St. Paul that caused me to view the whole place as some kind of magnet of universal malevolence, at least as far as I was concerned, which would not tolerate my presence. I knew then that I would have to attempt another hitchhiking escape—soon.

TUESDAY FEBRUARY 27, 1990 (Yesterday evening I ignored my own cautionary instincts and finished the pint of Gordon's vodka with a quart of Pabst beer.)

I must have waited a day or two before leaving St. Paul, because I know I had forty or fifty dollars in my pocket when once again I put my foot to the highway. So the check from the janitorial agency must have arrived in the interim. Three weeks later I landed in Tucson, broke and discouraged enough to stop there rather than continue on to California, which was my original intention. Along the way the usual assortment of fringe characters appeared on and receded from the stage. There was a preacher and his family who picked me up after I had waited for two days in a snowstorm in Lakeville, Minnesota. They prayed for me as we drove southward and dropped me off in Mason City, Iowa, where I slept that night in the icy shadows next to some culvert pipes in a concrete fabrication yard. There was a ne'er-do-well who managed to drive his beatup car from town to town only by hitting up on hitchhikers for gas money or begging his fuel from churches and local government agencies along the way.* There was a sailor on leave. There was an old man who dropped me off on a little-trafficked ramp in a desolate area where it was illegal to stand on the freeway—this far short of his actual destination exit—because I spurned his homosexual overtures. And there were many others.

In Wyoming I happened to be dropped off on a ramp near Cheyenne where a pretty young girl with delicate features and long blond hair was soon dropped off also. With her as bait it did not take long to get a ride from another truck driver who ultimately paid me twenty dollars to help him move furniture one day in Denver. Later, he dropped us off in Colorado Springs, where a snowstorm drove us to seek shelter at the local Red Cross homeless agency. The girl slept in a separate section of the building, and, getting up early the next morning, I managed to slip out the shelter door, walk to the freeway, and catch a ride out of town before she was awake, probably, leaving her in a place more suited to her lightweight garments and her need for companionship with other people recently disenfranchised by the Lord.

As long as I have been analyzing music it might be interesting to note a strange phenomenon with respect to its composition. Before the girl was dropped off on that Cheyenne ramp I had been waiting there for a couple of hours, just contemplating the majestic landscape that seems to stretch forever in the form of those great rolling swells of treeless terrain that characterize many parts of the country between Iowa and the Rockies. Having nothing better to do, I decided, for the first time in a year, to attempt a song, and in a little while came up with a snatch of passable melody attached to the words "Wide open, wide open, wide open dream; wide open, wide open, wide open scheme." Now during the time I was traveling with the girl and helping the furniture truck driver in Denver, I would sometimes revert in mind to the melody, changing a note here or there in an attempt to imbue it with a little more flavor, but I couldn't quite satisfy myself that it was right.

A little ways south of Colorado Springs I was picked up by a middle-aged man in an old sedan who was on his way to put a bid in at a hospital in Pueblo. He was of Spanish or Moorish

---

*It's surprising how many police departments and small-town social service offices will supply gas to these vagrants just to get them out of their jurisdiction.

descent, judging from his conversation, and possessed one of those classic profiles that seem to belong more to the nobility of medieval times than to modern, homogeneous America. His company manufactured trophies, awards, pins, and the like, and he was so confident of his bid to the hospital that he regarded it as a mere formality preceding the award to him of the contract. He related how alcoholism had ruined him a few times at least—how after successfully building up a company of one kind or another he had lost it all by resorting to destructive recreation in the bottle. He was open and amiable to a disconcerting degree and let me sit in his car while he walked into the hospital to take care of business. Later we drove into the central business district, where he bought me coffee and donuts. He said he wanted to get a book for me. He would not tell me which book, but referred occasionally to alcoholism and how I ought to take the cure. How he might have surmised that I was in need of rehabilitation is not vividly clear to me, even now. I did mention something to the effect that at times liquor had gotten the best of me, but there was nothing then in my general appearance or behavior or in my conversation to suggest that I was now anything other than a strict teetotaler.

We bounced around town in his car from one bookstore and residence to another in search of "the book," while he inveighed intermittently against my excessive consumption of alcohol and sympathized with the plight I was now in as a result of it, because, of course, he had been there himself. There were a couple of hours in failed inquiries and fruitless conversations with locals to gain directions, which, by the way, he presided over in a relatively exquisite Castilian dialect, one I can only assume had passed down to him through his family unscathed by the corrupting influence of New World linguistics. One of the Mexican-Indian men with whom he talked actually beheld him in an attitude approaching reverence as the finely articulated sentences flowed from his agile lips and he gestured in his dark, well-tailored suit in a manner reminiscent of a Venetian street merchant. It would have been interesting to know that man's family history.

Finally we pulled up to a clean modern brick building on the town's outskirts, framed by a vista of sunlit foothills and pine-clad peaks in the distance. He went inside, past a sign with diminutive lettering revealing the building as a treatment center for alcoholics. In a few minutes he returned with a large brand-new book with a dark blue cover entitled simply *Alcoholics Anonymous*. He gave it to me for nothing, and in a few more minutes, after I politely declined to attend an AA meeting with him later in the evening, he dropped me off near a busy freeway ramp and went on his way.

I did not attempt to hitchhike out of town that evening, since most of the daylight had been commandeered by our peripatetic mission in search of the Big Book, as it's known to AA insiders. I started to read it in a large abandoned lot by the freeway while sipping on a half-pint of gin and a quart of beer that I bought en route.

I thought it was one of the most engaging and fascinating books I had ever read. I kept it with me as I continued traveling the next day and dipped into it on ensuing days as I waited for hour upon hour on the ramps and shoulders of freeways heading south and west. It told about the handful of people who started AA and how it expanded over the years to millions of members. The bulk of its pages contained personal accounts of members' degradation by drink and their subsequent recovery through AA. Then one day while standing on a freeway shoulder somewhere west of Las Cruces, New Mexico, I opened the book to a paragraph that started out, "The day he died." I looked up from the book and put those words to a facsimile of that same Wyoming-begotten melody I had reverted to in my mind over the days, except that now it was in a different kind of rhythmic time and was somewhat rearranged notationally. I added another segment with the words, "I must have cried a thousand tears of sorrow," again based on that previously created melody, and I thought the result was excellent. I shut the book, for the time being at least, and for the next few days made up a long, very good melody based on that first tenuously derived phrase of notes. When I was in Tucson, and after I had finished the book and left it for another reader at a mission there, I realized that the first notes of the song I had composed were almost identical to the first phrases of the old song that starts out, "Try to remember the kind of September." It is not recognizable as such at first, because the number of repetitions of the notes is different and the melody is in a somewhat altered rhythm. But though I don't consider it one of my shabbier creations, to this day I have not put words to the song because of the resemblance of its first part to that old hit. The year following the composition of that one song, however, has turned out to be the most musically prolific I have ever had: fully half of the complete and partial melodies that are now in my repertoire were created in this period. I wonder sometimes whether, if I had not succeeded in breaking through the barrier of composing that first song, I would have gone on to exert the effort for the remaining twenty-nine.

SATURDAY MARCH 3, 1990 (TRY TO REMEMBER)   Today is my thirty-sixth birthday. If I don't want to renege on the diary format I must confess to a lapse in memory and a resultant omission in the last entry. Perhaps that I forgot such a significant occurrence is sufficient in itself to indict my recent habits. The fact that I still cannot remember the event's exact slot in the chronology probably warrants conviction. Anyway, at some time in my intermittent tenancy of the Twin Cities last winter, when I was staying at the YMCA in downtown Minneapolis, I decided to walk into a popular strip bar on a busy section of Hennepin Avenue. I hardly noticed the cop car parked outside the door. The instant I was across the threshold a huge, burly bouncer locked his arms around my neck and lifted me off the ground. He muttered something about "coming back" and wrestled me out the door while I struggled between desperate gasps for air. Once on the sidewalk the police took over with handcuffs and shoved me into the back of the squad car. I remember walking through the halls of the new subterranean jail and one of the cops laughing derisively behind me. "Hah, lookit that," he scoffed. "Whatya do, shit in your pants? Lookit that," he repeated to his sidekick, "the guy shit in his pants."

"Yeah," I retaliated, "you guys got enough demon spirit pourin' outa you to make up for a couple tons a shit."

There was a strange silence in the aftermath of that remark as the booking process was completed and I was escorted to a cell. Luckily I was released early the next morning and was able to return to the "Y" to change my soiled clothes. It was true: I had shit in my pants. But when and how it occurred is lost to my memory. It seems possible that, since I had been drinking before I even entered the strip bar, I was actually going in there for the purpose of elimination and that during the ride to the jail that function transpired exactly according to the premeditated timetable. Whatever the case, I was left with a very sore throat and an aching ear in addition to whatever viral maladies already existed. So this must have occurred shortly after my return from Des Moines, when I had money in my pocket from the hotel job, but before that first aborted flight by thumb down to Burnsville.

SUNDAY MARCH 4, 1990   Last Sunday I was in central Tucson arranging for a telephone message service when I stopped at a cantina-style restaurant near the campus of the University of Arizona. While finishing the diary entry for that day I drank four sixteen-ounce cups of draft beer. I went to another saloon after that on the dilapidated outskirts of the campus district and had a brandy and water. I bought a half-pint of whiskey on the way to the bus stop and drank most of it at my campsite later on. Except for yesterday, when I drank about a third of a fifth of Canadian whiskey, I have limited my daily consumption in the interim to a half-pint in the evenings. So far I have rented a storage closet a few blocks from my campsite (fifteen dollars per month), arranged for a mailing address at the Traveler's Aid Society (free) a few miles south of downtown, and contracted for the telephone service (twenty-five dollars per month). These things allow me to search for work during the day. Usually I "shower" and shave in the mornings, using a gallon container of water that I can fill up for a quarter from a machine in the nearby shopping center. There is an enormous Hilton Hotel right across the street from my campsite so I usually perform this daily toilet in a depressed wash a few yards away from where I sleep. A patch of stained soil and some discarded motor oilcans there would seem to suggest that my bathing area has been used previously for less godly purposes, but it hides me well from any tourists in the tower whose umbrage at sighting a nude man pouring water over his head might trigger a call to the police. I now have $250 left in the bank, and the balance will reduce tomorrow to $200.

Part of the reason I have not rented a room right away with the intention of searching at a frantic rate for work before the next rent comes due is that my work history is not such that it will win the ready admiration of potential employers. In fact, it is so replete with vast stretches of apparent inactivity and jobs quit after a few months or weeks that I have invented a new history just for the purpose of applying. So the universe of potential employers is now reduced for me from those who would be prompted to hire me to the subset of that group which will not take the time or expend the effort to call up the former employers I have listed. They are real employers, mostly, but I have expanded the duration of our association considerably in most cases.

I suspended the writing of the diary for a few days because it does not seem to be working. That is, although I am not imbibing to the extent I was a few months ago, writing, even of this simple narrative variety, seems to instill a further craving for booze rather than curb the desire that is there already. So perhaps I will take a new tack and compromise with the Devil. I am going to try to limit my daily intake during the week to one half-pint and my weekend consumption to a pint a day. I am aware that this approach would inspire a howl of derision from the AA-ers who, according to their own testimonies, have executed all of those strategies short of abstention only to find them lacking in workability.* This is so, they say, because, in every alcoholic, booze establishes a chemistry that overwhelms him with desire for more and more of the same. He loses control after the first drink because his "sickness" determines that his metabolism will interact with alcohol in a way that makes him utterly helpless to refuse another drink. Well, this ignores at least one important fact: that alcohol occurs naturally in the body even without its willful introduction. However, the AA perception might very well be valid. Perhaps the increase over and above the natural level is the triggering factor. Nevertheless, I am going to try (and possibly fail at) what they so stridently scorn, and future entries will concern themselves with different psychological aspects of my attempt, woven together with the history already begun and with accounts of my present attempt to climb up from the economic abyss.

SATURDAY MARCH 10, 1990   The first four days after resolving to limit myself to one half-pint daily saw me drink at least a whole pint each day in addition to three or four glasses of beer at a local tavern. Thus it can be fairly concluded that the strat-

*Besides familiarizing myself with some of the AA literature, I did, under compulsion from the law, attend a number of AA meetings in Minnesota in 1986. In 1985 I was the object of an "intervention," and I have talked with AA members here and there.

egy of moderation announced less than a week ago will likely not work for me. There is a paradox in consuming alcohol. We drink, ostensibly, to make ourselves feel good, yet each swallow only serves, it seems, to inflame the desire for more of the same. Does this mean that the liquor is actually making us feel worse? My own experience tells me that I sometimes feel a more aggravated state of loneliness or desperation after a few belts. But this might be due to a sedative effect that settles me and dissipates the tension which might have blocked my examining that state of empty yearning to begin with. The desert does not palliate this longing in the least, but no place can be said to effect a cure for an isolated soul. Loneliness transcends geography, I imagine.

The way heroin works might illuminate the mechanism of the paradox, or at least offer a psychological metaphor for why drinking leads to more drinking. With heroin, from what I have read, the addict craves not just that the substance be in his body. Rather, what precipitates his intense desire is the "rush" of exhilaration that accompanies the relatively sudden change in the metabolism upon introduction of the drug. It is the steep change in body chemistry that provides the pleasure and not any stabilized amount of drug in the system, which nevertheless might produce a continuous stupor of some kind. The way that methadone works in this regard is to quench the appetite for heroin while circumventing the body's clamoring for the rush or sudden metabolic surge of pleasure. Why methadone is considered an improvement over actual addiction to heroin seems tinged, to me, with overtones of puritanical hostility to pleasure, since both involve addiction to and continuous injection of a strong drug, except that one affords elevation into euphoria, while the other simply satisfies a habit.

I'm remembering all this from a *Scientific American* article from a number of years ago. However, even if my memory is faulty or if the state of scientific knowledge has altered since then, this metabolic scenario with respect to heroin can still furnish us with a psychological allegory for excessive drinking. For who is the drinker that can deny that a session with the bottle will be highlighted by a succession of euphoric rushes or flights into near elation? That the corresponding descents into more depressed moods might be more grudgingly admitted is perhaps less disproof of their actual occurrence than it is indicative of

27

the drinker's inclination to smooth over these troughs with great expectations of the next peak of jubilation and, attendant on this, his acceleration of his drinking to accomplish the ascent. So in one sense, then, getting drunk is a kind of perverse visitation by manic depression—a disease of intense emotional lows and highs—that one hopes does not extend into a more permanent residency. Of course, it is possible that, unknown to the heavy drinker, this pattern of highs and lows is already established in his daily life by his alcohol intake; or that the lows he feels during the day are more severe just because of the highs he imposes upon himself at night by drinking; or that the lows and highs he would experience even during a long stretch of sobriety would be more pronounced because of the trenches and concavities already dug into his psyche by long-term alternation between intoxication and temporary deferral.

This possibility is frightening, because it opens the door to the disease theory of alcohol, except with a greater emphasis on deliberately induced mental infirmity rather than a physical predisposition to excess. It is a theory which would claim that the alcoholic is intentionally subjecting himself to a mild form of mental illness. Whether it is true or not is a question I must leave to some future student of alcoholism who is perhaps more talented in practical scientific observation and who commits himself to experimenting with an eye to the possible ramifications that are usually so far from the minds of those just entering the field.

On the other hand, many episodes of drinking are simply a way to arrive at a mellow plateau as an escape from or an alternative to a more problematic sobriety. Drinking can dissolve the tensions and mental turmoil generated when one engages in creative efforts of many kinds. It can dispel the ennui or habitual concentration arising from tedious employment of either a mental or physical character. It can anesthetize, to a degree, the aches, and banish the fatigue resulting from hard physical labor. And in my case, at least, it can sometimes deliver me from the ghastly and incessant suffering inflicted by the Devil.

Now, whether you interpret the word *Devil* as adversity residing in an environment created by an angry, vengeance-conscious God, or whether you construe it to signify the beastly dimension latent in each of our personalities, or whether you actually take it to mean some kind of supernatural agent that comes down to earth to harass people and gall them and generally raise havoc with their lives, is not important. Because for the person who occasionally indulges in a religious perspective, any personal misery that seems gratuitous or extraneous to the operation of the universe assumes the character of an evil agent, at times, that can only be traced to the jaundiced machinations of the originator of the universe. Let me represent it, for now, by something that happened to me on Monday night last and caused me to break away from my resolution to limit my imbibing to half a pint a day. However, I will commence the reporting of this incident in tomorrow's entry, for it is getting late on this rainy Saturday afternoon and I long deeply to savor my third beer in this saloon into which I took refuge just a few sentences ago. Translated, this means I am getting a little too thirsty, for the moment, to continue writing.

WEDNESDAY, MARCH 14, 1990   On the Saturday afternoon following the last entry, I walked to the drugstore, bought a fifth of Canadian whiskey, and consumed most of it underneath the bridge that spans the Pantano Wash near my campsite. It rained liberally for a number of hours, and water flowed in rushing streams and rivulets down the wash. The overpass afforded only a minimum of protection. After a while rain leaked through the seams between the great concrete beams that lie atop the poles that traverse the wash. Confinement to a small patch of dry sand and fascination with the voluminous waters cascading from the street and the nearby hotel parking lot, down concrete embankments and through culvert pipes, to mingle at last with the animated network in the wash, occasioned the excessive consumption, I rationalize; and the next day I remedied the hangover with more of the same. Further delay in continuing the diary I trace to uncertainty on my part as to whether I should tell the truth concerning the reason I broke my resolution, made a week ago Monday, to keep my daily consumption to half a pint. However, since I have adhered to the truth so far, and committed myself to the diary format, I reckon I can't very well start telling lies now.

29

I awoke in the dead of night. To a tramp who frequents the more populated areas of the country this "eye" of the night, around two or three in the morning, is determined not by the position of the moon or the orientation of the Big Dipper with respect to the Pole. Rather, he deduces it by the deathly stillness of the roads, which even in the most populous areas will experience a decline in traffic to only an occasional lonely car whose soughing wheels will seem to penetrate to the most desolate reaches of the sun-deprived universe. I discerned this stage that night because I was sleeping right under the road where the decline in traffic had occurred. It had sprinkled earlier in the night, so I had packed up my equipment and abandoned my campsite by the edge of the wash in favor of the shelter of the overpass. When I awoke there during the eye, the dark profile of distending, turbulent clouds could be seen moving starkly against the clear night sky on both sides of the bridge, and occasionally the moon's bright image would be extinguished, to shine only on the fringes of those distant traveling cumuli.

It was very windy. Twice I sat up in rigid fright as some creature seemed to be loping swiftly across the sand just a few yards away, only to realize that it was just a paper bag or a tumbleweed bouncing wildly through the underpass. Then the wind seemed to pick up. A plastic bag I had filled with empty cans and paper trash suddenly jangled away across the wash, and sand peppered my face. A sound like squeaky wheels seemed to course through the air above me and concentrate in a point somewhere in the bridge toward the middle of the wash. I retracted my head from the sleeping bag to see a shadowy wisp of bats disappearing into the crevices between the concrete beams. Of course, I had seen this group of bats before, but only when they were leaving in the twilight, and now they were coming back a good three hours before daylight.

Then the wind accelerated, and a loud humming resonated on the lower edges of the north side of the bridge as if the passageway beneath were a huge bottle mouth being whistled on by a giant. A great rushing wall of sand and debris suddenly occluded much of the light on either side of the bridge. I had experienced dust devils in Arizona before, but this seemed more like the start of a tornado or something.

I stood up, half in panic, and tried to anchor down my groundcloth and sleeping bag while picking up bags of clothes and equipment. Finally, I swung the bedding over my shoulder and was starting away with bags in hand when there was a loud popping noise from up the street and a buzz and screech as if a transformer had blown. All at once everything was black. The pale light from streetlights and the nearby hotel was gone. I had never experienced such darkness. My cotton robe streamed away to the southeast as I bent into the wind and tried to walk down the wash toward the shopping center—but I felt as if I were trying to push against a stalled car. When the blowing sand allowed, I would open my eyes to a blackness so devoid of orienting features that I felt as if I was trying to swim through some kind of thick, resistant ether.

I plodded with difficulty through some softer sand, turning and crouching a couple of times in deference to the barraging gusts, and finally made it to the eroded slope at the edge of the wash. I could hear a metal sign clanging from somewhere in the shopping center, and I began groping up the hillside. About halfway up my foot slipped into a gulley and I tripped backwards, tumbled down the slope, and landed hard on my back on the floor of the wash. I felt dizzy and nearly unconscious. But somewhere, maybe blowing to Mexico for all I knew, were my sleeping bag, clothes, and equipment!

I pushed myself up in desperation, but as I stood, it was as if I were locked in place by one of the queerest sensations I have ever known. All the blood seemed to be rushing out of my head while sharp prickles covered my face and scalp. It was similar to a foot falling asleep except it was my head. I swayed momentarily. And then I felt it. A strong, calloused hand grabbed the muscle between my shoulder and neck and squeezed till it hurt. In my weakness I managed a terrified bellow, pivoted, and flailed my arms wildly in the darkness. But nobody was there!

Then, as suddenly as it had rushed in, the wind began to subside. In a moment I could see starlight through the settling dust and sand, and in another minute the air was almost clear, and moonlight bathed the wash and the gently rocking shrubs on the wash's edge. I stood, crouched slightly and arms extended in readiness for battle with a nonexistent foe. Was it just a fit of craziness or some peculiar perceptions brought on by alcohol? I know that the skin on my face has oftentimes felt numb in the last few months, and my cheeks have taken on the rosy hue of a drinker's flush. But I know one thing for sure: that sensation of a hand on my shoulder was as real as the paper on which this is written. But since no one was there, I have no choice but to ascribe it to a supernatural agent, a supernatural agent that I think might appropriately be labeled the Devil.

Now you might have thought that such an experience, especially since it seems related somehow to madness brought on by alcohol, would persuade me to stop drinking. But I had another notion. After I collected my belongings that night, scattered up and down the wash, and finally located the bag with my toiletries and the half-full pint of vodka just a few yards from where I fell, nothing but a little sedation was as dear to my heart and as comforting to my traumatized metabolism.

SATURDAY MARCH 17, 1990   In his essay *Compensation*, if I remember correctly, Emerson wrote that he had wanted to tackle the subject for a number of years. I sometimes think, perhaps fancifully, that the delay was due to his difficulty in finding in the real world those situations which would corroborate his argument that balance and a kind of natural justice are woven through the fabric of creation. At least this balance seems hard to find at those times when evil is relentless and is apparently unimpeded by any offsetting good. For the purpose of argument, let me posit the notion that some of the evil to which humans are subject is the result of the supernatural intervening in our affairs. This cannot be proved, of course, but it might be interesting to reason from the assumption that a certain pattern of events, or a succession of setbacks, or the suffering brought on by unusually severe diseases, or adversity of many kinds can be attributed to the supernatural. If this is so, the question arises, Why? The answer that comes readily to mind, especially since it mirrors man's experience in gaining a livelihood from a refractory earth, is that God is exacting a toll of some kind for our privilege of journeying through life. But when suffering of this kind becomes so unbearable and so unceasing as to cause us to prefer death over continued existence, then its source impresses us rather as a vindictive creator and not a great fountain of benevolence who is simply inflicting some token misery on us to remind us of His love.

Are these types of questions and observations legitimate? We are accustomed to think of God or the supernatural as akin to nothingness, or as close to nothing as you can get. But since Einstein, it is generally accepted that even empty space is something, in the sense that it can be manipulated. For example, according to these modern theories, any empty, evacuated space inside a vehicle moving at a significant proportion of the speed of light will necessarily be "less" empty space than contained by the same vehicle moving at a far slower rate, since the vehicle itself will have reduced dimensions at the faster velocity. Thus, in Einstein's world empty space cannot be regarded as "nothing." According to the big bang theory, space itself was initiated in a tremendous explosion at the beginning of time. Thus, modern science allows us to consider empty space to be a creation itself. How then can it possibly be "nothing"? In fact, there can be no such thing as "nothing" if empty space itself is regarded as the product of a process in which it did not exist prior to its initiation. In the post-Einstein world, "nothing" becomes a relic of erroneous thinking of the past. It is a vestigial concept that must be dispensed with in light of these latter, more enlightened developments. Philosophical integrity demands that a modern thinker erase the idea of nothing from his mind altogether, since it is a concept that represents something which does not exist in the real world. To advert in mind to "nothing," then, must be relegated to the province of the intellectually lazy who cling dumbly to an anachronism. In the modern world view, "nothing" is nullified and banished from the inventory of allowable concepts utilized to think about nature and the universe at large.

This can be extended further. From the earliest days of our youth, of course, we become familiar with the concept of nothing, and since God, if He exists, is spirit, we naturally associate Him with nothing. But now that we have advanced in history to the point where we know that nothing is an invalid concept based on excessively primitive views of the world, that nothing, essentially, does not exist, then God, if He exists, cannot possibly be nothing. God must be something. And I think I have discovered, after years of being subjected to the type of evil heretofore analyzed, something about this something that we think God is. However, before I write more on this subject, I better go have a drink to celebrate Saint Patrick's Day.

SUNDAY MARCH 19, 1990   This morning as I was emerging from my desert campsite two Tucson policemen appeared out of the brush and accosted me with the usual search, record check, and importuning queries about my activities. I was surprised I was not arrested. If this were California, a charge would have been invented, if need be, to keep me off the streets and in the missions. Presently there is one warrant out for my arrest in San Diego for "camping in the tidelands." In Santa Barbara I am expected to pay a fine of $211 by April for "urinating in public." There is an old warrant out for my arrest in Orlando, Florida, for "camping by a lakeside," even though this was on vacant, private land. In Minnesota, the charge of disorderly conduct arising from my previously portrayed attempt to walk into a strip bar was ultimately adjudicated last June, after one missed court date. The charge was dropped on condition that no further charges are brought against me in the Twin Cities area for a year. I have a few months to go before I am safe on that one.

Of course, when dealing with these cops, you divert their attention from those places where your record is tarnished by handing them an ID from a locality where you are clean. Although there is almost no chance that they would extradite you for a misdemeanor, it's better to keep them free of suspicion and lingering doubts about your status. From what I have seen, enforcement officers and social workers in this country do not yet utilize any nationwide clearinghouse of legal information stored in a centralized computer and communicated electronically, so that each state presently checks with the other for such important data as outstanding arrest warrants, unemployment benefits received, and one's history of participation in welfare and food stamp programs. From my point of view this is good, but the fact that the governments have not coordinated their efforts in an age when computerization would be easy and when faced with pressure from the law-and-order lobbies and the zealotry of the enforcers is nothing short of amazing. Where a government does not seize the available technology to further tighten its control and so behave in accordance with its proclivity to monopolize the supervision of all aspects of life, then there must be a check somewhere in the system preventing that spreading encroachment. Is it legal, moral, political, or spiritual in this case?

Concerning yesterday's entry, the question lingers: Why, if God is good, does He inflict pain sufficient to make us want to die? My own theory would assert that God is not only the creator of the universe, but also the sustainer of it, to an extent. Many people hold this view, I imagine. It becomes interesting when you consider that God might suffer, or at least endure something analogous to what we call suffering, in order to do the sustaining. Thus, when evil is dispensed by God, one of His motives is to wrestle us into the acknowledgment that, yes, if it weren't for You, I would not even be here. He wants to instill in us the realization that, again in an analogous way, He sometimes has grave doubts about continuing the painful effort that makes our lives possible. And He wants to make sure that we share, at least for a while, in that pain and doubt, by coercing us into despair and rendering our hope for life impotent in the face of His countervailing antagonism.

Why is our existence seemingly so onerous to the Spirit? We do not see mountains suddenly detonating or trees abruptly withering in response to the wrathful displeasure of the Lord. Here is an idea: The inert material world of elements can be placed at the bottom of a pyramid where rank indicates the degree to which the things so ordered are subject to the punishment of the Spirit. Perhaps combined with the elements, or at most one step above them, would be the plants. Above these would be the animals, and crowning the pyramid would be man. The animals are placed above the plants because, although they might not experience direct chastisement from the Spirit, still they have been placed in a setting where pain, fear, and hunger are incorporated into the web of daily life. If, for the sake of argument, it can be assumed that God intended that these negative sensations be enmeshed in the natural world as part of a network of compensations and hardships, then they can be regarded as being somehow spawned by the Deity, and animals are therefore more exposed to divine punishment than plants and are assured of a ranking place on the pyramid.

A theory can be constructed around the pyramid idea which might further elucidate the spiritual motivation for human suffering. It seems obvious at first glimpse that those material entities that have no consciousness, or awareness of their own existence, are not subject to supernatural reprisals because they have no capacity for pain. But the close connection between capacity for suffering and the existence of that suffering might mask some verities buried deep in the nature of things. The higher up the pyramid an entity is placed, the more consciousness it has and so the more it is exempt from what we call natural laws. Although the behavior of water when heated to 212

35

degrees Fahrenheit can be firmly predicted by reference to unchanging laws, the behavior of human beings under certain situations and conditions is so wildly uncertain that whole libraries of sociological, psychological, and economic commentary cannot suffice to explain it. So, then, if according to an earlier assumption, God acts not only to create the material world but also to sustain it, it can be posited as the first principle of this theory that those material entities which behave strictly according to discoverable laws, and which happen to be devoid of consciousness, require less suffering on God's behalf to sustain them than those entities which are not so subject to control by those laws. If this is true, it could very well be due to the fact that existence according to natural laws somehow eases the burden of the Deity in sustaining that existence. For example, gravitation acts according to the law that each material object will be attracted toward the earth's center in proportion to the mass inhering in that object. Thus, if God is the ultimate source of the powerful force we call gravity, even if some mediating mechanisms, as yet undiscovered, can somehow explain it, then He has essentially relegated the specific behavior of objects in relation to gravity to a natural law, while He simply sustains the centralized, outwardly radiating force without regard to its multiplicity of effects. Likewise, because the behavior of objects in motion, of substances in chemical ferment, of light reflecting from a planet or a moon, and a multitude of other phenomena can be reduced to fundamental laws of attraction, resistance, or

other mathematical arrangement, it seems likely that any supernatural sustenance required for the existence of the objects involved with those processes can be reduced to some kind of centralized or primal force that pervades the objects in conformity to the pre-established principles, much as water will soak into a sponge only by following the labyrinth of orifices and passageways already imposed on that absorptive body.

Under this theory, then, consciousness, and especially advanced consciousness, is what elicits the wrath of the Spirit, because consciousness must be sustained by spiritual effort without abiding by any known laws. The Spirit must instead conform to the conscious mind by propping it up, maintaining its existence, despite the fact that it does whatever it wants to do without the slightest notice of that to which it owes its very existence. In this scenario the Spirit becomes a slave to consciousness, so to speak, and inflicts punishment on it to somehow compensate for any supportive, supernatural role. Of course, all of the foregoing is only speculation on my part, and it is possible that as a rationalization for human suffering at the hands of the Deity it has the same validity as Christianity's chimera concerned with Lucifer.

When analyzing consciousness I am sometimes, especially when under the influence of alcohol, engrossed in the mystery of our individuality. If I had been born with a slightly different nose, for example, or destined to grow to a height two inches shorter than I eventually did, would I have been a different person altogether? Would "I" not then exist? Why am "I" not my younger brother, or my older brother who died at childbirth? If alcohol and other drugs can temporarily dismantle and rinse away all those memories, predispositions, and peculiarities programmed into our flesh and which determine our individuality, leaving our egos bald and reduced to a level of consciousness which could very well be transferred into another body, then does this mean that I am just a shell which encloses and stakes out as its own a small volume of the great sea of consciousness? Or do I, as I grow from infant to adult, generate my own consciousness, which might then flow back into that great sea of preternatural consciousness which made my existence possible to begin with? Does God punish us, not because He chafes at sustaining our existence, but because in growing up we acquire a complex of desires, aversions, and fears, in other words an ego that somehow leaches the vital element of individuality from the material world in direct conflict and competition with the more diffuse, less ego-concentrated consciousness of the Spirit? Or is it all just an elaborate enigma meant only to divert us simple mortals while we dissipate our days here on earth, never to see a life of any kind again?

These are the questions I cannot answer as I close this diary until after I find work. My scant capital has decreased to less than eighty dollars, mostly, I suppose, because I have squandered my days on eating and drinking instead of looking for work. Word from Minnesota tells me my father is on his deathbed with cancer, a development I find so disheartening that I can hardly bring myself to write it down. So I hope I am at a turning point in my life; I hope I find a job; I hope my father is cured; I hope and hope and hope; I hope I will resume this diary with more auspicious chroniclings than those with which I leave it.

TUESDAY APRIL 10, 1990   I am in Minnesota now, not Arizona. My father died on March 19 from an aggressive tumor that invaded his neck and salivary gland area in June of 1989. The growth apparently wrapped itself around his carotid artery very quickly after its inception, making surgery too life-threatening an option. I did not see him even once during his ordeal. A tube was ultimately inserted into his stomach to provide nourishment and the morphine that he was in continuous need of during the latter, extremely painful stages. To talk or to swallow became unbearable near the end, even with the drug, and at last he requested that the tube be removed. He died as much from starvation, likely, as from the cancer, early on the morning of the nineteenth. To me, the death seems more like a cruel murder than a demise from natural causes. He was sixty-two years of age, a lawyer still in vigorous contention with both life and his legal foes. True to his nature, he was not defeated by the affliction even when its ultimately lethal character became evident. From what my relatives and others have reported, he became involved in his own funeral arrangements, to an extent, fine-tuned the will in his office until bedridden, and queried those close to him about the possibility of salvaging the gold from his teeth before burial.

I was staying with my brother up until a couple of days ago, but I was drinking heavily enough on some days to possibly jeopardize his own sobriety, so I voluntarily decamped for the mission, where I pay four dollars a night for a bed and breakfast.

They say that man is the only animal that cooks its food, and I would have to concur, at least based on my own observations of dogs, cats, and other domesticated beasts, who are all cunning enough to get others to do it for them. But if man is the only animal to embrace the culinary function, then he is also the only one to saddle that task with an irksomeness that goes far beyond its original simplicity. To prepare a lettuce salad, for example, can be an easy and even enjoyable activity. One grasps the head of lettuce in the hand and firmly thumps the core against the cutting board or counter. After removing the now-loosened inner stalk, the chef carefully peels off any rusted or soggy leaves until only the fresh, crispy interior head remains. With his hands he might simply break the head into quarters and serve them in bowls with dressing and garnish. Or with a sharp knife he might wedge the head or chop it or slice it according to his preference and toss it with vinegar and oil in those same bowls. With a more complicated tool, a rectangular metal shredder, he might reduce the head through a simple back and forth motion against the grating holes to smaller strips and strings for use in a slaw or sandwich dressing.

Man, though, is apparently not satisfied with accomplishing tasks in a simple manner. Within his nature there must hide a propensity to balloon even the most elemental of chores into a complex system of technology and repetitive human labor that can be absolutely staggering to the imagination. Preparing a lettuce salad, for example, begins in the offices of the engineers who plan the layout of the factory where the lettuce is to be cut up. Their cerebral efforts are translated on the factory floor into the various loud and perpetually moving machines that perform the different complex steps in transforming a head of lettuce into salad-qualifying components.

From a large box a man shovels out heads onto a moving conveyor belt that bisects a long stainless steel table. Workers standing on grated platforms at the sides of the table grab a head at a time, punch it into a metal cylinder projecting from the table's edge to excise the core, tear off and prune away any blighted or sodden leaves, throw these into a refuse barrel at their sides, toss the head onto another moving conveyor belt above the table, and swiftly proceed to the next green unit of production. This the workers do all day long at a hectic pace.

The cleaned heads drop off the top conveyor into the mouth of one of various types of cutting machines, depending on whether the lettuce is being chopped or shredded and how fine a cut is desired. Inside the three-by-five-by-eight-foot-tall machines, a ring of blades spins very fast, drawing the head by centrifugal force against their extremely sharp edges and expelling the sliced lettuce into a gravity chute, where water sprays it clean. Near the upper mouth of each machine is a warning— a human hand with the fingers chopped off and bleeding at the first set of joints. From the gravity chute the lettuce falls into a large metal basket. When it is full, a worker from the shipping department operates a boom on wheels, which is furnished with cable, motor, and parts to attach the basket. The basket is lifted five feet into the air, wheeled across the floor, and dropped momentarily into a disinfecting liquid contained in a large stainless steel tub. The basket is lifted back out and lowered into a stainless steel cylinder nearby. The attachments to the boom are removed, the lid to the cylinder is clamped down, and a button is pushed to set the basket to spinning inside the cylinder to extract the liquid in an operation akin to the last cycle in a clothes washer. After this the dried lettuce is dumped onto another large stainless steel table equipped with open chutes at two of the corners. A worker attaches a plastic bag to the lower extremities of the chute, below tabletop, in such a way as to connect the bag also to an electronic scale hanging from the wall. He draws the lettuce into the chute until the scale indicates the correct weight, removes the bag, and places it upright in a nearby bin. He repeats this operation all day long.

Another worker lifts the full bag from the bin and attaches its mouth to a vacuum sealer on a tall stand. After kneading the bag and squeezing out some of the excess air, the worker activates the vacuum sealer and waits thirty seconds for that function to be completed, during which time he might construct a cardboard box, move a pallet, or tape up a completed box of those bags that are finally removed from the vacuum sealer. From here, of course, all the activities and middlemen necessary for shipment of the salad material come into play to assure that America's fast-food restaurant customers are adequately supplied with roughage and sufficiently stimulated by a variety of gastronomic delights.

I don't know. I think it might be easier simply to provision every household with a knife and a grater. If I had only eaten at McDonald's I would not have come to this conclusion, of course. It took a recent week and a half of working at just such a lettuce factory in Minneapolis to fully cultivate these ideas and grow them into a fully formed opinion. The job was through a temporary agency, and my good work had prompted the manager to ask that I return the following Monday, but it was difficult to bring myself to a task so out of accord with my newly formulated principles and beliefs. So I quit. Now I find myself in a position very much like I was in earlier in Tucson. My capital is just as paltry, but the weather will not reach outdoor sleeping conditions for another month, possibly, and rain here is always plentiful in the spring. So each night I brook the close, heavy atmosphere in a dormitory crowded with unsavory bums while trying to anticipate my next move.

My father's death caused me to realize that something I had gone through previously was very much like experiencing the death of everyone I ever knew or who was part of my family. So when it happens a second time it's not quite so traumatic, evidently. The experience might as well be related here since, most inadvertently, I have provided a background for its explanation in previous diary entries. The experience was the discovery, made in March or April of 1983, that my family—that is, parents, siblings, cousins, aunts, uncles, et al.—and everyone I ever worked with or ever knew was different in a spiritual sense from myself. I have already proffered the theory that consciousness is sustained by the Spirit. But the consciousness of everyone I know, up till now at least, is somehow combined with or penetrated by the Spirit, while my own has been allowed to grow by itself into an entity which does not share in that "consciousness of the Spirit." This, obviously, is one major reason for my present economic difficulties, and it was an impetus for many flights from Minnesota and near-penniless journeys around the country in search of "someone like myself." Alas, the spiritual fabric of the country has appeared basically uniform on these quests, but this does not mean that some "odd" fellows and females might not reside somewhere in the interstices. If and when they find out who they are in relation to even their nearest kin (if that, indeed, has not already happened), they, if they are like me in sensibility at least, will experience a fear of such profound intensity that it will be a wonder if their bodies survive it.

I cannot help but feel that I am the first of many people who will ultimately go through such an experience. If this is so, then I have an obligation, it would seem, to publicize myself to the world at large so that those who go through a similar epiphany of horror will have a beacon to guide them to the right place— where they can acquaint themselves with like people, if they so wish, or just know that those people exist. I believe that people like myself, who have been set aside and separated spiritually, should separate themselves physically as well, and should live in a place that is geographically different.

In an attempt to make myself known, I have done a lot of writing since late 1985. When I finally made it to Tucson in early 1989 (resuming now the history suspended after the entry for March 3), I had two and a half books under my belt and numerous unincorporated ideas and unattached narratives, all of which I had stored with a married sister living in St. Paul. One book was the product of a lot of independent scientific thought I had applied myself to from 1979 to 1986; it scrutinized and critiqued the way that physicists currently regard certain aspects of circular motion. The other book was a collection of stories, novellas, and narratives based on my nearly destitute wanderings around the country, and the half-completed book was to be a novel about an illegal immigrant from South America who comes to California to gain financing for what he fancies are revolutionary advances in technology made possible by his own renegade ideas in the field of physics. While I was in Tucson, then, I collected food stamps, lived outside, and wrote half of another novel about an ex-hockey player named Skoloff, who was starving himself to death in the California deserts. During all this time, of course, I felt as if I was being chased and harried to madness by the Devil. In the late spring I hitchhiked back to Minnesota and in desperation asked some people here if they knew if there were other people like me or if they knew of someone who might know of them. Those were inquiries which required overcoming an immense amount of fear, because they were so seemingly insane. Getting no reply from these people, but especially in response to the ceaseless antagonism of this ubiquitous tormentor, I did something I had contemplated as a possibility for a year, at least, but which I now regret doing at all. I took all my handwritten material, for which I had labored and lived so arduously for ten years, and carried it in its large canvas sack down to the shores of the Mississippi River near where the Lake Street bridge connects Minneapolis and St. Paul. There I burned every last shred of writing I had done and walked away from a smoky, ash-strewn glade of sand and cottonwoods less one decade's worth of mental effort.*

*The exact date of this conflagration can be determined by reference to the newspapers; by an interesting coincidence the headlines the next day announced the Supreme Court's magnanimity with respect to incineration of the U.S. flag.

Just before the burning I had gotten a part-time job at a janitorial agency and borrowed two hundred dollars from my mother to sustain me until I received my first check, but after the blaze I quit the job, packed up my stuff, and used the two hundred dollars to buy a bus ticket to California. I collected a welfare check in Oceanside and wandered up the coast to Santa Barbara, where once again I tried to extort cash benefits from the government, this time while living in a welfare hotel. To my surprise, I was found to be eligible for an interstate unemployment claim based on wages made over the previous nineteen months at various jobs around the country. Because the temporary agency through which I was last employed had not found work for me immediately after I had completed a specific assignment, I was endowed for the next six months with a check for $130 every two weeks. Of course, I was forced to move out of the welfare hotel and tramp along the coast, which, considering the beauty of that edge of the continent, was not unlike advancing from the dungeon to the penthouse.

One weekend I walked twenty miles or so up the coast to a state beach. Along the way I carried a plastic water jug by hanging its handle over my left hand, allowing its weight to rest on that hand's index finger. A blister developed there that did not heal promptly when I returned to Santa Barbara, so I visited a clinic in Isla Vista, near the University of California at Santa Barbara, that dispensed free medical services to the homeless. However, the antibiotics I received did not seem to cure the infected blister in the least. It healed, but only slowly, and at a pace seemingly unrelated to the intake of the doctor's prescription. Then my fingers on both hands began to erupt in similar blisters without any provocation whatsoever from an agitating weight or from an abrading pressure of some sort. For two months, I think, blisters formed and reformed on my fingers, turning into painful ulcers that healed over only very slowly and leaving red scars in their aftermath. I think maybe forty or fifty ultimately appeared and receded on the fingers of both right and left hands until they finally stopped. It was probably as much the thought that something had gone awry with my biology as the pain of the blisters that spurred me to unprecedented intake of liquor during this period and formed a very debilitating habit that has tapered off only very slowly to this day. This little sketch, then, ought to bring the diary up to the present as far as recent drinking history goes. I can now concentrate on more current feelings and ideas generated by alcohol or whatever else seems worthy of note.

FRIDAY APRIL 13, 1990   My quitting the lettuce job was actually motivated by less elaborate logic than what I have written. I was planning to go back to work there last Monday, the day after I moved into the mission. But the prospect of *always* being in the presence of the kind of people who surround you at such low-paying jobs or subsist with you cheek by jowl in the mission was just too damn disheartening. I would not have saved enough to escape the mission for a couple of months, perhaps, and even then I could lose the temporary job anytime and be catapulted right back to square one. Hiding this authentic motivation from even myself, I arranged for another temporary job as a janitor in an electronics company through a different agency last Wednesday. But when I was awakened by the mission attendant at four in the morning on Thursday, I could not bring myself to start the job. Throughout the night I had been disturbed continually by a perpetual chorus of snoring, wheezing, coughing, and by repulsive respiration in general. A few times during the night I nudged the man in the bed to my left to discourage his resonant breathing, which seemed to be directed in a perfect arc into my left ear. The man to my right, above me on the upper bunk, mumbled in a drunken half-sleep through the night, and on occasion lowered his head below the side of his mattress and delivered an unstifled cough into the narrow chamber between our beds. On one such occasion, he reared back for an especially profound expulsion, threw his torso toward the chamber to commence with the outburst, and through inertia and lack of sober equilibrium he slipped right out of bed and fell five feet to the hard floor. Lights were turned on, attendants called to inspect for injuries, and a general hubbub did not subside for half an hour. Elsewhere in the dorm, someone had regurgitated on the floor, and the faint odor wafted in random currents about the room to occasionally assault the nostrils with repugnance.

The next day, after calling up and quitting the unstarted janitor job, I reasoned that I could still work part-time and possibly withstand nights at the mission. But these last couple of mornings I have ignored the wake-up nudge by the attendant, and I have come to realize that I cannot live at the mission. Staying at the place at night has become for me like a slow dream journey through a dank tunnel lined by recently hung corpses and creviced along the floor with pitfalls into decomposing flesh. I am returning to my brother's tonight to get my bedroll and, with ninety dollars in my pocket, to find some other kind of arrangement, perhaps in another town.

I have confronted this kind of decision many times in the last five or six years. Essentially, what I have found is that my proclivity is to engage that option which is cleaner. If I worked at the lettuce factory or as a janitor all day long and returned to the mission at night, I would feel as if I could never get clean, notwithstanding a nightly shower and sleeping between freshly washed sheets. I don't mind working fifty or sixty hours a week at any kind of job, really, but if I cannot climb out of the sty at night, the situation is intolerable. I choose, then, abstention, if necessary, from booze and food, a cleansing mortification if that is inevitable, over constant immersion in a violated atmosphere, even if that is only mental or spiritual in character.

MONDAY APRIL 16, 1990   I am going back to the mission tonight. When I awoke this morning, on the clean sand next to the St. Croix River, about twenty miles east of St. Paul, I felt renewed by the rigors of sleeping outside during these bracing early spring nights. My outlook seemed bolstered somehow by the knowledge that I had recourse to this wilder, unconstrained way of life. After checking my wallet and finding only forty dollars left—a decline perhaps attributable to one fifth too many over the weekend—I could not help but feel that my refreshed perspective would easily sustain me through a few more nights at the mission. As some incipient raindrops turned to snow, and I hurried to pack my belongings and pace across the bridge into the town of Stillwater, I felt confident that I could isolate myself in mind and body from the squalor inside the mission and move through that world as if insulated from those corrupting influences shot through the surrounding atmosphere.

In the restaurant later, as the storm intensified and laid two or three inches of snow on the sidewalk, and as the radio announced temperatures plummeting into the twenties that evening, I realized that a night or two more at the mission would not necessarily commit me to a long-term stay. I always had the option of sleeping in any one of those outside spots I had haunted in earlier days that were close enough to the bus line to get to the daily labor office on time to obtain work. Yes, I know now that I will be able to wedge myself comfortably between those laundered sheets tonight in the full knowledge that I am separate from and above the tainted environment, that I can abide there in a removed, superior state, untouched by any filth or human offensiveness that one might otherwise encounter in a less transcendent state of mind.*

WEDNESDAY APRIL 18, 1990   Exactly how I quit the lettuce job is relevant to recent events. I was expected to be at that job on that Monday morning a week and a half ago, so I called up an hour before and notified the labor office in Minneapolis of my resignation. But I still had in my possession a time ticket from Saturday's labor, which, if I wanted to be paid on Tuesday, had to be handed in by noon on the very day I was quitting. So in order to make my leaving the job seem reasonable and to justify such short advance notice as one hour, I fabricated the excuse over the phone that I was moving to Rochester, Minnesota, at the invitation of a cousin to look for work and that I had found out about it too late on Sunday to give proper notice. So later that Monday morning, when I walked into the office to submit Saturday's time sheet, the two young office managers seemed rankled. One was on the phone with the manager at the lettuce factory trying to explain my absence, which, through a shortage of extra workers that morning and an excess of canceling employees, had not yet been made up for two hours after starting time. The other one gave me a sharp look and reproached me rather testily for not calling up earlier and leaving a message on the recorder, a system established to accommodate just such changes in plans. Sheepishly, I handed in my time sheet and took my leave. The next day, Tuesday, I was able to pick up my check without incident.

   Yesterday morning, desperate to shore up my position in that most liquid of assets, I finally made it to the other daily labor office in downtown St. Paul. At six o'clock, one of the office

---

*These remarks were not meant to slight the mission staff, which does the best job possible, considering the caliber of its clients.

managers called me up to the counter and asked if I'd like to go out to the lettuce factory to work that day. Of course, I knew that temporary employees from this particular daily labor office in St. Paul (a different company altogether from the temporary company in Minneapolis) had sometimes worked at the lettuce factory while I was there, but I thought the chances of my being sent there were nil. However, that is where I was being sent. I had been down at this daily labor office in St. Paul a few weeks ago while still living with my brother, and work was scarce enough that many, including me, had to go home that day without an assignment. So yesterday, after hemming and hawing, and glancing around the crowded office, I accepted the job.

On the drive out to the lettuce factory, a mild trepidation nagged me. Would they accept someone back who had so cavalierly thrown a wrench into their scheduling a week and a half ago? These kinds of considerations are magnified greatly by one's total economic dependence on those who ostensibly have been wronged. Particularly niggling was the transparency of my excuse. I am sure that Rochester is a very economically healthy municipality. But when I happened to look at a map of that town a few days ago, I realized it was not the kind of pulsating megalopolis that one might gravitate to in search of work. I used to have cousins there when I was a kid, but the only geographical feature I remember from our visits there is a small lake in the town that stays open in the winter and attracts thousands of those Canada geese who opt to forbear the longer flight south. (To be continued.)

THURSDAY APRIL 19, 1990   Anyway, nothing much was said by the managers when suddenly I showed up on Tuesday morning and told them I was now working for the temporary company in St. Paul. A distinct coolness seemed to shade their behavior toward me, however. I was not shifted so frequently from one task to another as the day progressed, and eyes would glaze over with indifference if they happened to meet mine in a passageway or while their owners were giving me instructions. Even the employees during break displayed a tenuous but discernible shift in attitude when in my presence or when I happened to make a comment during a lag in the conversation. I think I know why.

The forty or fifty people who work in the production area of that factory do jobs that can be learned within minutes. Within one or two days of engaging in a certain repetitive activity there, a worker will have attained his natural speed, which might even be faster than the usual rate of a longtime employee. So any satisfaction that derives from a job like that is due predominantly, I think, to the psychic fulfillment that comes from having persevered through a very long and tedious process in order to produce a large ration of supposedly beneficial and worthwhile goods for society. This satisfaction, however, will be present even if the product is scarcely tolerable in concept as a thing for which humans ought to work so mindlessly and frenetically (e.g., poker chips or dog biscuits). At least this seems to be the case in America, where many workers haven't the faintest notion or concern about what it is they labor for so diligently. No, the satisfaction can come even when the product's beneficial qualities are not known or are just assumed. It comes from a pride of sorts in enduring the job and from the rather impersonal bond one forms with co-workers who accompany you through the torture. So when someone like me comes along, works a week and a half, becomes proficient at several tasks, tells everybody he's moving to Rochester (a monumental life change requiring the termination of his present job), and then returns a week later and resumes production at normal to high levels and with undiminished skill and enthusiasm—well, it might engender a little resentment that I can understand perfectly well.

FRIDAY APRIL 20, 1990   Of course, the lettuce factory, to which I will return today to finish the week, is not as simple as the name suggests. Cabbage, broccoli, cauliflower, tomatoes, peppers, onions, melons, pineapples, potatoes, and apples are all processed there for use in restaurants and other hospitality facilities. Lately I have been working on carrots. I imagine that in ancient days, before factory canning and mass production of foodstuffs, there might have been women in the towns who made carrots the focus of their gardens and, in processing them in various ways for neighbors or a local market, could thereby lay claim to "knowing" carrots. After a few days of peeling carrots on a line, however, I feel I am qualified to usurp that reputation. I have peeled more carrots in these last few days than those women probably uprooted in a lifetime, and I will not tolerate their infringing on a valid claim to a knowledgeable closeness to that particular tuber. Thousands and thousands of carrots have recently passed through my hands or have been gazed upon by my harried eyes. I am as familiar with carrots now as I would be with a wife, if I had one, and I will not allow any ancient crone to eclipse the glow of our relationship.

Now a carrot is not exactly the most glorious of vegetables with which to claim an association. The potato, for example, will almost always win out over a carrot in a contest for public favor. Who, for example, would ever condescend to the title of a "couch carrot" or feel pride in having a black-eyed drinking mascot called "Carrots" Mackenzie? Why, the carrot is not even deemed worthy of a nickname. However, this bias might very well prove defective upon closer inspection of the two parties to the rivalry. If you took a miniature auger, for example, and bored through a carrot, you would encounter no material that is foreign or extraneous to the essential nature of a carrot, but would plough instead only through pure carrot the whole way. If you were to attempt the same feat with a potato, you would be doomed to disappointment, of course, since your auger would necessarily be required by that tuber's nature to drill through two thin layers of fraudulent potato, potato material that can only aspire to the genuine stuff—spurious potato matter, actually, which, if all pretenses were dropped, would needs be regarded as only an inferior, debased cousin to the authentic starchy substance which it encloses. Of course, I am talking about the so-called skin of the potato.

TUESDAY APRIL 24, 1990   I drank heavily over the weekend, finishing a quart of brandy on Saturday morning that I had bought Thursday evening and buying a fifth of Canadian whiskey that afternoon to ween me off the bout. I did not go to work Monday or today, not because of hangovers but because I could accomplish only an hour or two of sleep these last couple of nights. Yesterday I sold some plasma for $15 to be able to buy food. I have $6 left now.

There was a thunderstorm last night while I stayed at the mission. I think I will camp outside until Friday comes, when I will get a check for approximately $50 from the daily labor office. I will use part of that money to buy a windup alarm clock ($8.50) so that I never have to sleep at the mission again. Yesterday afternoon I was out at Stillwater and a cop out there did a check on my IDs (all clear)* and warned me not to sleep in the area, but I think I will be able to go out there for a few days now, eat ascetically, and hide out on the strip of vacated land on the Wisconsin side of the river. Then on Saturday I hope to start working again, and sleeping outside, since the weather has opened up now into more springlike conditions.

It is a curious trait of human beings that we experience a compulsion to act, to do something, to fill our days with some kind of activity in order to feel secure in the world and stake a claim of some sort to legitimacy. As history progresses into the high-tech era, this tendency could take on some aspects of the ridiculous, due to a lack of corresponding awareness on the part of men and women of how their activity might impinge upon their happiness or inure to their "true" economic benefit. Today, for example, I feel slightly adrift and assailed by a sense of economic insecurity because of my decision to postpone working for a few days. This is so despite the fact that full-time employment through the labor agency, living at the mission, and the drinking that seems to go hand in hand with that lifestyle, is absolutely a zero-sum game where I am concerned and is rivaled in economic logic by doing absolutely nothing beyond partaking of any free meal programs that might avail themselves to me in the course of my sabbatical. But this is not exactly the true economic benefit analysis to which I have referred, since eventually circumstances in no way ridiculous will compel me to return to work.

The true economic benefits that today's society gains from its workforce must be gauged from a broad perspective. Beyond satisfying everyone's basic needs for food, clothing, and shelter, for what does the majority of the modern American workforce toil? It does not require an elaborate examination of statistical records to infer the answer. Simple experience in a variety of jobs teaches me that a very small percentage of the work being done in this country today is given to growing food or building shelter or making clothes. Instead, we work here for automobiles, and for amenities such as tiled bathrooms and mecha-

*He checked IDs from Milwaukee, Des Moines, and the Twin Cities. Thus I was able to convey the impression of multistate virtue and perhaps provide myself some immunity from harassment while camping near Stillwater in the future.

nized kitchens, or for conveniences like preprocessed foods, or for providing the hospitality and service offered by restaurants and stores. I would estimate that only a very small proportion of the work Americans do can be said to apply to those minimum food, clothing, and shelter needs required for a basic level of human dignity and material comfort.

Now the problem with this kind of setup is that people do not have the option of devoting their workaday lives to gaining only those elemental material advantages considered necessary since time immemorial. Rather, if they choose to work, they must immerse themselves in activities oftentimes frenetic, tedious, or tension-producing beyond reason, which are dedicated to products or services that are either totally unrelated to those elemental needs or embellished way beyond the character of the original products or services that meet those needs. So, for example, if a man wishes to purchase a simple house for his family and have the resources to pay for basic foodstuffs and simple clothing, he is not allowed to work at a job constructing simple houses or growing basic foodstuffs or making simple clothes. Instead, he must work in a factory that coats chipboard panels with a film of simulated oak or maple paneling material, or work in a plant that converts potatoes into the powdered instant variety, or work as a stock clerk in a warehouse filled with the latest in trendsetting surfwear. Don't get me wrong. I am not necessarily identifying with that economic man who would opt for "plain living," and I am not maligning modern conveniences and technology. But a realization of the disparity between the goals of our present workaday activity and those earlier more primitive needs is essential, I think, to intelligent analysis of our economic system and for fashioning suggestions for its improvement or for forestalling harmful developments. I will be addressing this issue more thoroughly in further diary entries.

WEDNESDAY/THURSDAY, APRIL 25/26, 1990 John Kenneth Galbraith's book *The New Industrial State* is now over twenty years old, but the essential thesis of that work might still be considered arguable today, namely, that the particular interest group in society which possesses knowledge of technology and plans for its change constitutes a new, fourth factor of production in addition to or even eclipsing the historically conventional land, labor, and capital. Whether or not one agrees with

Galbraith's thesis, one must admire a man who, by adhering to one simple assertion, is able to illuminate a wide landscape of economic thought and do it in a way that captivates public attention and turns a profit in the process.

Perhaps the subject on which I have so innocently embarked requires a whole book for thorough elucidation, by someone of far greater scholastic stature than myself. But if I can point out the way to someone else or simply outline here those topics that might ultimately fructify in an entire book for myself, then I have succeeded for the time being.

One of the points reiterated by Galbraith is that those men responsible for operating the economy are deeply involved in making sure that the net savings of society are offset by a matching amount of expenditures. What he is referring to, I think, is what I will call the flow of capital. One way to view that flow is to spotlight the individual worker. Let us assume that a man earns his living by working in a vast, automated bakery, where he tends a stainless steel vat into which he pours the appropriate quantities of flour, yeast, oils, and additives for baking loaves of store-bought bread. In connection with his job he might operate a mechanical kneader, arrange and haul palletsful of ingredients, and finally dump the blended dough onto the conveyor of a machine that will divide it into loaf-size portions for eventual allotment into baking pans. For his trouble he is paid $12 per hour. It is not unrealistic to assume further that by the end of the year this average worker's income will have been routed into various expenditures, including his mortgage payments, car payments, grocery bills, clothes purchases, so that nothing is left over for savings.

This common situation is probably not what Galbraith had in mind when enunciating his principle that the economy's savings must always equal its outlays to achieve optimum performance. However, in a very broad way, the expenditures of this average man can be divided into those that ultimately go to remunerate capital and those that are cycled back to compensate workers like himself who make his purchases possible. For example, his mortgage payment is filtered first through a facilitating network of financial institutions that, in siphoning off interest, not only thus reimburse capital, but take a portion as well to compensate those workers hired to execute and arrange those financial transactions. The principal of his payment, however, ultimately rewards the former owner of the land and structure, or the sellers of the raw materials exploited in the construction of a newer home (that is, rewards capital), or it pays the carpenters, plumbers, et al. who assembled and shaped those raw materials into a house. After many years, of course, a house can take on the character of capital alone, since the workers whose toil brought it into existence have long since been paid for their productive activity. Each material component that initially goes into the house can likewise be divided, again in a very broad way, into labor or capital. For example, the money that ultimately pays for the wood in the house does not just go to the owner of the land on which the trees were grown, but is diverted also to the multitude of workers, from lumberjacks to forklift operators, who caused those trees to be transformed into the structural units of a house. Thus, although it would be a complicated project, it is possible to divide a mortgage payment into those portions which at length reward either capital or workers.

There appear to be at least two basic economic phenomena, besides interest rates, that can change the ratio between payments made to capital and those applied to compensation of workers. Both of these have been occurring in America for many years, and they both tend to increase, at least temporarily, the flow of money to capital at the short-term expense of the worker. The first phenomenon occurs when scarcity drives up the price of a raw material like wood, for example, and the owner of that capital—whether it be the forest owner or the lumberyard owner—suddenly finds himself the recipient of a windfall due to the price increases. The second way that capital co-opts a larger share of the average worker's payments is through the increase to capital made possible by technological advances. Whenever the owner of capital discovers a way to increase his cash flow, whether through a reduction in expenses or an increase in revenue, he will proceed according to the rule that he maximize his return on investment. To determine, for example, whether the reduction in expenses made possible by a new machine is worth the investment to purchase that machine is a decision process in which all business school graduates are well versed. Essentially that process can be reduced to this question: Will the cash flowing to a certain available amount of capital be greater if that capital is used for the purchase of this machine than if it is used for another purpose? The history of technological advance has been a long series of such decisions which favored the purchase of machines at the expense, very frequently, of labor. The dismissal of a worker is justified because the increase in cash flow to the business due to wages no longer paid represents the highest return to the capital used to buy the machine that replaced him. Thus, when technology or some other efficiency measure eliminates a worker, the share of the average man's payments to capital as opposed to labor increases. However, as I indicated, this shift in the ratio is not necessarily permanent.

Returning now to the issue of how work performed by modern man has drifted in purpose or goal away from satisfying basic needs, it will be useful to invoke Galbraith's algorithm that the managers of the economy strive to ensure that net savings are always consumed by an equal amount of expenditure or investment. If the individual capitalist can be regarded as an exemplification, in one man, of that group of economic managers to whom Galbraith refers, then their motives become clear. When the individual owner of capital sees his reservoir increasing in the form of cash, he acts according to economic principles which demand that he maximize his return on all assets. Thus, cash lying fallow or in a low-yield bank account is like a hot potato which must quickly be transformed into some type of capital investment such as land or machinery that promises a higher rate of return. Now it would be easy at this point to simply state that net savings accruing to capital due to technological advances are employed by the managers of the economy in enterprises less connected to basic needs just because those less basic industries now offer a higher rate of return. But a more satisfactory explanation resides in a deeper scrutiny of that analysis which chooses the machine over the laborer.

From the point of view of the owner of capital, the analysis that results in that decision is in essence a commitment to reduce his total cash investment over time in a particular process that results in a given output and revenue. That analysis, learned so well by business graduates, compares the lump sum of cash necessary to buy and install a machine to those cash payments that would otherwise be made to a worker over the life of the machine; and, taking into account any interest revenue lost by tying up the cash immediately versus extending the payments over time in the form of wages, and including in the calculation any other relevant expenses such as machinery overhead or loan-interest costs, it shows which cash investment is greater over the life of the machine and chooses the one that is less. In this sense it is unfortunate that economists have promulgated the rather arbitrary distinction between labor and capital. Both require a cash investment over time. The machine requires that a block of cash be immediately relinquished, while the laborer requires that the cash investment be surrendered slowly over time, usually out of the very revenues he assists in producing. The capitalist who is economically astute will always choose the lesser cash investment over time, the one which, taking into consideration all interest revenue either lost or gained by either arrangement and any differential in expenses between the alternatives, will result for him in less cash devoted to a certain revenue-producing process.

For a blue-collar worker who is in continuous association with expensive machines that seem to dwarf the productive capability of a solitary man, the realization that these machines actually require less cash investment over time than the labor that would produce an identical quantity of goods can come as a revelation approaching religious proportions. When a man works with large, impersonal machines all day long and observes their power and efficiency at close range, he tends to invest that technology with an awesomeness to which it does not hold a valid claim. The machine becomes a juggernaut of sorts, concentrating the resources of the jowly capitalist into a miraculous combination of steel and electricity and coming to represent all the might and muscle of the financial elite. So it is a surprise to learn that the formidable machine is actually the focus of fewer financial resources than the laborers who would produce an equivalent output over time. From the proper perspective, technology falls under the dimming shadow of economic logic, and the capitalist who instigates it is reduced in prowess to a mere shuffler of cash, a man or a group of men who, in a very academic and even nervous fashion, allot only those resources to a productive activity that are sufficient for its accomplishment.

So, then, we are finally in a position to explain why people prefer to cut up lettuce in a factory rather than in their kitchens. As technology has progressed across a wide range of man's productive activities—a historical development that has coincided remarkably with the history of the United States as a nation—the capitalist finds himself in possession of a surplus of investment cash due to the savings wrought by technology. But in surveying the financial landscape, he discovers that the very process of innovation of which he is a prime mover is shrinking opportunities for investment in those endeavors which are basic to human survival. This is so because, as we have seen, the same process of technological progress that precipitates his savings also *reduces the total cash investment needed to bring about a certain output in any given industry.* Thus, agriculture, for example, requires less and less a share of the capitalist's expenditures because technology, following the implacable compulsions of the marketplace, reduces the cash investment necessary to produce a given level of harvest. In the area of housing, for another example, the capitalist sees that the technology which has made the logging of trees and the milling of lumber and its delivery to the homesite less labor-intensive has also reduced the amount of cash investment required to produce and deliver a given quantity of that lumber. If this were not so, then the initial decision to invest in that technology would not have been made.

Thus, the capitalist concludes quite accurately that the circle of his investments must be enlarged to include products or services that do not just meet basic human needs. Instead of devoting cash to growing wheat, then, he devises a new bakery product like flavored cupcakes injected with a surprise creme filling for nationwide distribution. Instead of investing his money in a sawmill, he builds a factory to construct a fancier lamp or other household furnishing. Instead of building a textile mill and producing socks, he starts a glossy fashion magazine to trumpet the personal advantages of ever more elegant hosiery and evening wear. Meanwhile, he hires workers to run these undertakings and so takes up that slack in employment caused by the penetration of technology into the more primitive industries. The man who gains his livelihood mixing up dough in the bread factory finally sees his multiplicity of monetary obligations to the outer world brought back to an earlier equilibrium between his payments to capital and worker, and the world settles into a tranquil economic routine. But wait. In a few months the bread factory worker's job has been eliminated! His function is now performed by a computerized system that measures ingredients into the vat from automated bins filled directly from large trucks! The bread factory worker is shifted to another sector of the company and now operates a delivery truck that distributes creme-filled cupcakes to convenience stores all around town! "Where will it all end?" he asks himself. "I don't know," I tell him, but in future diary entries I will address some further ramifications of the phenomenon called technological development.

FRIDAY APRIL 27, 1990   One of the problems John Kenneth Galbraith addresses in another of his famous books, *The Affluent Society*, now over thirty years old, is the gulf between the opulence afforded by private wealth in a well-off society and the degraded condition of public life due to a lack of corresponding improvement in government services. I have not read enough of Galbraith's recent works to know whether he regards the evolution of government since 1958 to have rendered his book in need of modification. It is surprising, though, that a popular economist has not thoroughly examined the very similar chasm between the degradation inherent in millions of jobs and the luxurious or frivolous nature of the products or services those jobs provide.

Working through a temporary labor agency does not offer an impartial vantage point from which to assess that chasm, I would judge, since the pay is so low. The misery one endures in hauling warm cattle hides, coated with blood and still dangling dried dung, from a mountainous, slippery heap to a conveyor leading into the tanning factory is mitigated greatly by a wage which allows the worker to buy one of the leather jackets that his labor helps produce. But if his work does not even afford him the purchasing power to buy a decent fabric coat to forfend the biting winter winds, then his position in society is demeaned. So a higher wage can bridge the chasm if the object of his work seems somewhat worthwhile to begin with. But will a higher wage serve the same function, in the long run, if a man deeply questions the worthiness of the ultimate aim of his labor? Does the convenience of driving to market rather than walking justify that a worker stand all day long at a machine punching rivets into a small fiberboard plaque that will be incorporated eventually into a battery charger? Does the great personal betterment furnished to the consumer by a television set justify submerging oneself each day into the desperate tedium of working on a line which manufactures the cardboard barrels that will someday be used to store a future television's electronic components?

These questions are important. They ought to determine the fate of people's lives. But they are irrelevant in another sense because people's lives are determined by an economic system that does not accommodate the questions to begin with. As the economy evolves into a supplier of goods and services increasingly removed from rudimentary human needs, the individual is carried along as if by a strong tidal stream into the great sea of driving production and relentless activity. His situation is a mirror image of the capitalist's. Because those industries that serve more primary human needs require a shrinking proportion of the workforce to effect a given output, he has no choice but to enter into areas that are either unrelated to those needs or that serve an embellished, transmuted version of those needs. And why is he coerced into that choice? Because, first and foremost, he strives to satisfy those more primary needs. It is a paradox of the modern economy, then, that a man desiring to feed, clothe, and shelter himself must throw himself with enthusiasm into tasks that are either foreign to or greatly distanced from those more immediate exigencies. So, in order to buy a house or rent a room, he works in a factory coating wires that are destined to become components in a car telephone. To buy basic food products, he works on a line in a plant where racks of ribs are trimmed, seasoned, cooked, and packaged for household consumption. To buy unpretentious apparel, he delivers flyers announcing a sale at a suburban jewelry shop.

MONDAY APRIL 30, 1990   The following paragraphs introduced a short article in today's *New York Times*:

> New York, April 29—Despite a recent drop in prices, the goal of home ownership in the New York metropolitan region is far more elusive today than it was 10 years ago.
>
> While average incomes increased by half in the 1980's, the average price of houses and apartments escalated at three times that rate. Economists say the growing gap between housing prices and incomes is among the most serious threats to the region's vitality.

Later, the article explained that rising housing costs are not so extreme in other regions of the country. However, as population continues to grow on a fixed amount of American land, certainly the situations in such places as New York and California will prefigure the general pattern nationwide. This is an example, then, of a larger portion of a worker's income flowing to capital, rather than labor, because of a scarcity-driven price rise. Especially problematical is a general rise in real estate prices, because it is so resistant to a reversal. A succession of house owners each takes an incremental profit, swelling the value of the house to a high plateau and exacting blood from the final buyer, who will not calmly submit to a sale price less than what *he* paid for it. This process is one that might benefit from scrutiny of the gap between meeting needs and the work done to meet those needs.

Certainly there is no more basic need than a house or an apartment to live in. But as land and the dwellings thereon become more expensive, and as payments made to banks or former owners increasingly take on the character of remuneration to capital—since the fixed amount of land will ultimately limit or curtail the building of new homes—the worker finds himself in a position in which he must apply great energy to producing totally unrelated goods or services. At the same time that technology excludes him from more traditional industries, a larger portion of his income must be transferred to landlords, banks, and former house owners, and his production in pursuit of the requisite cash becomes ever more frantic, desperate, and absurd. Like a tight spring spiraling upward into paroxysms of irrelevant activity, the workforce finds itself in a hectic chase after the creation of ever more sophisticated electronic gadgets, the provision of ever more exotic innovations in gourmet dining experiences, or the devising of ever more effective methods of persuading the public to prefer one brand of beer over the next. All of this, of course, so they will be able to justly reward the capital which found their house or apartment to be such a handsomely lucrative investment to start with.

FRIDAY MAY 3, 1990   On Tuesday and Wednesday of this week I worked at a job through the daily labor office that is representative of the kind of gratuitous work with which our economy seems to be increasingly involved. The factory is located in one of the fine suburban areas north of Minneapolis. On the days I worked there, temporary employees were shipped in by the busload to expand the regular workforce to over three hundred people. The vast one-story building is divided by conveyor belts stretching the length of the floor. Very slowly, the products move along the belts and gradually assume a completed form.

At the beginning of one of these lines, it was my job to first lay a pair of cardboard sheets on the belt. From a rack I then lifted a blue plastic frame, in the shape of a kind of rectangular truncated pyramid, and placed this wide end up on top of the cardboard. From a couple of stacks on a table nearby, I grasped two end panels and two side panels and rested them at slightly projecting angles inside the frame, where they would be attached by screws at a station down the line. The side panels were also dark blue. They were made of some light, composite material, but protruding from each one was the word "Lite" in translucent, white plastic letters. Also protruding from each side panel was a perfect replica in plastic of a set of billiard balls, with a cue stick below. Impressed on the end panels, made of composite material as well, was the image of a cue ball and some other beer-hall designs. At the end of the line, each of these rectangular truncated pyramids issued forth as a lamp, complete with neon bulb and hooks for attachment by chain to a ceiling, so that their illumination would not only furnish conspicuous incandescence to a beer label, but would light up a pool table as well.

In another part of the factory, a similar lamp was being constructed by the thousands, this one with a more elaborate mantle, however, of a model of a coach and a team of Clydesdales to provide an acute reminder of another famous liquid refreshment. The pride of the factory, though, was a two-foot-tall plastic replica of a dog wearing a turtleneck (spray-painted green in one of a series of booths) that, on the flick of a switch, would dispel any surrounding darkness while simultaneously radiating the comforting image of your favorite drinking mascot, that inveterate, chummy jack-o'-lantern of beers, Spuds himself.

Now this particular job was not so easy to classify on a scale of necessary to frivolous as it might seem. Introspection on this matter has forced me to concede, however reluctantly, that my own needs probably exceed those three basics of food, clothing, and shelter by about five or six. Brandy, scotch, whiskey, vodka, and gin certainly deserve a ranking position on my list, but beer could lay claim to only a tenuous standing when I started this job. However, as those days at the factory wore on, and one repetitive movement blurred into the next, and my head grew heavy with the oppression of the tedium and my heart swelled with ennui, I realized that beer, as a list member in good standing, was, unfortunately, dispensable. In fact, work at the factory made me ready to deny that I had ever enjoyed playing a game of pool. This was not the reason I declined going in for the third day of work, though. As I scratched my earlobe at one point late on the second day, I heard a worker down the line yell, "Yeah, they ain't gonna let him work here!" Doubtless he was referring to someone else, but I was perfectly content to allow the prohibition to be applied more generally.

As I look over previous diary entries, I realize that a reader might gain the impression that I am anticapitalist or an exponent of radical reform of some kind. I am not. To advocate the overthrow of capitalism because it is too efficient at meeting our needs would be as ludicrous as arguing to cut down the apple tree because it bears too much fruit. The problem with capitalism is that it works so well. Accordingly, its adherents are staunch in its defense and chary of analyses that purport to reveal weaknesses or fault lines in its structure. If nothing else, what I am trying to advocate is a view of capitalism as a flexible tool rather than a sacrosanct religion. I think that more government spending ought not to be a prime ingredient in that flexibility, however. The experience I've had in government jobs, the exposure I've had to government bureaucracy, and my natural inclination to favor the clean energy of the entrepreneur over the sluggish inertia of tax-financed institutions all push me to the conclusion that capitalism's flaws should be remedied by imagination and an openness to innovation rather than by more government monopolization of economic activity.

This does not mean that government by genuine consensus could not play a regulative role of some kind in bringing those innovations into existence. The ancient Greeks might provide a model of flexibility to guide people in their modern predicament. If a city-state in those long-gone noble days, for instance, decided by majority vote that property was unequally distributed, they would just redivide the whole jurisdiction as easily as you reshuffle the deck and deal out a new hand of cribbage. If they thought that a certain class of people was unjustifiably receiving a disproportionate share of the income, the democratic throng would vote down the elite, redesignate them as slaves, commandeer and reassign their salaries with as much nonchalance as you might show when distributing the cheese and crackers at a cocktail party. If the plebiscite were suddenly assailed by a marked contempt for those presently holding political power, they would demote that cadre of officeholders to common laborers and reappoint their substitutes from the agrarian class just as swiftly and as unthinkingly as you might change a light bulb or rearrange the shoes in your closet. Well, I might be exaggerating. But I do seem to remember that the Greeks were not averse to sweeping reforms every few centuries or so.

SUNDAY MAY 6, 1990   (Stillwater)—The leaves on the trees have unfolded in the last two weeks so that the high banks of the St. Croix River have flushed out into a blanket of soft spring foliage. Just a few weeks ago, the cold rains painted the trunks and the crooked twigs of the riverside architecture a shining black against the dull, earthy walls of the bluffs, suffusing the winding river valley with a melancholy and dismal aspect.

The Friday before last weekend, taking the bus out here to Stillwater, I was trying to revive from a week of economic inactivity and all of the difficulty that entails in suppressing, evading, and parrying those impulses and drives to do something worthwhile, which have proved so vexatious to the modern economy. I realized that contending with those latent ambitions was actually a very trying, stressful experience, so I decided that the pint of whiskey I had already purchased that evening would need to be augmented by a quart of something the following day. This was the Friday, recall, that I had just gotten a check for what turned out to be $60 from the daily labor office.

On Saturday, after doing my wash and buying an alarm clock in a shopping center a couple of miles east of the river, I reasoned that it would be prudent in an economic sense to purchase a bottle of brandy on special for $7 at the nearby liquor store. Rather than buy half-pints each night as the ensuing work week progressed it would be wise, I thought, to invest now in a whole quart and drink from it each day so as to reduce my total cash commitment to an equivalent amount of intoxication. Well, as that rainy weekend progressed, I could see that my capital was being consumed at an unexpectedly high rate. Taking a local bus from the town of Bayport along the river back into Stillwater, I concluded that some kind of accelerated depreciation method might have to be invoked to account for the bottle's swiftly decreasing contents. That night I escaped the rain by sleeping in an empty railroad car sidled on the tracks next to a marina on the river, and at the end of the next day, Sunday, my capital was totally depleted. My wallet's contents had undergone a similar depletion so that I had less than five dollars remaining as I bedded down for the cold, rainy night under the covered entryway to an insurance firm along the highway across from the shopping center. That Sunday I made some phone calls I'd rather not remember, and I did not make it to work on Monday as I had planned. So I guess the whole financial scheme would have to qualify as a bona fide fiasco.

Today is much more pleasant, with a fine dry breeze from the west dispelling any haze and the sky emanating an exceptional blue. I do not have enough money remaining this weekend to invest in capital of any kind, so I am blessed with a sense of health. I did buy a pint of whiskey last night which I will polish off in a moment, but this was a deserved reward, I thought, after working once again on the carrot line at the lettuce factory yesterday to get the ten-dollar draw for the day. I have discovered one facet at least of an ongoing relationship with a vegetable. Absence does not make the heart grow fonder. Until next time, adieu.

63

WEDNESDAY MAY 16, 1990   Last week I worked over fifty hours at the lettuce factory. A check for around $100 will be mine this Friday. I worked Monday and Tuesday of this week as well, but I took today off. Yesterday afternoon, as I peeled lettuce at a breakneck pace, I began to fancy that I was about to merge into a socially acceptable routine and climb to success at long last. I resolved to quit drinking and so groom myself for eventual arrival into a respectable state of affluence.

Almost immediately, in a reaction as yet unexplained by medical science, my limbs went limp, and my torso slumped with weakness. My knees started to shake and buckle as I slowly crumpled toward the floor. Then, as my chest whirled with palpitations, I began to itch at an astonishing rate on a great many areas of my body. No smooth arch, hairy expanse, dark crevice, moist depression, sensitive orifice, airy passageway, handsome feature, or muscled appendage seemed immune to the onslaught. Hemorrhoids became inflamed, joints flared with pain, and a disorienting vertigo overtook me as I slumped to the floor. Realizing, however, that I would rather die than go back to a dog's life of drunkenness, I got up and decided then and there to remove myself from what the Catholic Church used to call a "near occasion of sin." I finished out the last hour of the day and then informed the manager of my leaving the job, at least for the next day or two, while "I helped my brother's friend paint the interior of his house." The "interior" component of the lie was necessary because it's been raining here for the last week and a half, mostly. (I've been sleeping under picnic shelters in a couple of different parks around Minneapolis-St. Paul.) My real intention, though, was to come out here to Stillwater and starve to death on the picturesque banks of the St. Croix River. I have made this resolution a number of times in the last ten or twelve years and actually carried it out to the extent of nine days of starvation at one point in 1986 in Borrego Springs, California. This time I started the interval of denial at about 2 A.M. after consuming the remainder of a half-gallon of chocolate ice cream in an interlude of wakefulness in the dry boxcar next to the marina where I spent the night. The abstention lasted about eight hours this time, as I have just completed a nice breakfast with coffee here in the second-story lunchroom of Brine's meat market in downtown Stillwater. I guess if I'm really going to quit drinking, I'll just have to pretend that I'm actually planning to get sauced each evening and so possibly contravene this strange psychological reaction to good intentions.

THURSDAY MAY 17, 1990   *The New Yorker* magazine dated May 14, 1990, contains a very interesting article by Catherine Caufield, which addresses the emerging national controversy over the harvesting of so-called old growth timber in the country's national forests. In one part of the article the author relays some figures which incidentally support the argument that technology effects a dual change in the structure of the economy:

Oregon's Department of Employment has reported that between 1977 and 1987 the state lost more than twelve thousand jobs in logging and wood processing, and that its timber industry now provides only about five percent of Oregon's jobs. . . . The reason for the job losses is not a shortage of timber from national forests; in fact, figures from Oregon's Departments of Employment and Forestry show that the amount of timber taken from the state's national forests has increased as jobs have disappeared. Oregon's fifteen-percent drop in logging and processing jobs accompanied a sixteen-percent increase in wood taken from the national forests. The main reason for the job decline is growing automation of the timber industry. In 1977, for example, it took 10.12 workers to process a million board feet of wood. Ten years later, only 8.2 workers were required to handle that amount—a rise of almost twenty percent in worker productivity.

Later, when discussing a similar situation in British Columbia, Caufield writes, "Formerly prosperous mill towns in the province, such as Nanaimo and Chemainus, have turned to other sources of revenue, from sponsoring International Hell's Angels conventions and bathtub races to covering the town's walls with murals of the glory days of logging. The layoffs have come at the same time that timber companies have been making record profits." Thus, she happens to have furnished an excellent example to support my earlier argument, namely, that technology not only causes savings to accrue to the owners of basic-needs industries and so encourages investment in unrelated areas, but also reduces the requisite employment in that basic industry, compelling former workers to engage in a similar pursuit of nonessential income-generating activities.

FRIDAY MAY 18, 1990   A front-page article in today's *Wall Street Journal* tells of the recent difficulties confronted by the Monsanto Corporation in introducing a new product called Bovine Growth Hormone: "A protein like one cows produce naturally, BGH is made by genetically engineered bacteria and then injected twice a month (into dairy cows). In farm trials, milk yields have shot up by 10% to 25%." Although "FDA officials say milk from BGH-treated cows is safe," opposition to the product has prompted temporary bans on its marketing introduction in both Minnesota and Wisconsin. The article provides only a sketchy portrayal of the anti-BGH group's motives, but they appear to be a combination of health concerns or distress over such a nonorganic method of farming and worries that a milk glut will further ravage the rural economy. I don't know if I would join or not in objecting to the hormone's use, but in my opinion the anti-BGH group's use of the economic argument is as foolish and fatuous as the French citizens' violent opposition to the introduction of Jacquard's first mechanical loom.

A cogent argument against the hormone might be obtained by reasoning out the natural human resistance to such a blatant manipulation of biology solely to serve the purposes of our species, but to argue against it because it makes the production of milk more efficient is as obtuse as refusing to feed the cow because it results in the production of milk in the first place. What these protesting groups should focus on, at least when addressing the economic aspect of the issue, is the more essential question of how mankind ought to use the capital and manpower made available when technology like BGH suddenly reduces the necessary commitment of those two factors of production to the satisfying of basic needs like milk. Unfortunately, this economic function has been relegated by default to the managers of the economy like the ones who run Monsanto. In their great wisdom they have developed, almost concurrently apparently, another product which will promote an increase in dairy product consumption and so take up some of that extra capital and labor released in the industry by the introduction of the hormone. Their new product is a substitute fat composed of milk and egg-white protein, which will be used to make a less fattening form of ice cream. Thus, Monsanto's marketing maneuvers this decade will reflect both the savings dimension of technological progress in basic industries and the application of those savings to less essential, more frivolous economic activities.

In my personal life I confront a predicament of less epic scope. I have not been back to work since Tuesday because a simple resolution to clean up my life, while engaged in the hectic pursuit of immense volumes of shredded lettuce, has brought on the most peculiar sensations of discomfort and debility. Plus, whenever I think of the refrigerated lettuce factory, I experience a hint of nausea. My music languishes in the dusty cubbyholes of memory, perhaps never to see the light of day; my earlier writings reside nowhere at all since I obliterated them in the blaze; and I am getting nowhere. I am sorely tempted, once I get my check today, to use part of it for a spree. But then, of course, I will just be hoeing the furrow of my destruction a little bit deeper and fastening myself more tightly to the cycle of ruin and despair. Yesterday I was apprehended by a St. Paul police-man in one of the downtown malls here and luckily he forbore from arresting me for drinking a pint of brandy in public. This did not stop him from depositing the remainder of the elixir into the nearest lavatory sink, however, an action I witnessed with the greatest of anguish and mental distress. The regret was that much more acute because the liquid disposed of had re-cently appropriated four and a half of my remaining six dollars. Oh, what cruelty will not be perpetrated in the name of the law!

Today, after getting my check, I will go down to the mission and take a free shower, an amenity available there each day after 4 P.M., but one which increasingly makes me want to heave as I wade through the oppressive corridor and then into the shower chamber, where old soap, rotten apple cores, and ciga-rette butts strewn on the floor greet the prospective bather with such a welcome invitation to hygiene and aquatic relaxation. Well, at least over the weekend I will have time to formulate a plan of some sort. I hope, like my prior withdrawal from sleep- ing at the mission, this plan will include an alternative—this time to employment through the daily labor agency. At this juncture grand theft looks pretty appealing.

SUNDAY MAY 20, 1990   This morning I was rousted from my refuge in the dry boxcar along the river by a Stillwater po-liceman, escorted in his car up the bluff to a bus stop along the highway, and told to have a nice trip back to St. Paul. I have left about seventy-five dollars of my hundred-and-six-dollar check.

About a year ago I had an agonizing experience in Stillwater. This was in the period between my return from Tucson by thumb and the burning of my papers. I was inebriated when I called up a cousin from a pay phone on a major corner by the bus stop in downtown. Almost immediately, as I slobbered some drunken nonsense into the receiver, a tall young man with shaggy, light-colored hair and wearing only a pair of shorts approached and hovered over me. As I continued the "conversation," he began to grumble about waiting too long to use the phone. When I turned to offer a retort, he swung a fist to my left jaw. I was so stunned I let the receiver dangle and watched momentarily as he stalked away toward a speedboat waiting at the edge of the river. When I began to follow, two young men passing by told me not to worry because they had notified the police. As I hesitated, a dark blue patrol car pulled up, and an officer accosted me with questions. What happened? Did I want to press charges? I said no. I knew there was a warrant out for my arrest in Minneapolis, due to my failure to show up in court the previous winter for the disorderly conduct charge stemming from my attempted entrance into a strip bar in the downtown section of the city. Of course, I did not want to alert the authorities to my wanted status. Unfortunately, the cop got out of his car and asked for ID. Discovering the Minneapolis warrant through the computers, he asked me to get into the squad car. He brought me to the jail in Stillwater, and later I was transferred to the Hennepin County Detention Center, where I spent a long weekend until released by a judge on my own recognizance. While I was there, a nurse looked at my very painful jaw and pronounced it a simple injury to the mandibular pad, which might be looked at by a doctor after my release. I did not have enough money for a doctor after my release, so I let the pad heal on its own. To this day, however, my jawbone is displaced sufficiently to the right so as to prevent a proper opening and closing of my mouth. The bones on the right side somehow obstruct one another and snap if the teeth are parted in a normal fashion. I now wish I had remembered the license number of that speedboat and pressed charges against that low scoundrel who saw fit to anoint himself overseer of the public telephone in downtown Stillwater on that beautiful spring day in '89.

MONDAY MAY 21, 1990   We are at a curious phase in economic history. At the same time that swelling population on a static amount of land is squeezing the fixed stock of humanity's natural resources, society is awash in a plethora of novel consumer goods that would have been marveled at only a century ago. At the same time that basic resources like arable land, minable ores, harvestable timber, and extractable fuels experience price increases due to the pressure of surging demand, the world's citizens are subject to daily assaults of solicitation for the most luxurious or trivial of products. As each person's share of the earth's natural bounty decreases, his personal stock of convenience items, toys, and gadgets accretes by the minute, by the day, and by the year into huge mountains of junk whose disposal is problematical.

The reason for the incongruity can be discovered in the same modern conundrum already analyzed. In order to provide for their most basic needs, individuals, families, and even whole nations must cater to desires alien to those needs, because those industries serving those needs command only a small percentage of the capital and labor available for the production necessary to satisfy those needs. Thus, although the resources required to feed, clothe, and shelter the world's population are being depleted at relatively swift rates, the populace finds itself in a frantic race to produce record quantities of sunglasses, surfboards, and sailboats; to sell unheard-of quantities of perfume, designer watches, and monogrammed luggage; or to promote a staggering number of purchases of diet plans, nouveau cookbooks, and exercise programs on the VCR.

I consider myself an objective examiner of this phenomenon in the sense that if I had the money I would be as inextricably involved in the crazed pursuit of these goods as anyone else. It is only my disenfranchised status at the moment that has given me variance, so to speak, to utter what many might suspect or fear to be true: that the eventual demise of society as we know it will be masked by the pervasive shine and intonation of television sets; by the ubiquitous charm of new briefcases, stylish business attire, colorful running shoes, and twinkling jewelry; and by the ease with which a frozen box is transformed into a steaming four-item meal.

One of the features of capitalism that exacerbates this modern problem is the two-dimensional nature of capital. If I adhere to a simple definition of capital as wealth used to produce more wealth, then capital can be divided between that which is created by man and that which is God-given or provided by nature. In this scheme, a machine that extrudes plastic would be capital created by man, but the iron ore from which it is derived would be capital supplied by nature. In a modern capitalistic economy like that of the United States, there is usually no distinction made between the two types. A man with money might just as easily purchase a factory as a forest, or a mine as a foundry, and use either one or the other in pairs to produce more wealth. However, when society finds itself in a shortage mode, when leaps in population put great demands on natural resources and a corresponding upward pressure on their market price, it becomes appropriate to examine the validity of private ownership of God-given or nature-provided resources.

One need look no further than to a country like Japan to discover how a deficiency in locally owned natural resources impels the population to a very energetic pursuit of products unrelated to basic human needs. In order to get wood for their dwellings and furnishings and rice for their tables, the Japanese invest extraordinary efforts in the manufacture of cars, electronic devices, and other recreation-oriented products. As a nation they are not unlike the individual worker in the United States who, lacking ownership of any of nature's capital resources, must proceed along in ardent compliance with the strong current of contemporary economic values. And, of course, for a nation like Japan, it is fortunate that those values are underpinned by the powerful marketing strategies of the industrial persuaders and by modern man's high receptivity to diversion through the purchase of more goods. For if Japan could not sell its cars and its radios, it would not be able to buy the food necessary to supplement its own insufficient harvests, purchase the wood needed to make up for its own lack of forestland, or obtain the petrochemicals that comprise a chief element in its population's clothing.

Now for Japan to engage in a very successful scramble after the creation of an awesome excrescence of stereos, VCRs, and copiers in submission to the whims of a worldwide marketplace which denies that nation sovereignty over the natural resources in other lands is not an economic configuration against which I can lodge any objection. However, Japan's individual counterpart in America is someone with whom I might sympathize greatly. And in order to better appreciate that individual American's plight, it might be useful to further contemplate and analyze the nature of capital.

In the beginning, capital was likely nothing more than

knowledge possessed by one person of an easier method to gain an elemental subsistence from the earth. If one member of a primitive society struck upon a way to make a digging tool by melting down ore into metal and recasting the molten material into the shape of a spade, he probably could use his knowledge to exact payment of some kind from those to whom he furnished its use. That the person conceived of the innovation at all might prompt the tribe to confer honor upon him or allocate to him an extra share of the available stock of goods. Discovery is always a wondrous process, and those excluded from its unfolding tend to endow its progenitor with mystery. Newton, after becoming famous for invention of the calculus and other scientific feats, was widely admired. Yet, when asked how he came upon his intellectual achievements, he answered simply that they were the result of much long and patient thought. Can we really assume that a similar application of mind to matter was the source of man's earliest discoveries?

Tuesday May 22, 1990   Whether or not early man gained his knowledge by dint of his own cerebral exertions is an aspect of history that will likely be forever lost. Is it possible to assert that man's capital in the form of knowledge was God-given or the result of natural impulses that lie outside the province of individual proprietary interest? Today, for example, any discussion of whether certain capital is man-made or supplied by nature would necessarily include consideration of the status of talent. Why should a person imbued with capital in the form of talent be accorded a higher flow of income if his gift is just that—a God-given ability? Naysayers would scorn this idea no doubt on the basis that any attempt to divide a person's abilities into given and earned in order to determine his income would result in a bureaucratic calamity. I don't think that is necessarily the case. People's basic honesty in matters like these would surely prompt them to a candid assessment of their own abilities. I, for example, if ever the lucky recipient of a record contract or other revenues arising from my songwriting, would not hesitate to declare that my abilities are the result of no talent whatsoever. Other people, like Edison, for example, might honestly declare that as much as one percent of their inventive output was due to something other than hard work. So the appraisal of naturally furnished talent should be no obstacle to a fairer way of dividing up revenues accruing to one's intrinsic personal capital.*

When capital emerges into the light of day and takes on the shape of buildings, lands, machinery, minerals, animals, and plants, then the division between God-given and man-made becomes less clear. However, there are some obvious, unambiguous examples of capital disbursed exclusively by Providence. Trees, precious ores, wild animals, fertile soil, oil, coal, natural gas, beneficial or edible wild plants, land itself as a space for a residence or the raising of crops, sunlight, oxygen, and gravity might all fall into this category. Is it appropriate that these kinds of capital goods be expropriated by individuals for their own aggrandizement? A reasonable solution is not so easily discovered.

What must be first recognized, I believe, is that long-term private ownership of land or other natural resources is a state for which man has a high affinity and which has the potential for the most sublime of returns. What could be more rewarding than the sense of dominion over a parcel of creation or the sense of being incorporated into the process by which soil, sunlight, and seeds interact to bring forth the sustenance of man or beast? Furthermore, permanent ownership of resources fosters an attitude of concern for their long-term productivity. In the enlightened individual a love of the land or of other natural creation will guide him to act as a steward of its riches and to preserve or enhance its beauty as well.

The owner of a resource will study and guard it in an impassioned manner that no governmental overseer or distant shareholder can equal. If he owns a piece of rolling open prairie in certain parts of Montana, he will not "bust the sod" for cropland because he knows that the native grasses, well regarded by cattle, will never rebound to their former erosion-preventing profusion. If he had owned an island in the Mediterranean in the days of the ancient Greeks, he might have stopped the sea traders from stripping his domain of timber because he would know that trees would never grow there again right up to the present day. If his ownership of the land where he resides is rigidly guaranteed by society and if any increase in the proper-

*This is facetious, of course. Also it ignores the reality that one's field of talent must be cultivated by very hard work and at times by long and patient suffering. Only money, in my opinion, is an incentive sufficient to carry one through those trials.

ty's value inures to him, then he will be that much more inclined to effect improvements that contribute to the beautification of the entire neighborhood.

In the early days of the United States, it was inconceivable that any arrangement other than private ownership of natural resources could elicit the ambition necessary to build a prosperous country. Adding to that faith in private ownership was a closer similarity then of the economy to a true free market. One of the required components of authentic free enterprise is that the market consist of a great many buyers and a great many sellers. And so it was, then, even in the case of the sellers of natural resources. When the population was small relative to the vast trove of resources in the far-flung lands beyond the homestead, then the proprietor of a mine, a forest, or a plantation was in direct competition with the bounty of nature just beyond the horizon. If a man didn't like the price charged for timber or coal by Mr. Jones, he had the alternative of moving down the road a piece and extracting those resources on his own. Thus, the price of those goods was likely kept very close to the actual costs incurred by the vendor in wrenching them from nature's embrace and preparing them for market.

Today, on the other hand, the number of sellers of natural resources is dwarfed by the number of buyers. There are at least two reasons for this. First, obviously, is the fixed amount of land that is forced to host an ever-growing population. Second, technology drives the smaller proprietors out of business. When a technology is first introduced into an extractive industry, its owner enjoys a certain number of years of savings due to his reduction in labor costs. However, after a period of time—perhaps the life of a patent or until news of the innovation spreads through the industry—his savings begin to shrink as competitors begin lowering their prices in accordance with their new, reduced costs due to the innovation. This process drives out the smaller competitors because many are not able to afford the initial capital investment to procure the machine in the first place. Also, it is possible that certain technologies are only suited to large-scale applications and so their cost-cutting benefits are not available to the small proprietor. Thus, after many years of technological advancement, the sellers of natural resources, the owners of farmland, and other proprietors of nature's bounty are thinned out to a relatively small number.

Therefore, technology acts not only to reduce the total of capital and labor committed to basic extractive industries, but, over time, to reduce the number of business entities engaged in effecting a given output in those industries and so takes that sector of the economy out of a free-market configuration altogether.

WEDNESDAY MAY 23, 1990   A thought for the day: I look upon a woman as an object only in the sense that she is a vessel of desire waiting to be tapped.

Advanced economics, continued: An industry does not necessarily become less competitive just because the advent of technology sifts out the great majority of concerns. The very process by which that winnowing occurs would seem to belie any assertion of oligopolistic price inflation. So even though the market in that industry no longer conforms to a strict free-market definition, the dimension of competition can still exist. Generally, society does not recognize that technical innovation is the driving force behind the contraction of an industry; they tend to regard the ascendancy of the large producer to the detriment of the small as some kind of unfair exclusion of the helpless and weak by the big and brutish. Nowhere is this perception so commonplace as in the public's attitude toward the ongoing disappearance of the so-called small family farm.

An article by James Bovard on the editorial pages of yesterday's *Wall Street Journal* blasts current federal farm policy as "Welfare for Millionaire Farmers."* He writes that the government "has a choice between subsidizing rich farmers or inefficient farmers," and he argues for the abolition of farm aid programs altogether. He says that statistics which "state that the total number of farmers shrank from 2,440,000 in 1980 to 2,197,000 in 1988" are an illusion based on the diminishing numbers of part-time, noncommercial farmers. He writes that full-time farmers (with sales over $100,000 per year) actually increased in numbers, from 271,000 in 1980 to 323,000 in 1988. These statistics make clear that technology favors the larger farms over the small; and technology is not unkind to those who accommodate its suitability to large-scale enterprise: "the average full-time farmer in 1988 (a drought year) reaped

*This is the title of the article.

an income of $168,000. . . . [he] is a millionaire, worth, after deducting debt, $1,016,000 as of Dec. 31, 1988."

For the public to resist the evolution of farming into an industry with fewer numbers of larger-scale enterprises ignores the fiat of technology. In fact, when looked at from a correct perspective, that antagonism assumes the character of ignorance. If mankind can produce his food with a lesser commitment of capital and labor, why should he not do it? Perhaps what fuels the hostility is not so much opposition to efficiency as a resentment of the loss of control represented by the ceding of the most basic of human productive activities to a relative handful of worker-owners. For if a shakeout of an industry does not result in oligopoly-like pricing, it unarguably results in oligopoly-like manipulation and control. When land and the function of growing food is surrendered to such a small percentage of a population, then the remaining workers are no different from a nation like Japan, which must rely on foreign countries to feed it. Like their Oriental counterpart, American workers are hostage to circumstance and must engage in a spectrum of unrelated production in order to put food on their tables. So the proponents of saving the family farm seem to have missed the point. The issue should not be big farm versus small farm, but worthwhile activity versus stultified activity. Should displaced farmers be coerced by the economy into manufacturing video games and selling baseball hats, or should their lives be devoted to worthier pursuits?

I am going to wrap up this whole economics section of the diary by stating that I do not have an answer to the problem on which I have spouted so profusely. To some it would seem that I am analyzing no problem at all since they consider the fruit of modern work to be an optimum mix of necessity, luxury, and the mere diversionary. I am not even sure that I would not agree with them. So perhaps my prolixity on the subject should be deemed only a shout from the wilderness—not nature's wilderness but the one created by man, where people endure long sunless days in drudgery in the bowels of factories, plants, and warehouses, only to bring forth in many cases a product or service of the most questionable benefit to themselves and their fellowman. As I look across the main floor of Hill Reference Library in downtown St. Paul, through the tall window on the opposite wall, I think I detect a glint of sunlight on the trees in the park across the street. I think I'll go have a drink over there now and soak up a little of God's free capital.

SUNDAY JULY 1, 1990   In the last two weeks I have been the happy recipient of around $600 in insurance money stemming from my father's death. I have been paying my brother $75 a week to live in his house and working sporadically at different jobs through temporary agencies. My monetary assets are down now to approximately $350. This morning I told my brother I did not feel right about the occasional bouts of intoxication I have indulged in while staying at his house and that I intended to leave after one more week. This might sound like a strange or gratuitous motivation for exchanging the comfortable embrace of a clean room in a very nice house for a less secure domiciling within the black walls of a mosquito-infested night. However, I cannot imagine a more burdensome feeling than that which comes from the knowledge that you are a drunkard in the province of the sober and the diligent. Waking up with a hangover in his house, tormented by the memory of an impertinent remark I might have emitted the previous night in the company of some upright family visitors, is enough to make my self-image sink to the floor. I become a dog, mean and humiliated, or a viper winding along on my belly through my carpeted domain. Of course, this kind of self-punishment ought to stop, and the only escape from my degraded state appears to lie in living outdoors and drinking only when outside of the relatively pristine moral atmosphere of my brother's house. His tolerance of my habits is amazing; he has not so much as uttered a solitary word in reproach. However, sometimes I cannot help but feel like the lowest beast alive when in his presence, so I will go.

SATURDAY JULY 7, 1990   I have borrowed enough money to rent an efficiency apartment and, finally, after six months' delay, to hire a musician to accompany a trio of my songs for the purpose of making a demo. On Tuesday I hope to hear one of my songs with accompaniment for the first time. Tomorrow I will move into the one-room apartment. It's in a large house in an old neighborhood of St. Paul where the aged yet stately homes of the long-established wealthy meet what was once crumbling decay of a small ghetto-like enclave of blacks and the poor. In one of my burned manuscripts I satirized the spreading enlargement of this particular deteriorating area and its slow penetration into the more sumptuous neighborhoods by depicting it as a war of sorts between the minority and the majority. If, by some miracle, those writings were restored to their preburnt condition, those particular passages would likely be considered inflammatory nevertheless.

I have to admit that my attitude with respect to black people was kindled in the sparks of a more heated, volatile era. Fifteen years ago, tension between blacks and whites, at least in this town, seemed higher than today. I remember walking down the aisle of a bus about that time and accidentally brushing against the foot of a young, lanky black who immediately scowled an angry rebuke. I shouted back a provocative rejoinder, and the simple unintended nudge just about erupted into physical violence. Another time during that period I was driving a school bus in Minneapolis on a route that took grade-school children from an integrated school in a well-to-do neighborhood back to their home in the "projects." One of the black kids was so hostile to my presence—throwing spitballs, calling me names, inciting the other kids to unruliness, and challenging me to actually use physical violence in order to subdue him—that I quit that route altogether and started looking for another job. Today, blacks seem more calm here. Their children are well dressed and even friendly, and everyone seems to have settled down to the difficult business of coexistence.

My own flare-ups of prejudice have softened, not, perhaps, because I have discovered any new affection for minorities, but because my hostility toward others has expanded outward to embrace the whole of human society. I am in the peculiar position of holding a prejudice against my own race. Largely this is due to my lack of certain spiritual accoutrements that evidently inhere in all humans but me. My position might be above all others if their common invisible bond is construed to be an undesirable glue of some kind against which they are constantly straining in futile attempts at self-extrication. Or I might be deemed below the great throng of spiritually endowed people if their absorption into that hidden life is regarded as an existence in which they dwell forever on a high plateau with the Deity. Either way, it is unarguable that in a psychic sense I reside outside of the vast contingent of contemporary humanity. And yes, it does get difficult at times holding racist sentiments against your own kind of people, kin included. It is a lonely experience to know that your bigotry extends to your parents, cousins, and ancestors back to time immemorial. It is one of the reasons I drank almost a fifth of brandy last night in disregard of my own more cautionary instincts. Perhaps I am just a lush and the salvation of sobriety will not be visited upon me even when I find those people against whom I can hold no prejudiced attitudes. But the isolation of regarding all races, including your own, as inferior to yourself certainly does not contribute to a morally outstanding life. Of course, the solitude of deeming everyone else superior to yourself can prod one into debauchery as well. If you mix these two attitudes with an ample portion of confusion as to which one ought to be adopted, then your corruption is a foregone conclusion. So . . . I better go have a drink now to confirm my reasoning, stabilize my viewpoints, and embolden the more precarious of my opinions.

SUNDAY JULY 8, 1990   I am a sad man, yet I have never experimented with cocaine. I am a man to whom ennui comes as naturally as play to a child, yet I have never dropped LSD. I am oftentimes overcome by a deep yearning for a happier state of life, yet I have never shot up heroin or indulged in the gratuitous intake of tranquilizers or speed. However, I did take marijuana at an earlier stage of my life, and I took enough of it then to qualify me to declare that it is an unfortunate addition to society's recreational resources. It dulls the mind, it accentuates any latent effeminacy, it makes one lazier than he normally would be, and it stays in the body for days and weeks after its consumption.

I am provoked to record this opinion now because yesterday I listened to a portion of a radio show presided over by William F. Buckley Jr. He was interviewing an expert on the issue of legalizing drugs. One of the expert's claims was that the existence of bars in Amsterdam where marijuana is freely available (although officially illegal) has not contributed to a higher incidence of marijuana use in the larger population. There used to be a beer tavern here in St. Paul where marijuana could be smoked or purchased without fear of legal reprisal. I am glad that it is now closed down. To provide easy access to a substance that can so radically alter a person's basic outlook and change him as an individual is not prudent for the simple reason that the person who is on the edge of succumbing to temptation will find it that much easier to take the fall. I know, because I was that person for a number of years.

If marijuana had not been easily available through that saloon or through acquaintances, I would not have expended the effort to obtain it through other less convenient sources. Marijuana is a deceptive lady. She invites you to explore her puzzle. She beckons with the promise of unraveling her mystery. But you never do. The only thing you learn is that she is harmful, and you pay her the price for that knowledge by experiencing the harm yourself in the form of lost strength and an increased propensity for self-indulgence.

SATURDAY JULY 14, 1990   This is Jacques Therapy anchoring our roving camera. As you can see on your sets, our mobile camera is now nudging open the door of a small apartment in a large house on Ashland Avenue in St. Paul, Minnesota, and zeroing in on the chef in residence. In a corner of the room, we see . . . can it be? Yes, without a doubt, our camera has fixed its sights on the incomparable Chef Donohue! He appears oblivious to our presence as he bustles about his small kitchen pouring ingredients, measuring spices, and stirring his dishes with grave concern and commitment. Our camera rises in a slow arc and peers into a pot of thick, gently bubbling white sauce. What kind of palate-delighting concoction has Chef Donohue come up with now? Oh no! Yes . . . well . . . yes. Okay, there it is now. Ladies and gentlemen, the inquisitive eye of our roving camera has finally settled on a fuzzy object on the nearby counter and is swiftly closing in on its target. Oh yes! Oui, oui, ladies and gentlemen! Chef Donohue has chosen to take his sauce from a can this evening, and yes—oh there it is, yes—oh magnifique, ladies and gentlemen! Chef Donohue has chosen a can of soup à la Campbell's for his white sauce! In fact, yes, he has chosen the unparalleled clam chowder à la Campbell's! But wait—our roving camera has abruptly transferred itself to stovetop and is now peering directly down into a large saucepan of boiling pasta. Could Chef Donohue have a surprise up his sleeve? Quickly shifting to focus in on a box at countertop, our camera reveals the chef's extremely gratifying choice—a box of macaroni à la Creamette! Oh! Chef Donohue has outdone himself this evening!

Later we interviewed Chef Donohue as he sat down to enjoy his dinner. Propping the plate in one hand, Chef Donohue lowered his steaming white concoction to camera-eye view and explained to us that he was now about to savor one of the best fettucine Alfredos anyone could ever hope to taste.

"But . . . but Chef Donohue," I inquired through the speaker incorporated into our roving camera, "do you mean to tell us that you can put together a sophisticated dish like fettucine Alfredo with just two simple ingredients?"

"Oh certainly," replied Chef Donohue between colossal spoonfuls of sauce and dangling noodles. "You see," he continued, turning toward camera and licking some remnant of chowder from his beard, "I have a philosophy about food, especially Italian, which says that in modern days we've complicated what was originally a very simple process. Italians, you see, started out dressing their pasta very simply. Perhaps just some olive oil and a quartered tomato and its juices would be enough to really add some vitality to a plateful of noodles."

"Ah, very well said, Chef Donohue! And now of course you are applying your philosophy to fettucine Alfredo!"

"Exactly," said Chef Donohue. "You see," he continued after abruptly rising, going to the kitchen, and returning with an empty can and box in hand, "these two simple ingredients, clam chowder à la Campbell's and macaroni à la Creamette, are all that a modern chef really needs to return to the wholesome simplicity of original Italian cooking!" As Chef Donohue displayed the two empty containers to our audience, I could not help but be overcome by admiration.

"Ah magnifique, Chef Donohue! Perhaps next time you will share with us some secrets of the simple and original cooking of the Chinese?"

"Oh, of course," said Chef Donohue, as he rushed back into the kitchen. Unfortunately, our roving camera dissolved the scene and started heading down the hallway of the apartment before Chef Donohue could reappear. But as our camera emerged into the light of a summer evening and raced down the street, I could hear Chef Donohue's clamoring voice in the distance. "Rice à la Uncle Ben's," he was shouting, and "chow mein à la Chun King!"*

SUNDAY JULY 15, 1990   Two thoughts for the day:

Alcohol does not make the world a less painful place, at least in Minnesota.

God made food, and he made hunger, so that men and women would have at least one schedule upon which they could agree.

MONDAY JULY 16, 1990   I am through with the diary. For its stated purpose of reducing my intake of liquor, it has proven the most ineffectual tool imaginable. In fact, if I had known from the start that I would have to drink as much as I have just to keep a diary, I never would have tackled the project in the first place.

*I had forgotten, when I wrote this entry, that tomatoes are native to the New World.

Part Two

Saturday July 21, 1990   I have decided to take up the scribe's habit once again. Abstaining from writing the diary does not seem to make sobriety easier. In fact, I have reached a point where resolutions are becoming less effective. A couple of years ago, if I wanted to quit drinking for a couple of days, I would have to take a personal vow to not touch a drop of liquor for a month. Now, in order to stop for twenty-four hours, I have to commit myself under oath to a lifetime of sobriety.

Loneliness is one spur to excess, although it is not necessarily the factor that tips the balance. It is, however, part of an insidious cycle. The heavy drinker alienates friends and relatives by his intrusive and overbearing conduct when inebriated. This is the most harmful effect of the poison we call alcohol. Each bottle ought to have a warning label stating that "contents can cause extreme social isolation by inducing repulsive behavior and so disaffect those people whose regard is most sought after and desired. This effect can be permanent and is more damaging than any health impairment this product might cause, including death. You only get one chance to cultivate social relations with any one group of acquaintances, friends, or kin. Are you sure you want to risk the permanent rejection of those people by flirting with the abuse that consuming this product might entail?"

The cycle is completed, then, when the initial social quarantine coalesces into a permanent ostracism. I have reached this point, I believe, perhaps out of a subconscious desire, in my peculiar case, to effect just that result. Perhaps without consciously adverting to it, I have utilized alcohol to adopt an offensive posture with respect to the world at large. It comes as a shock, nevertheless, to discover just how successful that strategy has been. When I moved into this rented housekeeping room, I gave the hall phone number only to my brother and requested that he furnish it to others only on an emergency basis. I guess I was thinking that in this way I could preempt the deluge of calls that my emergence into a conventional housing arrangement would somehow elicit in the general public. Of course, there was no need to keep my number a secret. My brother has not called me once in the last two weeks, and I strongly suspect that my message board at his residence is blank. So drinking precipitates social isolation, which causes loneliness, which promotes more and heavier drinking, and the cycle continues like a vortex pulling one down through the toilet bowl of life.*

MONDAY JULY 23, 1990   Today was my first day on a new temporary job that might last for two weeks or a month. I work in a large plant that publishes, among other things, glossy advertisements, small trade magazines, and small newsletters for organizations and clubs. Today I stood at the end of a conveyor where finished Yellow Page telephone books for St. Paul arrived shrink-wrapped in packages of six. I and my partner loaded

*This last image was not meant to imply any further analogy, in which I would be incorporated, than that of sinking into oblivion.

them onto pallets at a brisk pace, so that by the end of the day we each probably lifted and placed approximately nine thousand books apiece.

I like keeping busy and the exercise is beneficial, so the job goes pretty well. I've noticed that work like this comes very easy to me. From 1980 to 1982 I worked for a local retailer delivering and stocking furniture. My fingers grew large, and I apparently developed some kind of muscular ability to perform that kind of work that has never left me to this day despite the otherwise enervated condition of my body from excessive boozing and a dissipated lifestyle in general. What I find especially amazing is that the strength in your hands, once developed, never leaves. Still, the floor of the plant is a dreary, gray concrete, the machines are loud and dull in color, there are no windows, and the atmosphere will, I know, eventually overpower me with deep melancholy. So I must ask myself that incessant question: Is the object of my work worth the trouble?

Well, with telephone books it probably is. They are not a yearlong, unending project, and, as everyone knows, they are now considered—like telephones—a basic need, since they fall under the category of "Requisite Components of Modern-Day Shelter." But if I had to work in that plant permanently and handle items like coupon packets for fast-food restaurants and soap flakes, or advertisements for a Bugs Bunny anniversary TV special, I would become disheartened. In all likelihood, other workers feel the same way. But they do not bond together and refuse to work on the more frivolous items, partly because they know those items are the source of some long green for the company and themselves and partly because they do not communicate to each other their distaste for suffering in order to bring stupid products into existence.

I have been reading a book called *Natural Resources* by Stroup and Baden, put out by the Pacific Institute for Public Policy Research. The authors set forth some appealing arguments, maintaining that common ownership or government control of natural resources results in gross mismanagement, depletion, and abuse of those resources, and that private ownership is the only way to effect their most valued use while simultaneously preventing pollution and other harmful side effects. For example, they write that pollution would not occur in a stream if it were privately owned. They discredit the myth of superior Indian stewardship of natural resources by pointing out the perilous decline in the buffalo herds when the Indians' "cost" to obtain that resource decreased due to the introduction of horses and firearms. They argue that special interests sway the government into allowing deleterious uses for grazing land and irrigation sources. They assert that the Rural Electrification Administration (REA), founded in the 1930s to subsidize the delivery of electricity to the country, essentially annihilated any endeavors at the time to develop alternative energy sources like wind power, and that these effects have reverberated into a modern-day dearth of energy options.

The authors are a couple of western intellectuals who do a good job of devising a rationale for getting the government out of the resource management business. If I subscribe to their viewpoint, then I must engineer a solution to the "frivolous products" problem which does not rely on common or government ownership of resources. One of their most telling arguments in this regard is that any artificially low price for a resource dictated by government results in inefficiencies and/or ultimate depletion of the resource. Which outcome will actually occur, they do not make crystal clear. On page 56 they address the regulation of natural gas by the federal government between 1954 and 1961:

> First, fixed prices caused unprofitability of all but the most easily accessible gas deposits. As a result, exploration was dramatically retarded and production dropped. Second, the real price of natural gas declined relative to market-determined prices of energy alternatives, leading to sharp increases in natural gas usage.

Thus, the federal government's intervention had the extremely unfortunate effect of causing both a decrease in production and a sharp rise in usage of an essential natural resource.

With damning evidence like this of government ineptitude, it would be foolish for me to advocate further encroachment by the offending entity. I think it was Timothy Leary who said that in the end our problems will turn out to be psychological and spiritual in nature. Perhaps therein lies the only solution to the problem that obsesses me: If workers were more open and less hard-wired to accepting the rigid practices of modern-day business, they might do something daring, like demand higher wages for work that strikes them as unnecessary or demeaning in purpose.

MONDAY AUGUST 13, 1990   This business of drinking abusively is attended constantly by a hideousness and degradation that is almost too depressing to put into words. I am living outside now in a tent on the land across the St. Croix River from Stillwater, Minnesota. It is an exquisite summer day. The sky is a splash of large fluffy white clouds drifting ponderously across a bright blue firmament, and the air feels generous and warm. Yet my personal life is like a concentrated distillate of failure, frustration, and despair.

I moved out of the rented housekeeping room after only a month because it was the focus of a preternatural antagonism—the antagonism of cockroaches and bedbugs, the antagonism of sleepless nights, and the antagonism of John Barleycorn, who tripped me into the consumption of more than five liters of brandy per week near the end. I was drinking even more, and spending money like a madman at the bars and nightclubs along a nearby commercial avenue, so that my bank account of borrowed funds was sinking at an alarming rate despite my working full-time at the printing house.

That job could have lasted another three and a half weeks through the temporary agency if I had wanted it so. The pay was five and a half an hour—high for a temporary position— and they shifted me around to a satisfying variety of tasks, like supplying the stitching line with tall, heavy stacks of unbound white pages or rebuilding pallets in the warehouse. But how can you work steady at a job like that when you wake up in the morning, if you have slept at all, with a quaking, sweaty body and still half-immersed in an alcoholic stupor?

My skin has developed into a veritable litmus test of abuse. The left half of my face is like a bulb that brightens slowly to a fierce red as I imbibe. This exacerbates a painful, blistering rash that has spread over a considerable percentage of my body in the last six or seven months. Doctors' prescriptions have been feckless. I have an appointment with a dermatologist next week. Likely he will tell me that there are underlying causes for these kinds of afflictions—specifically alcohol. But how can I tell him that I drink for reasons that transcend natural, underlying causes? It is not probable that "preternatural antagonism" is included in the doctor's compendium of allergens or diseases.

On the intellectual front, I continue to be intrigued by the "frivolous products" problem. One obvious difficulty in studying it is that one man's frivolous product can often be another man's sacred necessity. Take hash brown potatoes, for example. One of the temporary jobs I had a couple of months ago was working in a huge plant where potatoes were culled, cleaned, boiled, shredded, and packaged for restaurant or retail sale as frozen hash browns. The secret, I learned, of manufacturing hash browns that will brown evenly on the grill is to freeze or cool-dry the whole potatoes just after boiling but prior to shredding. This and a hot grill are, I think, what most consumers omit when their kitchens suddenly become redolent of burning carbon or the "brown" portion of their hash browns clings longingly to the pan. Still, it is possible to make decent hash browns without resort to their production in a factory, and many restaurants succeed winningly in that regard.

Nonetheless, I can understand why a smaller restaurant might find it economically attractive to simply purchase the frozen variety of hash browns rather than hire extra help to make their own. Two levels of frivolity, then, are discoverable with respect to manufactured hash browns. First, it is not necessary that a restaurant buy them rather than make them on the premises. Second, the consumer could prepare them in his own household rather than go out to eat at all.

Now all of this is scientifically correct, and it ought to convince me that the hash-brown factory should be demolished immediately. This is especially true of the particular factory where I worked, because it seemed to me that management made a conscious effort to make the jobs of its thousands of employees as miserable as possible. The place is hot, close-quartered, and loud as hell. To do the job I did—sweep up the millions of potatoes that fall off the shredding line, load them into wheel barrows, and dispose of them into a chute across the floor where they are ground up for animals—one must bend over repeatedly under a jungle of dangerous machinery and withstand a constant shower of potato flakes while contorting oneself around pipes and conveyors like a monkey trying to free himself from the bowels of a nuclear reactor. After an hour your clothes are absolutely drenched, your socks are soaked from immersion in standing water, and your nostrils are seething from the perpetual assault of the foul odor of rot that originates deep down in the tubed bowels of the ancient, decrepit, and still deteriorating three-story building.

Despite this particular reprehensible case, though, I cannot bring myself to condemn the manufacture of frozen hash brown potatoes. They might be a frivolous product, but when a mound of them is served to me on a plate, hot, crisp, and garnished with a pat or two of butter at the counter in the local greasy spoon, then they transmute into one of the most necessary frivolous products ever invented, in my opinion.

When, in an earlier entry, I suggested that common or government ownership of natural resources might at least be considered as a possible solution to the twin problems of declining natural resources and the proliferation of superfluous or extravagant products, I was thinking that a system wherein access to resources was strictly democratic would ensure that people with little or no capital would not then be forced into the degrading situation of working to supply luxury items for others or otherwise providing society with items extraneous to simple survival. If they so chose, those people could subsistence farm, for example, or cut down and mill enough timber for their own dwellings, or lay claim to enough coal or natural gas to heat their homes without regard to the market mechanism. On a less naive level, government ownership of natural resources could at least assure that price inflation due strictly to a growing scarcity of a particular resource would not occur. Or the government could dictate that a particular resource be used for only certain designated essential products. At this point, though, I am very reluctant to commit myself to an opinion on this issue. I have discovered that it is a complex question that has been addressed down through the centuries by writers much more learned than I am. So, in approaching the frivolous products problem, I have put the issue of public versus private ownership of resources to the side and attempted to formulate a solution that is more neutral in that regard. Recently, this search has led me to read the book entitled *Theory of the Leisure Class* by Thorstein Veblen. He addresses one dimension of the problem that was perhaps more pertinent to the earlier era in which he wrote, namely, that useless or not entirely functional products are procured by those who can afford them for the sole purpose of displaying to the outer world one's ability to pay, or one's power, or one's lack of dependence on useful work to gain a livelihood. Veblen, it seems to me, had a gift for language. He could bend a single idea into a thousand subsidiary thoughts and express those in such a multifaceted convolution of abstractions that one might be fooled into thinking that he was actually operating from more than just a very elementary base of premises. How else can I account for the absence in my memory of all except a few of his more essential arguments?

Unfortunately, Veblen did not address the issue of the disparity between the degradation inherent in many jobs and the frequently capricious character of the merchandise produced. Nor have any other books I happen to have selected focused on the more long-range predicament of dwindling resources accompanied by the rising production of nonessential goods. One of the books I read many years ago, however, combined with some ideas I got from Stroup and Baden's book, have led me to uncover what might be the seeds of a solution, or at least a solution on paper. (To be continued.)

TUESDAY AUGUST 14, 1990   Many years ago I read a book, whose title I forget, which discussed the various attempts to build utopian communities down through history. In the case of those American communities based on communal farming that populated the countryside by the hundreds in the last century, the author attributed their eventual decline to a disintegration of the rigid religious convictions held by members of the communes in their most successful days. He predicated the success of any attempt to live on a communal basis on a tight religious structure that would keep the members motivated to maintain those habits and routines thought necessary for sufficient production. Without that religious devotion, members would soon drift off into the more enticing and colorful secular world, and the commune would go the way of history.

What this analysis ignores is the role played by the advancement of technology in rendering those early American communes obsolete. The author of the unnamed book would have us believe that as those communes aged, their members somehow became less devout or more inclined to embrace the profligate and wayward ways of a less virtuous secular world.

But it seems to me that any particular member might have possessed an equal amount of piety as time moved on and, observing the growing chasm between his own lean consumption and the amenities offered by the outer world, bolted the commune nevertheless. Religion did not become weaker in those days; the Devil just got stronger.

Reinforcing the temptation provided by the retail marketplace was the observation, made by any relatively perceptive commune worker, that their methods of producing goods were constantly becoming less efficient in relation to the mechanized processes of the secular world. Laboring over a steaming vat of vegetables and surrounded by glass canning jars, a kitchen worker would not be utterly oblivious to the higher and higher incidence of the use of tin cans among the population at large. A worker straining at the handle of a manual gristmill or butter churn would certainly notice, sooner or later, that flour and butter seemed to be proliferating with magic ease on the grocery store shelves in town, courtesy of a larger, more automated facility a few miles down the road. The man toiling under the hot sun to mow his grain with a scythe could not help but become aware of the mechanized harvester in his neighbor's field, cutting and taking up grain at twenty times his own speed, while the machine's operator sauntered in the cool shadows of the horses and gazed about with calm, supervisory assurance. Well, of course, the commune could always buy a harvester, too. But what would commune members Henry, Jonathan, Michael, Roger, and Charles do then, whose movements are following a similar primitive harvesting pattern in the fields on the other side of the barn?

No, it was not deteriorating religious conviction that did in the communes. Under the circumstances their members would have required a substantial increase in piety just to maintain the status quo. No, it was simply the ongoing divergence between the efficient production provided by the outer world's technologies and the lesser output afforded by the static, more traditional methods of the commune.

Thought for the day: Drinking teaches patience in the sense that its practitioner must wait to engage in many worthwhile activities until he is sober.

(Economics to be continued.)

SATURDAY AUGUST 18, 1990   I am in the second day of a "water only" fast. I do not know how long it will last, maybe just until this evening. But deprivation is economically sensible now because it curbs, to a degree, this intolerable torment, this sense of being hounded by a mysterious and demanding adversary. Sometimes, though, it's just as bad as when I'm eating. So I am prompted to carry on by the promise of ultimate death. To live as I have been, with the drinking and the constant sense of inadequacy, is not the image I envision of the good life. In a way, I feel as if the decision is out of my hands, since these peculiar psychological sensations seem immune to amelioration by others means. So far I feel strong, although very hungry. This morning was tough. I was half nauseous, and my body was pervaded by a deep craving for some kind of consumption. But after a shower of cold water from a gallon container, I felt fortified and got on with the day.

If I don't die, I plan to research the feasibility of applying certain features of the old American communes to the food-processing sector of the economy. In particular, the three features of common ownership, shared work, and payment in the members' own output could conceivably be harnessed ·by a large group of people to "communize" the production of food-stuffs from the time it leaves the farmer to the time it is shelved in a warehouse, or "store," or even up to the time it is introduced into the member's household. I have an "ideal" case in mind for people with a certain amount of money to invest and a desire to have greater control over and contact with the food-processing system, and a more "realistic" case for those who are less well-off.

I have left the farmer out of the scenario for several reasons. One, despite the recurring reports that the family farm is defunct, many if not most farms today are managed by one or a few individuals who possess a formidable variety of both general and technical knowledge about farming. (This conclusion was garnered very informally from farmers who have picked me up while I hitchhiked around the country.) For a group of idealists to attempt to assume the role of an experienced large-scale farmer today is not prudent for the same reason it became economically unreasonable in the days of the erstwhile American communes: it does not require a whole group to perform what one or three knowledgeable, well-seasoned farmers can do on their own.

Furthermore, if members of the proposed commune were to attempt to assume the role of farm worker rather than farm manager, they would be compelled to work at the mercy of the weather, the type of crop being grown, and the different methods of planting or harvest being employed that season by the farm manager. One summer, for example, I worked on a small farm just south of here which grew hay for a small herd of beef cattle. The owner had to wait until the hay was sufficiently dry before harvesting it, so my job of stacking hay on the wagon behind the baler and later storing it in the barn was postponed or rescheduled on several occasions until the weather became more agreeable. Moreover, farms are widely dispersed geographically and so are not suited to the needs of those who are part of a revolving force of temporary workers—a facet of the commune I would consider essential for its sustainability and appeal. Lastly, a food-processing commune that is severed from the farming function would enjoy the benefit of a continuous supply of farm-grown produce, commodities, and livestock and so would not be subject to the fluctuations in yield of any particular group of farms or parcels of land. The commune would have access to the same worldwide supply of "raw materials" that is made available to any other commercial processor of foodstuffs.

It is later in the second day of my fast now, and I have decided to abandon it for one reason. It is not working. The purpose of the desired banishment is still annoyingly present. What's more, sometime in September I expect to receive a check for $15,000 as my portion of the distribution of my father's estate. If dying by starvation will require forty to sixty days, I might as well wait until I can afford to kill myself with a gun or by asphyxiation from carbon monoxide before the starvation deadline even arrives. So I will go have dinner in town now, perhaps accompanied by a glass of wine, or whatever else it takes to quell this implacable demon.

Thought for the evening: It is conceivable, at least, that the proclamation "In God We Trust" was inscribed on the coins and currency of this country by its founders in anticipation of that day when the United States would join with the rest of Christendom in adopting a free-floating currency, unbacked by any intrinsically valuable metal like gold. It is just as conceivable, too, that those founders had little realization that it would take a full two hundred years for their declaration to be fulfilled.

SUNDAY AUGUST 19, 1990   People are reacting strangely to my music. Their initial appraisal is always congratulatory and laced with encouragement. They compare me to certain well-known extant folk artists or to certain singers of the 1940s, or they put the music itself on a par with the best of early American or as outstanding in certain genres like bluegrass or 1950s rock. Most gratifying of all, they say they like the music. But after this the situation deteriorates. They get sick and sell all of their equipment. They commit themselves with avid enthusiasm to compose an elaborate accompaniment to a specific song, and six months later not a single complementary note has been discovered.

The hired musician mentioned in the entry for July 7 was very disappointing. First, as I walked into his elementary basement studio, he informed me that his base rate for recording would be ten dollars per hour and that his guitar work would be five dollars per hour extra. This was five dollars per hour more than what we had agreed on over the phone for the whole package, but it was still cheap, so I acceded. Then he pulled out a large reel-to-reel tape and told me that this necessary technical component of the session would require an extra outlay of either eight or twelve dollars, depending on whether the tape was new or used. I opted for the used. For the first forty-five minutes of paid session time, he busied himself pushing buttons and pulling a miscellany of knobs and tinkering under consoles with different connections and wires until he finally became satisfied. Turning a button, he smiled radiantly as the first song on my tape played over the speaker. However, it was marked by a great distancing effect, as if I were singing in a dark tunnel opening onto the river. "See," he said delightedly, "we can get an echo effect on your songs here too, if you want." I nodded, trying to keep my disgruntlement from rising to an audible growl of displeasure.

Finally we got down to trying to secure a basic chordal accompaniment to a song called "Bells Will Ring." To my surprise, he listened to the whole thing through only twice before attempting to find the chords. It was obvious he had not learned it, either. A number of times I had to correct him on the melody itself, which he sang in discordant opposition to the tape, which was playing at the same time. He tried to play the song in the wrong time as well. It is more like a melodic waltz, if anything, but he attempted to play it like rock and roll. If you can imagine the song "Scarborough Fair," composed in the Middle Ages but made famous by Simon and Garfunkel, being interpreted in the vein of something like "Street Fightin' Man" by the Rolling Stones, then you have an idea of my astonishment.

After a while I persuaded him to simply listen to the song and just strum the appropriate chord. But even this proved impossible. We would go through and review five or six chords without once hitting a harmonious middle ground. A couple of times we argued over whether a chord should be major or minor, because he seemed to think that a song without a certain minimum of minor chords would not contain enough interesting musical variations. After two hours, we probably had secured two agreeable chords out of the whole song, and he announced it was time for a break. I announced it was time for me to leave. I paid him the thirty-eight dollars and told him to keep the tape in the event I still might require his services as a studio engineer. But I have not been back since, and soon I will call him up to request that he return the tape and erase the reel-to-reel. All in all a wasted endeavor.

The last musician I worked with cost me forty dollars. Although he tried hard and applied his classical training to "Bells Will Ring" in order to write down the notes on lined paper and obtain some harmonious chords, the sound was just not right. If anything, each chord was just a minute tonal quantity off so that the entire accompaniment was in competition with the melody rather than in support of it. So out of five musicians now I am batting a big fat cipher. Am I wrong to suspect that five additional musicians would produce the same disappointing results?

Reverting momentarily to some of the ideas expressed about songwriting, I have perceived over the months that those songs that seem to come so mysteriously or suddenly from the heart are actually what might be called an articulation of the heart's "ideas" or, as it's worded in the Bible, of the "imagination of the heart." It's as if the state of one's heart can only be translated by means of a song. Like a mind ready to burst with an idea or a discovery, the heart swells with a longing to make apparent its inner structure of desire, expectation, or dejection in any particular situation or locale. This would explain also why songs seem to take on the character or mood of the geographical area in which they are composed.

SATURDAY AUGUST 25, 1990   A commune that confined its members to ownership of and working in the food-processing industries might at first seem impracticable or contradictory. The primary purpose of the commune would be to supply its members with finished food products that they had manufactured themselves in facilities owned in common. However, because each individual's annual food requirements, even if dependents are included in the computation, are much less than what that individual can manufacture by himself each year in combination with efficient technology, then the only kind of employment possible for each member would be temporary or on a part-time permanent basis. This, of course, would preclude managers, engineers, skilled mechanics, and other valuable and necessary full-time personnel from active membership in the commune.* Essentially, membership would be confined to unskilled production workers whose tasks on an assembly line or in a warehouse could be learned in a matter of hours or even minutes. The contradiction arises, then, because that part of the population whose skills and proclivities suit them for production work is also that part of the population least able to afford a proportionate investment in those companies, whether extant or not yet constructed, which process food. Similarly, those skilled or highly educated personnel who work in the food-processing industry have no incentive to stoop to factory work in order to earn foodstuffs of less value than the corresponding money wage they would make as part of the hierarchy of management or engineering. Despite this basic drawback, however, it might prove valuable to examine, in a comprehensive way, what such a food-processing commune would be like in struc-

---

*That is, unless these employees took only a small percentage of their salaries in the form of communally produced foods, in which case a certain egalitarianism among the communal ranks would be lost, I would think. But anything is possible!

ture and economics in order to extract ideas that might work in a slightly altered or less complex conceptual arrangement.

That individual productivity would be greater in a modern food-processing commune than in the farm-based religious communities of yore is a conclusion borne out by statistics. The best and most recent data available in this regard in the J. J. Hill Reference Library in St. Paul is a small booklet entitled "The Latest Scoop," published by the International Ice Cream Association. It portrays, in statistical and descriptive form, the frozen desserts industry for the purpose of expanding consumer awareness and promoting ice cream and its related products. The objection might be made that ice cream and ice milk, which together comprise 90% of frozen dessert production in the United States, could themselves be judged frivolous products, extraneous to a utilitarian-oriented diet, and so would not be included in the menu of food products manufactured by any commune purporting to focus only on satisfying basic needs. According to the booklet, for example, it was not until the late 1600s or early 1700s that ice cream in its present form was even known to mankind. It was regarded as such a sensational novelty in 1812 that its appearance on tables in the White House that year under the direction of the First Lady, Dolly Madison, is commemorated even to this day by a popular dessert company bearing her name. The first hand-cranked freezer was not invented until 1846, and the first commercial ice-cream plant did not appear until 1851. How then could ice cream be accorded a legitimate place in the list of strictly necessary foodstuffs? In a way it is fortunate that this most recent and thorough data pertain to ice cream, since consideration of that product's history casts light on the vast changes in the nature of foodstuffs that have accompanied the industrialization of food processing, which has been proceeding inexorably for well over a century.

A farm wife of two and a half centuries ago would be struck with amazement on walking into a modern supermarket and observing both the abundance of storable, preserved items that she had known all too well in her working days and those new or offshoot items that she might be hard-pressed to recognize at all. So the question becomes not whether ice cream is a necessary element in a modern diet; it is whether any of the foods you buy in the supermarket are required at all. If you contend that ice cream is a frivolous product, for instance, and that only whole milk should be incorporated into the prospective scheme of communal production, I might counter that peanut butter ought to likewise be eliminated and that only the raw, unsalted peanuts be approved for entry into the scenario. If you argue that baked bread is dispensable, and flour even, and that only bushelfuls of the whole, unviolated grains of wheat should be permitted, I might retort that the meat-packing plant be similarly discarded and that only the whole cow be allowed admittance into the system. So the point becomes moot. The fact is that the whole range of victuals has evolved from the time of the genuine family farm of two hundred years ago and has been transformed into an entirely new array of goods to be used for satisfaction of gastronomic whims and desires. So why exclude ice cream?

The statistics I will use from the booklet for ice cream and related products are industry wide. Thus, the productivity they convey is an average only and does not reflect the efficiency of the most up-to-date and well-run plants. In 1988, the total output of frozen dessert products in the United States was 1,387,271,000 gallons (prepared from data published by the United States Department of Agriculture, USDA). According to another table, in 1988 the number of man-hours for production workers in the frozen desserts industry totaled 22,700,000 (from an estimate by a branch of the U.S. Department of Commerce). Dividing gallons by man-hours yields an output per man-hour of over 60 gallons. Now, the nature of these statistics prevents one from obtaining a similar figure for ice cream alone. But since ice milk and ice cream together comprise 90% of all frozen dessert products, it is not unrealistic to assume, for the sake of analysis, that the 60-gallon figure can be applied to ice cream alone. Using this approximation, the average worker in an ice cream plant can be said to have produced, in conjunction with the attendant machinery and white-collar personnel, over 60 gallons of ice cream per hour in 1988. This is not 60 gallons per hour for the whole plant. It is 60 gallons of ice cream per production worker per hour.

Another way to view this statistic is to consider each production worker as just a "job," or a human slot in the manufacturing process. In a year's time each production job in an ice cream plant will therefore produce 52 weeks × 40 hours × 60 gallons = 124,800 gallons of ice cream. Another statistic tells us that there were 765 plants producing ice cream in the United States in 1988 (USDA) and that they produced a total of 881,522,000 gallons of ice cream that year. Each plant therefore produced an average of approximately 1,152,000 gallons apiece. If each production employee was responsible for 124,800 gallons of output that year, then the average number of production employees making ice cream in individual American plants in 1988 was 1,152,000 ÷ 124,800, or approximately nine per plant.

Now what if the production employees in that average plant decided to approach management with the proposition of producing a level of ice cream in any particular year that would exceed the firm's marketed production by an amount equal to that which would be consumed by all of those employees during the year in question? The object, obviously, would be to allow the production workers to consume at home ice cream they made at the plant rather than purchase that item in a grocery store. Let us assume that the employees and their families are real ice-cream hogs. If their families consist, say, of four ice-cream-eating members apiece, who each wolf down a half-gallon every week, with a two-week respite, then the employee and his family will consume 100 gallons of ice cream per year. But we have already seen that those nine employees can produce at the rate of 60 gallons per hour per employee. Therefore, each employee need work only a total of 100 ÷ 60 = $1^2/_3$ hours or 1 hour and 40 minutes to supply his household with enough ice cream to last an entire year. This is something of an advantage in productivity over the methods employed by the more primitive communes of the past. Those nine employees would in all probability spend more time at lunch, on breaks, and in commuting on that particular day than they would in producing enough ice cream for their families for a whole year. But alas, things can never be so simple in reality, for we have omitted all the costs intrinsic to the ice cream production process, other than labor, that these nine employees have ignored in so furtively absconding with their year's worth of just desserts. These will be addressed in a future entry.

TUESDAY AUGUST 28, 1990   Since 1983 I have been very wary of the written word. The problem is that since most of

99

what a person reads in a highly complex international society is not personally verifiable, it becomes easy to slip into skepticism. Combined with a cynicism regarding the motives of writers and communicators in general, that attitude can transform very readily into absolute disbelief of any and all written or broadcast reports. This reaction becomes especially pronounced when the written material involves complicated reasoning or subjects that entail challenging mental exertions like higher mathematics or difficult scientific concepts. I know that if I happen to pick up an article whose first paragraph requires a sudden concentration of mental effort, I will usually place the magazine back in the rack and assume that its contents are pervaded with falsehood. If a book begins with subject matter any more arduous than, say, an advanced grade-school sociology text, I return that volume to the shelf and dismiss it as bald prevarication. My reasoning in the past has gone something like this: If an author has already constructed a web of complexities or a difficult conceptual structure that serves to shield his main ideas from unbridled scrutiny, then why should he bother telling the truth? All of this is only to warn the reader that the upcoming entries concerned with communal economics might initially seem overly convoluted or shaded too much by mathematics or other unreasonable forms of logic. But, alas, I think that the writing will be proved to be all too true in the long run, so bear with me.

As usual, my personal life is a shambles. I am in "detox" now in Hastings, Minnesota, a town about twenty miles south of the Twin Cities. My memory of last night is sketchy. I do remember drinking a pint of brandy rather quickly at my campsite and repairing to a saloon in Stillwater, where I spent another $20 on drinks and tunes from the jukebox. On the way back over the bridge, I apparently stripped off my clothes and cannonballed twenty feet down into the St. Croix River. The problem was that a cop was in the audience. I got a ticket for disorderly conduct, requiring a court appearance September 11, and a free 72-hour hiatus in this rural county-operated detoxification center. I don't know if my tent's rain fly is on or off. If it rains in the next three days my belongings might very well be written off as irreparably waterlogged. Plus, who's to say what kind of vandals might avail themselves of my absence? I am going to move from my Stillwater site as soon as possible.

WEDNESDAY AUGUST 29, 1990   The standard length of residence at the detox center here turned out to be only 48 hours, not 72, so I will be released tomorrow morning. Through meetings and reading the AA literature, I have reacquainted myself with some of the accepted guideposts to sobriety. The first of the "12 steps" out of drinking says that "we admitted we were powerless over alcohol—our lives had become unmanageable." What this means is that the alcoholic loses control after the first drink and the cycle downward to destruction is resumed. It is very possible I have reached that stage where I cannot take even one drink.

The weekend before last I was drinking fairly heavily. Then, the next Tuesday morning I walked into a bar in Stillwater to kill a hangover and, with encouragement from the bartender, drank five strong brandies before leaving. I walked to the liquor store then and bought a fifth of Canadian whiskey. I took it to my campsite across the river and drank half of it before returning to town for lunch. After two manhattans with a Reuben and french fries, I returned to the bar I had been at earlier. For the next four or five hours I drank one strong brandy after the next, while freely slipping dollar bills into the jukebox. I know that I left in time to get to the grocery store, but I don't remember what I bought or how I got back to my campsite. I remember being surprised the next morning to find that both of my gallon jugs had been filled with water. How they got that way is a mystery to me. I was disgusted with myself, so I poured the remainder of the Canadian fifth and some vodka I had left over from the weekend onto the beach and vowed not to touch another drop.

Well, a few days later—on Saturday afternoon—I was sitting on the ground at my campsite, trying to endure the haze and the humidity and the constant streams of sweat trailing down my torso, when I decided to walk up the steep highway on the Wisconsin side of the river to buy some beer from the liquor store at the crossroads. I brought the six-pack with some ice cubes to my campsite and drank four before heading over to Stillwater for dinner. I drank three or four manhattans while dining on fried walleye and french fries. Later at my campsite I drank the remaining two beers.

The next day I felt pretty satisfied that the quantity I had drunk the day before signified total control on my part, despite a slight hangover, so I had no compunctions about heading up the Wisconsin hill again to buy a pint of brandy. I drank that pint at my campsite and, betraying my original intentions, returned for another and drank that also before the sun set. So the cycle was already in motion, starting right from that first beer on Saturday.

The next day, Monday, I was in Minneapolis for a doctor's appointment and while waiting I had two glasses of burgundy and a bottle of beer at a pair of bars by the University. After the appointment I returned to the first bar for two brandies on the rocks. Later, back at my campsite, I drank a pint of brandy purchased in Stillwater. I returned across the bridge then and searched for a place to eat. It was rather late on a weekday night, and the only place serving food was a rather trendy upstairs bar that catered to the younger set and served free tacos between 11 P.M. and 1 A.M. During this "power hour," as they christened it, their bar booze was priced at only a dollar a shot. I plunged right in, ordering doubles, eating an occasional taco, and wasting dollars on the jukebox. At closing time I had three doubles lined up on the bar and drank them quickly at the urging of the bouncer.

My memory of the ensuing calamity is spotty at best. I vaguely remember the galvanizing jump into the river and emerging nude from the water to greet the cops, but the actual arrest and the drive down to detox is episodic. I do remember being in the Stillwater police station and shouting "Fuck you!" very loudly at an attending officer. The experience ought to convince me not to take that first drink. But what can you do when the Devil's got you by the ass?

It hasn't rained here yet during my stay, so I am curious if my tent and belongings are still intact.

FRIDAY AUGUST 31, 1990   My tent was intact and undamaged upon my return from detox. Some wild men had had a party on a slab of concrete a few yards away. A big burnt log, a collection of beer bottles, and some discarded clothing testified to their presence. But all they did was loosen a corner stake of the tent, possibly just to let me know they were there.

Saturday September 1, 1990   Now I am going to set forth the ideal food-processing commune configuration, in order to more fully elucidate the costs and benefits involved in the "payment in kind" process and to provide a conceptual paradigm from which a more realistic model might be extrapolated. The utopia I envision would not be bound to any particular geographical location. Both the members of the food-processing commune and the production facilities themselves would be scattered far and wide over a vast area such as Canada and the United States. The first step in establishing the commune would be to identify the food requirements of prospective members. At least to start with, currently available marketing studies might indicate a typical basketful of the processed foodstuffs most often purchased. For simplicity, let it be assumed that this typical basketful of groceries contains fifty distinctly manufactured items, ranging from fresh meat and poultry to canned applesauce and dry roasted peanuts. The next step would be to identify factories and plants that produce those fifty items. This might require finding fifty such individual facilities, but more likely fewer would need to be searched out due to the manufacture of multiple products at a single location. Cheese, cottage cheese, sour cream, and butter might all be made under one roof. Ideally, only the most modernized, well-run, and efficient facilities would be regarded worthy of entrance into the communal scheme.

Another important determining factor in plant choice would be its proximity to population centers. Presumably, prospective commune members would demonstrate residence patterns that mirrored the demographics of the population at large. Thus, care must be taken that factories are located close to where potential members currently live and work.

At this point objection might be made that to impose the commune over most of the continent is too ambitious in scope. Sooner or later the commune members are going to want to consume their earned edibles where they live. This would entail a large distribution system of some sort, whose complexity and expense would preempt any benefits the system was originally intended to provide. This might be especially true when perishable items like milk and fresh meat are shipped halfway across the country despite their availability through a local producer.

I have no argument with this objection. It is perfectly valid and serves to point out that any actual establishment of the type of commune under consideration might require an initial stage in which a number of regional communes are organized in widely dispersed geographical areas around the continent. These regional communes would necessarily be restricted in their choice of food items to those manufactured in their domain. Perhaps only twenty items, including dairy products, fresh meat, and locally processed fruits and vegetables, would be incorporated into the local system. But examining the commune as if it were implemented on a large scale at least simplifies it and exposes its essential structure.

Presumably, the local communes would be erected under the same principles, and a fully developed commune would only come into existence on a continental scale. Its consummate form would be international in scope. Chickens grown and butchered on the East Coast are consumed around the country. Cheese from Wisconsin makes its way as far as California and Hawaii, and vegetables canned in San Francisco are distributed to the farthest reaches of the North American land mass. Only by aiming for widespread production will the proposed commune be able to offer its members the whole range of choices in food products that one finds in a typical grocery store.

The main goal of the commune would be to employ its members in those facilities whose aggregate output in "payment in kind" wages would result, for each member, in a typical food basket. Of course as time went on any divergence in taste between the members of the commune and the general public would become evident and their productive activity adjusted for that shift. A system of warehouse stores would be established around the country, where members could buy food based on credits earned by working in the selected factories and plants. If a manufacturer of canned soup, for example, agreed to use commune members as either all or part of its production workforce, then the wages of those employees would not be in money. Rather, the soup company would ship to the various commune warehouses around the country an amount of soup whose value was equal to the wages left unpaid. Exactly what this value is will be the subject of further analysis. The amount shipped to each particular warehouse would necessarily depend on the number of commune workers who patronized or were assigned to that particular communally operated facility. The ideal scheme mentioned earlier would entail actual ownership of the production facilities by the members of the commune, but that is not practical for the reason already mentioned: those people most in need of the benefits of communally produced goods are the very people least able to afford an investment in such an extensive operation. What's more, it's possible that the incentives intrinsic to a communal arrangement could very well lure producers into hiring employees on a communal basis without those employees possessing the actual authority of ownership.

WEDNESDAY TO FRIDAY SEPTEMBER 5 TO SEPTEMBER 7, 1990   The incentive to hire workers and pay them "in kind" would be a substantial reduction in the cost of wages for the employer. This savings would accrue to the employer despite those "in kind" wages constituting an equal or greater value to the production workers than the money wage they would otherwise earn. To see why this is so requires some rather detailed scrutiny of "communal economics."

Essential to this argument is the distinction a business recognizes between variable and fixed costs. The fixed costs of a business are those which the entity would incur whether production was high, low, or even nonexistent. They are costs such as the salaries of a minimal staff of white-collar personnel thought necessary to keep the business open and viable as an ongoing concern, or certain depreciation or overhead costs that would be sustained whether production was maintained or not. They are costs that are independent of the quantity of the plant's output and that would remain constant whether record-breaking sales occurred or not a single finished item rolled off the assembly line. Variable costs, on the other hand, are expenditures directly attributable to added production or sales. Wages, depreciation of machinery due to use, certain overhead costs like additional outlays for energy due to higher production, or the cost of higher commissions payable to salesmen as revenues rise would all be labeled variable. They escalate in proportion to production and sales, and a definite quantity of these costs in cents or dollars can be attached to each unit of production as it moves through the factory to completion.

To help identify the cost to the company of compensating "in kind" rather than in money, it will be helpful to ask this question: What portion of a given amount of production would be allotted to payment-in-kind wages and what portion would be made available to sales if it is assumed that the value of the payment-in-kind wages is equal to the company's standard or base wage for all of that production in question?

Let X be equal to the total production per employee. (In the case of the typical ice cream plant already illustrated, this would be 60 gallons multiplied by the number of hours worked.)

Let K be the part of that production in number of units, such as gallons, cans, packages, or pounds per employee that are used to pay that employee in kind.

Let O be the output, in units per employee, made available for sales during the arbitrary period of production under consideration.

Then, $$X - K = O$$

Let W be equal to the standard or base wage, in money, normally paid to the production workers.

Since the payment-in-kind (PIK) wage will be equal in value to the money wage, W, then each employee's PIK wage per hour will be W/P where P is the wholesale price charged by the processing company for one unit of its output. It is readily seen that this term simply yields the number of units of output that the standard wage is capable of buying after one hour of work. Confusion might arise as to why the price, P, is not the retail price. After all, wouldn't an equivalent wage in goods be the number of those goods that one hour in money wages is capable of purchasing at the retail level? The answer is an emphatic no.

First of all, the value added to the products manufactured when they are installed into a retail setting has not yet come into existence. Immediately after the output comes off the line and is stored in the plant's warehouse or shipping area, the value it has on the open market is just what any other purchaser is willing to pay for it. All of the shipping, handling, accounting, sales, and management functions that come into play in bringing the items to a customer-accessible status have not yet occurred. And, since these yet-to-be-shipped items are the stock from which PIK wages will be paid, their value in the computation must reflect their lower-than-retail cost. Second, if the plant or factory workers must provide a sufficient PIK wage to those fellow commune members who work in warehouse or distribution functions and who do not actually contribute to the production of the foodstuffs, then the additional units per hour earned by using the lower wholesale price, P, can be used for compensating that work, which would normally be performed by an organization like a retail grocery chain. Later, it will be seen that this way of computing the PIK wage will still result in a lower wage cost to the company than a corresponding hourly compensation made in money.

If each employee's PIK wage is W/P, then K, the total PIK payment per employee for the period in question, will be $W/P \times H$, where H is the number of hours worked during this period. If T is defined as the productivity per employee per hour (such as the 60 gallons per employee in the ice cream example), then X in the above equation, representing total production per employee, will be $H \times T$. Therefore, the equation $X - K = 0$ can be rewritten in this form:

$$ HT - \frac{WH}{P} = 0 $$

This relationship will be helpful later on when the company's normal money cost for any particular quantity of output available for sales is calculated. This then will be compared to the cost of the PIK wage now to be derived.

One of the main differences between the PIK wage and the money wage for identical output available for sales per employee is that the PIK wage will necessarily be applied to the higher number of hours required for the manufacture of those very food products which will compensate the workers for both their output that will be sold and that which will be cycled back into PIK wages. It is interesting to note that, despite this increase in man-hours, the total PIK compensation applied to the longer time period will still cost the company less than the money wage normally paid out for the fewer hours required for only the output available for sales. The total PIK wage per employee has already been derived as WH/P. This term, it will be recalled, is in units of production, whether those units are in gallons of ice cream, cans of soup, pounds of chuck steak, or packages of macaroni. If V is defined as the company's variable cost per unit of manufactured PIK wages, then at least one part of the cost of the PIK wage per employee will be $V \times WH/P$. Essentially, this term is a computation of the variable costs incurred by the company in producing the additional output per employee made necessary by paying that employee in kind. Since no money wages are paid for any of the PIK employee's production, the only cost for wages will be the extra expenditure associated with that added production needed to manufacture the PIK wage.

Now, whether or not fixed costs ought to be incorporated into the formula can be ignored for the moment. Assume that the company in question has no fixed costs whatsoever. Then V in the above mathematical expression will simply be the wholesale unit price less that particular component of ordinary variable cost per unit which would normally go for wages. Wages, of course, are not being paid in money, so they do not enter into the dollar figure for PIK variable costs. This formulation also ignores any profit as a percentage of unit price. This can be regarded as a negligible error for two reasons. First, the profit margin for technologically advanced food processors is often relatively small. In the ice-cream processing industry, for example, it is only 1.4%. Second, the argument being propounded here is that the cost entailed by a company in PIK wages is less than the money wage for an equal quantity of "available for sale" items. If a small number of cents per item that ought to be regarded as profit is actually included in the money cost of the PIK wage, this is a bias that militates in favor of the opposing argument. The miscalculation actually increases the estimated money cost of PIK wages by a small amount. It is a concession I can live with in order to more clearly and conveniently present the main argument.

The portion of ordinary variable cost per unit normally attributable to wages is W/T. This term shows the hourly wage over the employee's productivity per hour and so gives the cost in wages per unit of output. The variable cost associated with each item of output, then, when wages are not paid in money, when there are no fixed costs, and when profit margin is ignored will be $P - W/T$. The cost of PIK wages, to repeat, will be the cost to the company of the added production needed to manufacture those wages. WH/P is the quantity of those wages in units of output. Thus, the cost to the company of PIK wages per employee, assuming no fixed costs, will be

$$\left(P - \frac{W}{T}\right)\left(\frac{WH}{P}\right)$$

$$= W\left(\frac{H}{P}\right)\left(P - \frac{W}{T}\right)$$

$$= W\left(H - \frac{HW}{PT}\right)$$

Any fixed costs have been assumed into nonexistence for reasons that will become evident momentarily. But now it is possible to compare this cost of PIK wages to the cost that otherwise would be incurred for money wages for O alone. Again, O is only that output per employee that is made available for sales. The money wage normally paid for that output would be $O/T(W)$. Since T is the productivity per employee per hour, O/T simply expresses the number of hours devoted to producing O. When this term is multiplied by the wage, W, per hour, the total wages per employee for O is discovered. Earlier, O was expressed in this way:

$$O = HT - \frac{WH}{P}$$

The second part of this equation is an expression for the amount of output per employee that is made available for sales when wages are paid in kind. Therefore, to find the money wage that would normally be paid for that amount of output, the second part of the equation can be substituted for O in the term $(O/T)W$ to give

109

$$\frac{\left(HT - \dfrac{WH}{P}\right)}{T} \times W$$

$$= W\left(H - \frac{WH}{PT}\right)$$

This term is identical to the term derived above, which is an expression of the company's cost of PIK wages per employee for the period in question. Therefore, if fixed costs are not existent and if profit margin is ignored, the cost of the added production undertaken to manufacture the PIK wages to pay for total production will be exactly equal to the money wages normally paid for the "available for sale" production alone.

Of course, every company will have fixed costs in addition to variable. One way to view the device of assuming that all costs are variable is to think of it as a semantic trick. To say that only the cost of wages shall be omitted from the unit price when calculating cost per unit is another way of stating that *all* the costs normally associated with production, including fixed but excluding wages, will be embraced in that unit cost. Therefore, the equality of the PIK wages when calculated using this comprehensive unit cost with the wages otherwise paid for salable production is something like a worst-case scenario. It is a warranty, directed toward the most begrudging and miserly of stockholders and managers, that the PIK wage cannot possibly exceed the money wage otherwise paid for marketable production alone.

Now, however, we are in a position to chip away at the resistance of the most wary and unyielding of decision makers. First of all, that rigidly skeptical board member or executive might insist that a proportionate amount of the company's fixed costs be allocated to the added PIK production, because variable costs alone do not contribute to a fair portrayal of the cost of that additional production. For example, if variable costs account for 90% of the price of a unit of production, then I would maintain that the cost of PIK wages is something less than the cost of wages otherwise paid. We have already seen that if the cost to produce a unit is the same as its price less the variable costs due to wages alone, the cost of added PIK production will equal 100% of money wages normally paid. But if only 90% of the cost of a finished unit is deemed variable, then the 90% figure will be incorporated into the formula set forth for PIK cost, $W(H - HW/PT)$, in such a way that this cost will be less than the comparable money wage for the same marketable production. I would argue that the PIK production is essentially marginal in character in the sense that such production only takes place if the communal system is in operation. It is strictly additional production that is over and above what would normally take place under a money-wage system only. Therefore, fixed costs, which will be present whether or not PIK is adopted and which will be constant in amount, should be ignored in the computation of PIK wage cost. However, I am perfectly willing to address this particular financial curmudgeon's objection.

In the "Latest Scoop" publication there is a diagram entitled "1988 Breakdown of Ice Cream Processor's Dollar." It is a picture of a dollar bill in the form of a block that has been sliced up into slabs that are proportionate in thickness to these percentage figures:

Raw Material Costs	52%
Processing and Packaging Costs	30.5%
Distribution and Sales Expense	11.4%
Administrative Expense	3.3%
Income Taxes	1.4%
Net Profit	1.4%

I am not familiar enough with the ice-cream industry to judge what portion of these various costs would be considered fixed. An arbitrary estimate might take 2% from the administrative expense and, say, 10% from the processing and packaging costs and call them fixed. Probably these would be largely in the form of salaries for personnel such as engineers, accountants, technicians, and managers, whose attendance to the plant's operation is indispensable, whatever the level of production. Or they might consist of costs for energy and depreciation due to certain mechanical processes that must occur at any level of production. So ordinary variable costs, according to this guess, will be 88% of the wholesale price of a gallon of ice cream. Another /// statistic from the booklet tells us that the average wage for production workers in 1988 was $10.17 per hour, which I will round off to $10.00. Dividing the "value of product shipments" for frozen desserts for 1988 by the gallons produced that year results in an approximation of $2.80 per gallon as the price charged by processors. Once again, for the sake of more convenient analysis, it can be assumed that this wholesale price applies to ice cream alone.

I have transcribed these figures in order to first discover what the cost of PIK wages would be if fixed costs do indeed exist, but only variable costs are included in the calculation. From that platform, it will be easier to view the effect that inclusion of fixed costs will have on the PIK wage expense. It will be recalled that the formula $(P - W/T)(WH/P)$ yields the cost of PIK wages per employee when it is assumed that there are no fixed costs. The first term is simply the variable cost for each unit of PIK-manufactured wages. The wholesale price, P, less that component of unit variable cost normally due to money wages, W/T, gives a PIK unit variable cost that ignores both profit margin and fixed costs. If it is assumed, however, that only 88% of the wholesale price can be regarded as variable cost, then the first term becomes $(.88P - W/T)$. Once again, if none of the existing fixed costs are allocated to the cost of the extra PIK production, then the cost of those manufactured wages per employee becomes

$$\left(.88P - \frac{W}{T}\right)\left(\frac{WH}{P}\right)$$

Plugging in figures obtained for ice cream production in 1988 gives

$$\left[.88(\$2.80) - \frac{\$10.00}{60}\right]\left[\frac{\$10.00H}{\$2.80}\right]$$

where H is the total number of hours worked by the employee for all of his production under consideration—that is, both PIK and production available for sale.

It will be interesting at this point to use the $1\,2/3$ hours figure obtained earlier that was found to be the total number of hours of production needed to supply a typical plant's workforce with enough ice cream for the entire year. What is the real cost to the company of that $1\,2/3$ hours of work, and what wage can the employees expect to receive in the form of their own output? If existing fixed costs are assumed to be inapplicable to the period under question, then the cost to the company of the $1\,2/3$ hours can be obtained by using the above formula, so that

$$\left[.88(\$2.80) - \frac{\$10.00}{60}\right]\left[\frac{\$10.00(1\,2/3)}{\$2.80}\right]$$
$$= \$13.674602$$

and the cost per employee is therefore approximately $13.67. What this figure represents is the cost to the company of the ice cream paid to each employee for that $1\,2/3$ hours of work. The second term of the formula, WH/P, provides the number of gallons paid for the time period in question, which in this case works out to approximately 5.95 gallons per employee. Why is this so much less than the 100 gallons that the employees produce during this period? Because the wages paid to production workers are just one component of the total outlay needed to produce those 100 gallons. If all of the factors that enter into production of the ice cream were paid in kind, then, according to the breakdown on page 111, the suppliers of raw materials, for example, would receive 52 gallons for every 100 gallons of sold output, the federal government would receive 1.4 gallons, and so on. Another facet of advanced technology is thus revealed: its very nature lends itself to a system of exchange rather than self-sufficiency. Technology demands that its products be sold in the marketplace because the costs involved in its purchase and operation cannot be paid in the product it manufactures. The vendor of a refrigeration unit will probably not be appeased by even a whole warehouse full of ice cream.

This does not mean there are no advantages to a system of payment in kind. On the contrary, both employer and employee stand to benefit from such an arrangement. First, the 5.95 gallons of ice cream earned by each employee represents a significantly higher wage than otherwise would be paid in cash. The cash wage normally would be $1^2/_3 \times \$10.00$, or $16.66 per employee. But the wage earned in ice cream must be evaluated in relation to the expense that normally would be incurred by the employee in purchasing that amount at the retail level. In "The Latest Scoop," statistics from the Bureau of Labor Statistics, U.S. Department of Labor, inform us that the 113 average retail price of a half-gallon of ice cream in 1988 was $2.46. If I round this off to $2.50, then the price of ice cream at the retail level that year war $5.00 per gallon. Thus the employee's wage for the $1^2/_3$ hours of work under PIK becomes $5.95 \times \$5.00$ or $29.75, almost double the wage in cash. Of course, this calculation is applicable only if the employees took their ice-cream "wage" directly from the factory where they worked. If they picked it up at a warehouse or store, part of that wage differential might be diverted to cover the expenses involved in that more extensive distribution process. This aspect will be addressed further in a future entry.

Payment in kind is economically attractive to the employer as well. Because that product which is used for wages is distributed to a ready-made market of PIK employees, a portion of distribution and sales expenses, advertising in particular, will be obviated, and a reduction in the variable cost per unit of output used for PIK will result. For example, if advertising accounts for 2% of the ice cream processor's revenue (out of a total of 11.4% for distribution and sales expense), then the unit variable cost of that output used to pay PIK wages is reduced from 88% to 86% of the unit wholesale price, and a savings in wage costs results. But even if this incentive is ignored, the employer still realizes a reduction in wage costs under PIK, assuming that fixed costs do not apply to that marginal production. Under that assumption it has already been shown that the $1^2/_3$ hours of PIK work in the ice-cream factory would cost the company $13.67 per employee. Now, the output per employee made available for sales during that period will be total production less wages paid in kind or 100 minus 5.95, or 94.05 gallons per employee. What would normally be the cost to the employer, in cash, of wages paid for that saleable output? The formula already derived, on page 109, $W(H - WH/PT)$, yields the answer, which in this particular case becomes

$$\left[\$10.00 \right]\left[1.66 - \frac{\$10.00(1.66)}{\$2.80(60)} \right]$$

or approximately $15.67 per employee. This shows that the cash wage for the marketable output resulting from that $1^2/_3$ hours of production would be $2.00 higher than the cost of PIK wages for both that same marketable output and the extra production of PIK wages itself. This is a differential of over 12% in the cost of wages and represents a large potential savings for the company. However, as already noted, our scholastic forward progress has been obstructed by an objection from that stingy old codger in the stockholders' gallery who insists that fixed costs should be allocated to the cost of PIK wage production in addition to variable. I refer him now to the case of the Twin Ice Cream Production Plants, in the entry immediately following the next one.

TUESDAY SEPTEMBER 11, 1990   I was in court today for arraignment on the disorderly conduct charge. Before actually pleading guilty or not guilty, I talked with the judge, trying to determine what kind of sentence would be imposed if I pleaded guilty. I asked him if a guilty plea would constitute an admission that the police report was true. His answer was not unequivocal. I asked him if, in the case of a fine being imposed, it could be paid later. He said that shouldn't be a problem. Then he directed me to an office in the hall outside the courtroom for an alcohol assessment. The counselor there was a typical state-sponsored crusader for AA and legally compelled abstinence. After conducting a very cursory interview with me and talking to one of my relatives on the phone, he wrote up a recommendation to the judge that I be committed to a state-funded, thirty-day in-house treatment program at a center like Hazeldon. I then informed him that I had not yet entered a plea to the judge. He seemed a little surprised. I accompanied him back into the chambers, but the judge was gone. After waiting a while in the courtroom and filling out an application for obtaining the services of a public defender, I was escorted through a hallway into the judge's office. I pleaded not guilty, asked for a jury trial and a copy of the complaint, and tendered my application for a public defender. It was approved forthwith, a pre-trial conference with my attorney was set up for October 18, I was handed a copy of the police report, and I left the courthouse with more than a month available to prepare my initial defense.

A lot of people, I think, in similar courtroom situations, are steered by the seeming urgency of the situation into making a decision detrimental to themselves. All across the country public defenders are harried and overscheduled. In San Diego the docket is so full that public attorneys talk to defendants and arrange plea bargains before the arraignment even begins. In Minnesota the procedure is not so streamlined, but the state is overzealous in forcing people into alcohol group therapy and treatment programs. One of the multitude of self-anointed personal behavior experts makes a sweeping judgment that compels treatment or long-term AA attendance based on a half-hour personal interview and a phone call to a family member. The victim might have seen this relative only three times in the last year. But if he was drunk during those three visits (his condition possibly being the only state in which he would make the call), and if he happens to express a liking for an occasional glass of beer to the counselor, then he is packed off to a court-ordered treatment program of varying intensity and duration. This has already happened to me once in this state for driving with an open can of beer in the car. And I have come close to being "sent away" on numerous other occasions by a state-inspired program that apparently is incapable of recognizing the line between personal behavior that, although self-destructive, is not harmful to others and behavior that is genuinely hazardous to society. In California, two of my run-ins with the law have involved alcohol-related offenses. Yet I was not so much as referred to an alcohol counselor or warned about excessive consumption. I have no doubt that the situation would have been otherwise if those violations had involved driving a vehicle, for example. But California at least leaves that man alone who opts to destroy himself in a socially benign fashion. Unlike Minnesota, it holds out for a kind of pacific forbearance with respect to those who only go so far as jumping off bridges in the nude. Of course, I might pay a fine, go to jail, or do public service work for that transgression along the coast, but they would never go to the extreme of sentencing me to thirty days of confinement with a bunch of reformed alcoholic counselors who demand that I evaluate myself in relation to my "higher power." Maybe Minnesota is jealous of the ocean.

WEDNESDAY SEPTEMBER 12, 1990   The Twin Ice Cream Production Plants—Assume that there are two identical ice-cream plants with cost structures the same as the typical plant already analyzed. If each plant had a sold output of 1,000,000 gallons for the year in question, then these are the profit and loss statements for those two plants, given that one plant paid the production workers PIK wages and the other plant paid wages in cash (see table 1).

The cost of PIK wages includes only variable costs in this illustration because those are the only costs incurred in providing those wages. There is no issue in this example over whether fixed costs should be incorporated into the cost of PIK wages. Fixed costs are deducted once and only once in each statement to obtain the respective net incomes. To deduct them again just because wages were paid in kind would falsely inflate the expenses for the statement that encompasses PIK production. That production entails no extra costs other than variable. And so it is seen that a system of PIK wages results in a truly impressive increase in income before taxes. In this example, $20,028 is added to the company's pretax profit, a 51% differential over

TABLE 1

	Plant 1 (Cash Wage)	Plant 2 (PIK Wage)
Revenue:		
1,000,000 @ $2.80	$2,800,000	$2,800,000
(Less):		
Fixed costs:		
$2,800,000 × 10.6%	($296,800)	($296,800)
Variable costs of sold		
output without wages*	($2,297,333)	($2,297,333)
Cost of cash wages*	($166,667)	
Cost of PIK wages		
(added production)**		($146,639)
Net income before taxes	$39,200	$59,228
Savings due to PIK		$20,028

* Variable costs including money wages .88 × $2,800,000

$$= \quad \$2,464,000$$

$$\text{Less money wages of } \frac{1,000,000 \text{ gals.}}{60 \text{ gals./hr.}} \times \$10.00/\text{hr.} = \underline{(\$166,667)}$$

Total variable costs of sold output without wages $2,297,333

**PIK wages:

Necessary total production, X, assuming 6% $KX - .06X = 1,000,000$

$$X \quad = \underline{1,063,830}$$

Therefore, added production, K $= \quad 63,830$

$$\text{Added costs due to } K = 63,830 \left[\$2.80(.88) - \frac{\$10.00}{60} \right] \quad = \underline{\$\ 146,639}$$

(Note: The 6% figure is an approximation of the 5.95 gallons per 100 calculated on page 112. The fixed-costs figure of 10.6% is the earlier estimate of 12% less the 1.4% profit margin.)

income earned when wages are paid in cash. The incentive to this hypothetical ice cream company to adopt PIK is substantial indeed.

FRIDAY TO MONDAY SEPTEMBER 14 TO SEPTEMBER 17, 1990   There has been a break in the weather here, finally, after months of unrelenting heat. The skies are darkly clouded and swirling ominously, but the strong breezes are tinged with a welcome autumnal coolness. I stayed at a cousin's house last night, and he lent me $50 until I pick up my inheritance check next Tuesday morning. I feel as if I am on the threshold of a division in my life. After almost eight years of rootless wandering, marked by swings between grim destitution and ugly overindulgence, I might at last be able to achieve an even keel. I am hoping desperately that this sought-after state of equilibrium is not just a uniform procession of dissipation and economic extravagance. I am hoping I will be able to get and keep a job. I am hoping I will stop or moderate my drinking. Mostly, I am hoping I will not squander the $15,000. If I were to try to save that amount on a $6-per-hour job, I figure it would take me anywhere from five years to infinity, depending on whether my frugality was cruelly prohibitive or just tolerant enough. So I have the wisdom to know the value of this bequest. I just don't know if my behavior can comply with my great store of sagacity and prudence.

On a more impersonal economic level, I return now to the envisioned commune. The foregoing mathematical analysis further illuminates the route that would be taken by those who seek to establish such an organization. The first step would be to identify those companies whose product lines and production job characteristics are suitable to the payment-in-kind process. Then each individual company's cost structure would be studied to determine a range of possible PIK wage outputs given varying levels of employee participation, hours devoted to production that is paid in kind, and differing wage rates. The amount of that production to be paid in kind would then be chosen by reference to that company's product as a proportion of the typical food basket. For example, if the company manufactured canned corn, and if canned corn made up 1% of the food basket's total value, then the company in question would have to produce PIK wages equal to 1% of the value of all of the foodstuffs provided by member plants. So the individual plant would have to be examined as part of the overall network of communal production.

Who would be the founders of such a communal network? It appears that a strong incentive resides with food processors themselves. Similarly, those capitalists looking to invest in start-up ventures might find it attractive to pool their resources in order to build a consortium of food processors that would harness the tremendous competitive advantage of payment in kind. When the feasibility of such a commune is being determined by its founders, an analysis like the one set forth in this diary would be performed for each prospective company to demonstrate the savings made possible by adoption of PIK. These savings, due to the marginal nature of PIK production, will represent one component of the financial resources made available to run the communal distribution network.

Another component of this resource pool would come from the "spread" between the employee's PIK wage and the lesser wage otherwise earned in cash. It has already been shown that in the ice-cream industry this spread is significant: one hour of work under PIK would provide a wage of $10.00/$2.80 or approximately 3.57 gallons of ice cream worth $17.85 at the retail level, compared to a cash wage of only $10.00 per hour. Of course, this differential is due to the use of the lower wholesale price, $2.80 per gallon, in the PIK wage computation. The "spread," in the form of manufactured foodstuffs, and the money savings that flow to the company as a result of the marginal nature of PIK wage production would converge, then, into a pool of resources that would be available to finance the operation of the communal warehouse and distribution system. And this is really the hinge on which the decision to establish the commune rises or falls: Will the expenses entailed in the process of communal distribution be less than the savings that accrue to the companies upon implementation of PIK? Or if an investment in a retail facility is required, will it be justified by the projected savings due to PIK?

Many factors will enter into the algorithm that determines just how the pool of resources will be used. Employees, including factory, distribution, and retail workers, if they are astute, will lay claim to all of the spread and quite possibly to a substantial portion of the company's money savings as well. Because they would be the owners of the warehouse stores' inventory, they might be willing to forgo some of the more gaudy frills and marketing devices found in a typical retail food setting and so have a basis from which to argue for higher wages. The owners of the food-processing companies will of course do all they can to counter the employees' claims and to appropriate PIK savings for themselves. Thus, an adversarial relationship of some kind would probably be an important determinant of the final disposal of any windfall due to PIK and so influence accordingly the decision of whether to implement the system at all.

Where will the employees come from and how will they be recruited? I would like to think that the goals which prompted this foray into utopian economics would be kept paramount in the minds of those who might organize the labor system of any communal production network. If the employees cannot use the commune to escape torturous employment in industries that cater only to the yen for frivolity or luxury, if they cannot gain a more valuable income in the form of goods received than they could earn in the cash economy for the same effort and time, if there is no possibility for control over the conditions of the workplace or influence over the methods of production, then the raison d'être of this whole argument will be washed away in a scramble to exploit by those who perceive this innovation as just another supporting constituent of the bottom line.

Fortunately, prospective employees are not so lacking in discernment that they will rush to embrace a system with no advantages over the money economy. One major incentive to join a commune would be the opportunity to work only part of the year or just part-time throughout the year while being allowed to change jobs frequently, moving from one communal producer to another (perhaps after a specified minimum time commitment), and, in the process, earning enough foodstuffs for one's family for the entire year. In the ice-cream industry, for example, if $1^2/_3$ hours of **PIK** work results in 6 gallons of ice cream per employee being shipped to the communal warehouses, then approximately 28 hours of work will produce the 100 gallons per employee desired by the most voracious of families. Of course, products and companies will demonstrate variations in this respect, differences that will be reflected in the number of credits a particular job provides at the communal warehouse.

The nature of the industry, the type of work, the wage rate normally paid, the amount of the spread in the PIK wage rate that is allotted to the job in question, and any savings due to **PIK** that the company is willing to use to increase employee compensation will all contribute to a determination of the credits earned at the warehouse by a particular job. Presumably, some kind of equilibrium point will be attained for each job where the credits it earns are sufficient to lure enough commune members to fill any available openings. For example, if a particular processor pays an especially low wage in the form of relatively small **PIK** contributions per employee or if the job is relatively miserable in relation to other communal positions, workers will tend to avoid that producer until he raises the credits of that job at the warehouse. Conversely, if a particular processor offers a position that pays a strikingly high wage in credits and thereby attracts the interest of a large number of potential communal workers, that producer might find it to his advantage to lower his PIK wage to a level just sufficient to draw an appropriate number of employees. This might, however, be one of those dimensions of communal employment that members would like to see subjected to negotiation in order to exploit any spectacular savings accruing to a company that finds itself especially rewarded by a system of PIK.

One of the costs that would likely be paid with cash is the outlay necessary for an office of some type which would be responsible for recruiting and scheduling employees. It is possible to envisage this function being modeled after a typical temporary employment office, and it is conceivable that that task could be opened up to bids by existing temporary employment companies. From what I have gathered in my contacts with these firms, one of their significant expenses is selling the idea of temporary labor to the companies that hire their workers. This is one component of the communal employment office that would be absent since the companies would have already established a large number of PIK positions. And once the PIK employees are recruited, they would likely be a much more stable pool of employees than the typical temporary workforce. These factors and the important difference that the PIK employment office (whether contracted out to an existing temporary firm or wholly run by the commune) would not be the actual employer of the commune workers would quite possibly *121* render it much more efficient than the average temporary employment office in business today.

The potential membership of the commune is shaped by certain constraints. Someone already working full-time and making a good wage in the money economy will not be attracted to communal work. Only those people with time to spare or those compelled by ability or outside demands to work at unskilled, relatively low-paying jobs will find the scheme appealing. And these characteristics point to one obvious sector of the population: housewives. I know that the publishers of women's magazines and successful women executives would like to convince us that the liberation of women into economically useful roles is a desirable social goal. But they are an elite who ignore the reality that for many women "liberation" is a passage into a condition not far removed from imprisonment. The vast majority of women go to work not because they seek fulfillment in some lofty and ethereal realm of self-realization. No, they go to work because they have to buy food and shoes for their children, help their husbands pay down the mortgage, or supplement their child support payments with money to rent a decent apartment. They are liberated into standing eight hours a day, five days a week, at a station on an assembly line where they bolt clamps to one part of a high-technology printer. They are liberated into a nightly routine of bouncing between deferential service at table and hectic excursions through a smoky kitchen and a crowded service bar. They are liberated into sitting eight hours at a desk each day with their eyes in continuous focus on filing cards or typewritten pages. When they are done being liberated for the day, they walk along an oppressive city street, limp and smelling of stale perfume and coffee, and liberate themselves further into the thick air of a crowded city bus. When they finally reach home, they tell their kids to go buy some Kentucky Fried Chicken for dinner, flop down into bed, and, when awakened later by their husbands or boyfriends, tell them they've been too busy engaging in liberation for any further activity. So housewives and single mothers represent a potentially prolific source of communal production workers.

Up to now the depiction of the commune has been necessarily sketchy and hypothetical. I suppose that it would require an actual experiment to thoroughly establish the workability of it and elucidate the procedures needed to build and maintain a PIK commune. There is a good possibility that the specific scenario just set forth, wherein food processors originate and finance the communal production and distribution system, will not be feasible for financial or other reasons. Unions or other entrenched employee groups might demonstrate great resistance to a continually changing pool of employees who learn their jobs in minutes, perform them for a few months, and then leave. Sometimes the smallest change in technique—a different way to twist the hand while trimming meat or a certain way to move the body when throwing or stacking heavy items or the proper way to use a tool—can result in an increase in a worker's efficiency that places him on a par with the most senior of veteran employees. But those entrenched workers who are able to impart that information may balk at helping a workforce they find threatening, strange, or disagreeable in principle. So for one reason or another a producer-initiated PIK system must be relegated to a status of only "possibly practical."

Trailing behind the "ideal" and the "possibly practical" comes the "practical" scheme alluded to in earlier entries. The incentive to a producer to form a commune might be great. Savings might be tremendous, but still not enough to overcome philosophical objections or to offset the necessary costs of distribution. One institution in society, though, would appear to have a substantial motive to share any financial burdens with the processors in order to realize a tremendous financial windfall itself. I refer to the federal government. In 1988 the food stamp program cost the federal government $11,149,000,000 and served 18,600,000 participants. In many states these stamps go to able-bodied men and women who are under no compulsion to work for their benefits. In other states and localities a system of make-work has been established wherein participants might rerake a park ten times a week or dally around a flower bed with spade in hand for another forty hours to gain their foodstuffs. In either case, the federal government pays the cost of the stamps. So there is ample incentive for the government to approach private processors and arrange some form of combined financing of communal warehouse and distribution systems. In this case a recruitment office is obviated; the workers show up automatically at the welfare office. And once assigned to a producer for work, the food-stamp applicant would receive credits for his labor like any other commune employee and pick up his food at the communally operated warehouse-store. The government pays nothing for the welfare applicant's food, the processor saves on the cost of wages, and the applicant is saved the humiliation of pulling stamps from his billfold at the grocery store. Thus, if the possibly practical alternative is found wanting, the practical route that invokes federal financial cooperation must certainly be judged worthy of a long hard look.

WEDNESDAY SEPTEMBER 26, 1990   Until 1983 I had flirted with destitution on at least a few occasions. But that year I embraced it unqualifiedly for the first time. I had taken a bus out to San Jose, California, and, walking along a crowded sidewalk in the central business district, I pondered over my finances with trepidation. If I were to buy a meal and a quart of beer, my cash resources would sink below the price of a bus ticket "back home." The prospect of roaming through a strange town without enough money to rent a room or return to my more familiar origins was frightening. So I wrestled in anguish with the decision until finally, stopping in front of a deli, I succumbed to the darker side of destiny and went in and bought some cold cuts, potato salad, and beer.

Now I was at the point of no return. The rest of my stay in San Jose was a typical exercise in attempting vainly to establish myself on little or no resources. For a while I slept outside in the ravines of a community college campus and on the roof of an abandoned building. I managed to get a temporary job through an agency near the end. But by then my resources were so low that I could not afford an alarm clock to awake me on time for work. I came in late a couple of days to the factory where they manufactured book covers and came in even later on day three. I realized then I had to give it up. I gave a forwarding address to the employment agency and hitchhiked to a friend's house in Arizona. That time I went hungry for a few days before dragging myself into a precarious state of bare survival.

That was more than seven years ago, and since then I have become much more adept at dealing with poverty. I was in a state approaching terror back then at the possibility of running completely out of money. It is not like that now, of course. Now I can say that I am capable of going broke anywhere in the world without considering it even worthy of a passing conversation. I have descended into pennilessness so frequently in the interim that a misfortune like stubbing my toe is an occurrence of more noteworthy importance. Part of this equanimity must be due to my having learned how to use resources like missions and meal programs. But a lot of the sangfroid is derived from an indifference to the kind of pain that comes with an utter depletion of financial resources. I think that repetition must inure the human animal to certain kinds of agony.

I'm remembering all this now because I've just been prompted to move away from a place by memories of experiences like the one just related. The place is the Santa Barbara area in California. Last Friday I took a jet plane out to Los Angeles from Charles Lindbergh Airport in Minnesota. I slept outside that night for a couple of hours on a small strip of vacant land next to Los Angeles International Airport. On Saturday I took a bus up to the Santa Barbara area. My intentions were simple enough. I wanted to relocate to one of those smaller towns like Santa Maria or Lompoc north of Santa Barbara. The rents are cheaper there, and I thought getting a job would be easy enough. I had always wanted to explore the islands in the Santa Barbara Channel and living in one of the beautiful mainland areas nearby would afford great opportunities for seafaring adventures. So on Saturday morning I camped at a state beach in Carpenteria on the coast and took a city bus into Santa Barbara proper just to inquire casually about charters and organized trips to the islands.

As I ambled along the shop-lined streets of Santa Barbara and walked out onto the long piers and observed the boats rocking gently in the glistening harbor and the people milling about under the warm sun, I became almost nauseous. My memories of the place, you see, are not good. They are not of tragedy or excruciating pain, but only of a six-month sojourn there between July and December of last year when I collected $130 in unemployment compensation every two weeks while wandering up and down the adjacent coastal areas. This and another stay there of two or three weeks in 1987 when I was broke enough to rely on the Salvation Army for sustenance are the sum of my memories of that place.

But the whole time I was different from other people. Always with bag draped over shoulder, always uncertain of a place to sleep that night, always wary of the police, always the focus of scrutiny as I soaped up and washed under the cold spray of a beach shower, always drinking to excess in flight from real or imagined demons, I felt for those long months that the whole of Santa Barbara must be watching me from behind their reflecting glass windows in their mountainside houses. Sure I was surviving. But I was so out of wavelength with the ample lifestyle of the typical Santa Barbaran that I began to feel I was under the sanction of a kind of unofficial ostracism, like a fugitive from normalcy or an outcast from a conventional existence.

There are many reasons that people either refrain from moving to California or leave it once they've arrived. Some people attribute their avoidance to fear of earthquakes, fires and floods; some people cite the high cost of real estate and the increasing congestion; others say it is difficult to make friends and acquaintances there; an acquaintance of mine back in Minnesota who had spent time in L.A. told me he did not like the "consciousness out there." Yeah, right: "Yes, Mr. Roberts, when making your decision be sure to keep in mind that the consciousness is not too good out here at times." (Real estate agent to potential customer.)

My reason for leaving the state is one I first read about in a slim novel by Richard Brautigan. In *So the Wind Won't Blow It All Away* he wrote that people move to new places to escape bad memories. It was not only my experiences in Santa Barbara. Similar bad memories emanate to me from San Diego, Oceanside, San Clemente, L.A., and Borrego Springs, California. They are especially tormenting because the places are in all other respects unspeakably beautiful. So now I have come to a place where I intend not to have any bad memories: I am staying in a hotel in Waikiki on the island of Oahu in the state of Hawaii. I am very serious about this place. I can't afford to have bad memories in any place anymore because I am running out of places. And if I can succeed here, I can see no reason not to stay in this region of the world for a long time to come. I believe that I am getting closer to home.

SATURDAY SEPTEMBER 29, 1990   On Thursday I boarded a jet plane that carried me even farther south to Kailua-Kona on the Big Island of Hawaii. A combination of shuttle bus and hitchhiking has brought me to this remote town of Waiohinu, where I rent a room in a nearly deserted hotel at the base of a steep, jungle-clad slope. This morning I hitchhiked down the one-lane road that leads to the southernmost point in the United States. The point opens to pastureland and windswept prairie as its immense mass descends to the sea. Starting at the cliffs on the western side of the point, I followed the upper edge of the land around the southern extremity and down to the wave-pummeled, bouldered shore on the eastern side. The water around that remote point is a pale blue of such pristine clarity that it almost elicits an embrace. Looking down from atop high, black lava ledges, one can discern great boulders shimmering in the blue depths as bright orange and black, and lemon yellow tropical fish glitter and flash in the shifting pools of submarine light.

I went to that windy and barren outpost to mark this sought-after division in my life. Like a dreamer in antiquity, I wished I could throw off the shackles of gravitational constraints and fly unaided through the veil of blue mist on the southern horizon there and emerge into the ancient enchantment of the tropical Pacific. But whether or not I ever reach that maritime frontier, I have come to realize that dreams are only an extension of the reality one makes for himself day by day. Drinking to excess is a way to clothe everyday reality in the impractical mists of a dream. It is an indulgence that is childish in the sense that it is an evasion of the day-by-day operation of working to make your dreams come true. So beyond this hoped-for division, I see a more mature Tim Donohue. I cannot guarantee that I will never again get drunk or never again drink to excess. But from now on drinking too much will be like a reversion to childhood for me, and I cannot afford going back too many times. So I will close out this diary on that hopeful note. It is an optimism born of circumstance, so perhaps the only contribution this work will ever make to the literature on alcoholism prevention or to the body of advice to those wishing to quit drinking is this: writing a diary doesn't help.

Part Three

Saturday December 15, 1990   A three-month perspective allows me to view the concept of PIK with a more critical eye. In particular, the analysis of PIK in the diary confines itself almost exclusively to what economists call microeconomics. That is, PIK and its effects are examined there only as they pertain to the individual worker or firm, or a small group of firms. The larger question of how PIK might interact with the economy as a whole—its macroeconomic role—is ignored altogether. But this role is important if any actual benefit from PIK is to be realized by society.

Basically, PIK will work only if it is not adopted on a relatively wide scale. For example, if all of the food-processing firms in America suddenly instituted a program of PIK for their production employees, the marginal nature of PIK production would be lost. Presumably, the employees brought into the program will already have been purchasing something approximating the typical food basket even before their initiation into communal production. For the economy as a whole, then, there will not really be any extra production due to the manufacture of wages as opposed to their payment in cash. Since the entire food-processing industry will be engaged in the PIK system, the communal warehouses will display and sell the same foodstuffs that its members were already purchasing before the advent of communal distribution. The industry as a whole will simply be exchanging production that once led to revenue in cash for an equal amount of production that now serves as a substitute for wages. The industry's actual production will not increase by the amount of PIK wages paid; that overall production will remain constant, and any financial advantage the companies would have enjoyed due to PIK production's marginal nature will have disappeared.

This "nullifying effect" might occur even if the industry as a whole does not embrace PIK. If a company is large in relation to its competitors, and if it commands a significant share or even a majority of the market for its product, then a large number of the communal employees it pays in kind will likely already have been purchasing that product before the commune was founded. Let it be assumed, for example, that the Blue Bell Soup Company has acquired over the years a market position so exclusive that virtually 100% of the soup bought at the retail level bears its brand name. What would happen if this company adopted PIK? The same thing that would happen if the entire food-processing industry adopted PIK. First, revenues in cash would fall by an amount equal to the wholesale value of the soup once purchased by commune members in the grocery store. Second, however, production would remain exactly the same as before, as an amount of soup equal to that lost in sales is shipped to the communal warehouses. Third, the cost of cash wages would drop by an amount exactly equal to the loss in revenue, causing net income before taxes to remain identical to its prior amount. I am not even going to venture into an examination of the possible tax repercussions under this particular scenario.

So PIK holds an advantage over money wages only when

the producer's output is small in relation to his industry's total market, or when a company is newly founded, or when a product is newly introduced. In these cases, essentially what occurs upon establishment of a PIK commune is an enlargement of the member producers' output by an amount equal to those warehouse purchases of member employees that were previously different brands purchased in a grocery store. A new soup company, for example, that used PIK would be able to pay wages out of production that is truly marginal because all of the production employees of the various producer-members of the commune would now be consuming the new brand of soup rather than their old brands. So PIK could very well be a strongly effective competitive tool for those companies just starting up or for those smaller companies wishing to take away market share from the larger firms by denying them the patronage of communal employees or for those smaller companies suffering financial difficulties and in need of a boost in cash flow from the lesser wage cost of marginal PIK production.

Now, whether or not the federal government would deem it appropriate to cooperate exclusively with the smaller companies that would benefit financially from PIK depends on how it defines its own role in society. Already the government assumes a somewhat maverick posture with respect to very large companies: the Small Business Administration, for example, and those legal departments which initiate antitrust actions are ostensibly active in promoting smaller-scale enterprise at the expense of larger. If a greater number of relatively small businesses is truly a goal of the federal government at this stage in history, then a program wherein the food stamp program was merged with a communal network of smaller food processors would not appear to be contrary to any current policy.

/3/

MONDAY JANUARY 7, 1991   If I can stop my hand from shaking, I will recommence the diary. Liquor has not been kind to me during my stay in Hawaii. It's treated me fairly good in the interval right after drinking it, but after that it transforms into a rather cruel and demanding comforter. I went on a ghastly binge here about two weeks ago when for three or four days I would wake up and drink a fifth before noon just to subdue my trembling bones. I know that the great number of people involved in AA would seem to signify that many have flirted with the ruination that can originate in the bottle. But I think the severity of my abuse must be rare. I cannot otherwise explain why I never encounter anyone else who's in as bad a condition as I am. I was glad, though, to read recently that ultimately the alcoholic drinks to become normal—to allow him to climb to a level of feeling that is equivalent to the state of a nondrinker and to settle his metabolism to a more placid level of operation; the whole time I thought I was acting drunk toward people.

It's hard to sort through the effects of alcohol versus those consequences that might come from one's lifestyle in general. Would I be slimmer and healthier if I didn't drink? Would I accomplish more in the creative arena? Would my bank balance be experiencing a less precipitous decline? Would I be able to plan for my future without quaking in panic at the prospect of dissipating my liquid assets on self-indulgence and wasteful habits in general? One possible effect that has been slowly becoming more manifest as the years progress is the loss of a great part of my ambition to learn. I no longer search eagerly through volumes in the library for interesting works in science or philosophy. Usually I am lucky if I can sit down and dedicate a few minutes to paging vacantly through the glossy photographs in magazines like *Vogue, Town and Country,* or *Arizona Highways.* But is this loss of scholastic ardor due to progressive alcoholism or to a deeper, more devastating shift in my psychological outlook? In the long run I suppose that question hardly matters, for if alcohol doesn't take away the desire to learn, it certainly detracts from one's ability to do so. I can no longer apply myself to extended periods of concentration upon any moderately difficult piece of writing. This might be due to brain damage, of course, but it seems just as likely to be caused by my practice of adjourning most study sessions prematurely in order to go have another drink. At those times I can at least tell myself that I will soon subsist under the illusion of clear thinking that alcohol sometimes confers upon its user. It was during one of these interludes of perceived mental clarity that I first realized the fear, since confirmed, that my newly won financial resources would initially experience a horrendous rate of depletion. So at least alcohol is not pulling any surprises. It lets you know from the start that it aims to destroy.

FRIDAY JANUARY 11, 1991   Hawaii does not disappoint those who expect a kind of paradise on earth. At least if you consider only the geographical aspect of existence, then it is hard to imagine a more exquisite atmosphere or a more beautiful setting. The "aloha" spirit can mean many things to a Hawaiian, but to me it connotes a certain fine, gentle feel to the air, the striking clarity of the surrounding waters and skies, the sense of cleansing in the daily cycles of rain and sunshine, and the impression that the hand of God has bestowed a kind of special bounty on the lands of the tropical Pacific.

Palm trees here are full and healthy; unlike their scrawny, transplanted counterparts in California and Arizona, the numerous species here seem to almost glow in the salutary light of their native habitat. Along the boulevards in California it is not uncommon to see palm trees whose slender trunks stretch up to the skies in a slow majestic arc, as if nature were involved in some mighty but graceful attempt to stake out and lay claim to one small parcel of the sun's benevolence. However, on top of that meritorious reach of bark and wood, only a few anemic fronds will be seen to have sprouted toward the heavens. Below that feeble efflorescence, a curtain of dead, dried-out stalks hangs down in listless apathy, as if in disregard of the natural force which strove so arduously to thrust it to such an honorable height above the city. Frequently a pile of these dead fronds will obstruct a pedestrian's way as city crews labor in unceasing efforts to prune away the boulevard's generous yield of vegetation.

/33

In Hawaii, the palm trees are topped by a round bouquet of dark green fronds that gleam in the dazzling sunlight and whisper and sway in the tender solicitude of mild, oceanic breezes. There is no need here to chop off tons of yellowed fronds each year or to saw and prune away undesirable stalks just to promote the growth of a few barely satisfactory branches. No, Hawaiian palms are, apparently, self-pruning. At least I have never seen one being subjected to that operation by a human being. Nor have I ever seen the multitude of date and coconut palms here being deprived of their abundant fruits by a human being. Such is the plenty of this land that millions and millions of coconuts and a similar quantity of dates are left to age on the trees and fall off only after reaching an inedible stage of ripeness.

Signs in the public parks say "Beware of falling coconuts." Shorelines are strewn with the gray, dried-up husks of the coconut palm's surplus offerings. Dates scattered and pulverized on the roadways are routinely blamed for accidents when rain combines with them to lubricate the pavements. Similarly, banana trees, their long, solid, dark green fronds arching over the upper edges of jungle-choked stream gorges or hanging over stone walls along the roadside, are not uncommon sources of overripe fruit. Great bunches of blackened bananas, their meat the consistency of mush, are encountered regularly as one walks along little-traveled roadways or stalks through the shaded pathways above a clear, silky-smooth jungle stream. Squashed papayas are common sights along the highways. Oranges and lemons are left to rot on the school grounds and in the back yards of houses. And the cloying fragrance of fallen passionfruit often pervades the immediate surroundings in the countryside.

On the northeast coast of the Big Island, and around Hilo on the east, great tracts of sugarcane, the plants' tall, grassy stalks waving in the breeze, descend on long slopes to abrupt cliffs by the sea. On small patches of land adjacent to these cultivated acres, a sugarcane plant will many times have taken root accidentally and grown to a harvestable stage so that the hungry passerby need only snap off a mature section of cane and gnaw away to his heart's content. Of course this method is invoked only in emergencies, for all the sugarcane fields are unfenced and available for picking to the passing traveler at any time of the year. Avocados and macadamia nuts offer similar year-round availability, of course, and a walk through an abandoned cattle plantation in the heart of the real estate boom on the western or "Kona" coast will likely reward the visitor with the discovery of an old shack next to a former garden where a variety of leftover onion, taro, and yam plants can be uprooted for the taking.

The ocean here is similarly munificent. By the lava reefs on the Kona coast, one can watch as the incoming swells slowly rise to a wall of glasslike translucence and then smash down into a sputtering mass of brilliant white foam. It is not uncommon to see, as the breaker crests and forms a "window into the sea," a large school of reef fish battling the surge as if in demonstration of a kind of prehistoric surfing. The reef fish along the coasts of these islands come in a great variety of shapes, colors, and sizes.

There are black fish with splashes of orange along their torsos and white lines along their fins and gills. There are flat yellow fish. There are big fluorescent blue fish. There are slender gold fish with billed snouts. There are fish that radiate the variegated pattern of a parrot. There are fish with bright green tails and a veritable rainbow of hues along their main bodies. There are smooth fish. There are rough fish. There are dark fish and there are light. There are red fish and orange fish, huge fish and tiny fish, ugly fish and handsome fish, dull fish and brilliant fish, skinny fish and bloated fish, and so many other kinds of fish that it would take a lifetime to learn how to identify all of them with unerring accuracy. But what is more, almost all of them are edible and all can be caught. You do not need a license to fish in Hawaii, and you can do it with a pole, a net, a spear, or an arrow.

The "bottom-dwelling fish"—those found in deeper waters—are plentiful as well. Ono, mahimahi, many different kinds of tuna, and the infamous marlin are hauled in by the ton each day by both commercial long-liners and the more recreation-oriented trollers and casters. One local fisherman has written a series of books that instruct the less knowledgeable on some of the finer techniques of Hawaiian game fishing. In one book he wrote that he has never been able to tell how long an opelu (a mackerel-like fish used as bait) will stay alive on the hook because within half an hour of immersing his live rig, a monster game fish invariably mounts a furious assault on the hapless lure. So why, given all of these paradisiacal characteristics, am I seriously contemplating leaving Hawaii? Because it's too expensive to live here, that's why. I will address this paradoxical situation further in future entries and perhaps chronicle my efforts, so far futile, to find a reasonably priced place to live.

SUNDAY JANUARY 13, 1991 In fairness to the citizens of Hawaii, I have to admit that I was exaggerating somewhat in the last entry when describing the great surfeit of unwanted fruits and vegetables to be found on the islands. I will leave it to the reader, however, to cull and set aside those statements that could actually be elevated to the status of a lie.

Like many other parts of the United States, Hawaii today sees its land escalating in price due to the pressure of rising population. In Hawaii, of course, the upward trend in prices is magnified immensely by the demand provided by resort developers and those purchasing for only part-time residence. What happens, then, is that land once put to agricultural use is converted to condominiums, golf courses, and hotels. This phenomenon is evident along Alii Drive on the Kona coast, where rocky land, thick with long grasses and vine-strangled trees, has been emptied of its cattle herds and rezoned for tourist-oriented development. Now, a drive along that low coastal road reveals dilapidated wooden cattle chutes and water stations in an irreparable state of disuse next to signs offering the land for millions per acre. Since I have been on the Big Island, a story in the local papers has related the saga of a large island sugarcane plantation, employing thousands and covering miles and miles of territory, that was granted zoning variances by the local governments to sell off some cultivated sugar acres for tourist development and housing in order to offset recent financial shortfalls. And tourists beware! This phenomenon does not always have just a remote, dismissable impact. Another story in the local papers has disclosed that many of the macadamia nuts packaged here and labeled "made in Hawaii" are actually grown in and imported from South Africa!

The lava flows here, of course, compensate to a degree for those lands that are diverted to non-food-producing uses. The lava rocks are not much different from what one might expect: a jagged jumble of stones and boulders, some still intact enough to evidence the wrinkles and ridges formed when they congealed to a solid state after their slow, boiling slide from the summits. From a distance, the newer flows look like vast fields of clumpy black soil that has been recently bulldozed into mounds to clear the area of vegetation. But they are solid clumps, actually, and although plants will grow readily right out of the pores and cracks in the volcanic rocks, a farmer will not usually convert the flow into a field or an orchard until a few hundred years have elapsed since the eruption. The older flows are covered with forests of a kind of primeval, forbidding character, but they are lava flows nevertheless, and don't let anyone tell you they are anything other than hard, jagged rocks.

On the island of Hawaii you cannot go camping as you would in a forest by Lake Superior or by the ocean in California. Unless you are lucky enough to come across a rare patch of sand or a clearing with soil, there simply are no places level enough to sleep on. The camper tells himself that there has to be a spot just beyond the next ridge of rocks or group of trees. But that is not the case. It is all rocks, and they are all sharp, unremitting, and contrary to the natural shape and posture of a sleeping human body. You will not find a suitable resting spot just beyond the next rise or down that slope a little ways or a few hundred feet along the shoreline. You will not find one at all if you are on a flow that has come into existence as recently as the last two or three millenia, and you will end up reconnoitering a substantial portion of the island before realizing that you should have stayed home and harnessed the simple advantages made available by a house and a bed. After a long time, however, the flows somehow evolve into arable land—a process that has resulted in a rich dark soil base on many parts of the Big Island—that can make up for those acres lost to the tourist trade. In this respect, Hawaii is more fortunate than the mainland United States, which must rely on innovations in hybrid technology and more efficient methods of farming in general in order to offset those losses in yield due to the vast quantities of land that are converted each year from soybeans and cornfields, orchards, and truck gardens to suburbs and shopping malls.

TUESDAY JANUARY 15, 1991   I have been told by some that the Big Island of Hawaii is like Alaska in the sense that there is a high rate of growth, a shortage of labor, and a high cost of living. On the Kona coast that is true. It is possible, though, to get a job there in a restaurant or hotel that pays a wage that not only pays the rent and the grocery bill but leaves some money left over for savings as well. This is a situation almost unheard of on the mainland, where a job as a houseman, maid, or dishwasher frequently results in a weekly compensation that is barely enough to scrape by under the stingiest of budgets. How many of those unskilled workers who have augmented the population of Alaska in the last decade or two in the hope of "making it" in a more dynamic economy would instead have flown out here to Hawaii if they had known that a similar financial opportunity awaited them in a less bracing climate? Of course everything is not all candy and orchids here, and in order to demonstrate some of the difficulties that might be encountered by a newcomer, I will present some features of my own failed history as an example.

MONDAY TO TUESDAY FEBRUARY 4 to FEBRUARY 5, 1991   I am in Las Vegas, Nevada, now, after having taken a jet from Kailua-Kona on January 19. I write this at the outset in order to eliminate any residue of suspense that might surround the question of whether my visit to Hawaii really was an economic failure. Of course, I started out with the intention of succeeding. My first day on the island of Hawaii I took a local shuttle bus down Alii Drive on the Kona coast with the idea of searching out a campsite to avoid the stratospheric nightly charges of the island's innkeepers.

It was still autumn and the air was very hot. Even the slightest exertion during the daytime brought beads of sweat to my brow and backside. But the wall of heat seemed to vanish at intervals as the miraculously cooling breezes swept up from the light blue ocean. I had never experienced a kind of heat which at once seemed so torrid yet was so vulnerable to being completely dissipated by the wind. It was not a stifling heat in the least, but one which seemed to be conquered itself by the cooling, ubiquitous aura of the sea. This, and the sense that the physical surroundings—whether the forest-covered land that rose in an awesome slope toward an angry mantle of purple and white clouds, or the clear blue sky just overhead, or the sparkle of the black rocks as they were washed by the crystalline surf—were somehow more vivid than in other places contributed to an atmosphere of strangeness and novelty about the place that kept me almost entranced as I rode the bus and disembarked finally at a new shopping center high above Keauhou Bay.

I walked into a grocery store and wandered spellbound through the air-conditioned aisles, where a mixture of dark Hawaiians and whites examined the array of fresh tropical fish or ordered native dishes like Kalua pig roasted in an envelope of taro leaves from the deli. Innocent that I was, I bought less exotic fare at an unexpectedly high price and then headed down toward the ocean. That shopping center is perched on a flat niche of land that has been carved right out of a frozen cascade of lava, and the road connecting it to the sea winds down steeply between the sculpted lawns of a handsome golf course that has likewise been reclaimed from a sea of rigid lava. Farther below, I passed some expensive housing and then came to the water at the edge of Keauhou Bay. That inlet is singular for

138

its almost rectangular shape, as if the ancient lava had man's orderliness in mind when jutting its lapping frontier of smoking, liquid land into the sea. The landward edge is sufficiently wide to encompass only a sand volleyball court and a diving and snorkeling cruise outfitter. The inlet runs outwardly perhaps only four or five times that length before opening to the congenial blue waters of the Pacific. There are ten or twenty boats of various sizes that moor there—a refreshing contrast to the tightly packed harbors along the coasts of California. I passed a small park at the inner corner of the bay and made my way past the volleyball players and around to the wall of black rocks that defines the bay's southern edge. I stepped carefully over the chasms and gullies in the rocks, nodding to the relaxing tenants of the small cottages that overlook the water there, and came out to a larger expanse of black rock near the mouth of the bay. I ate and drank there while studying the clear ocean as it ebbed and flowed in the chambers and concavities of the boulders at water's edge.

After a while I thought about where I should camp. There was a cold shower at the park I had passed, so I decided to stay somewhere close by. There was a large hotel right behind me, and dwellings surrounded the bay, so I would have to find a spot removed somewhat from the water. I lingered on the black rocks until after twilight and then headed back up the sloping road leading from the bay. On the left side of that road balconied condominiums crowded the sidewalk, but the right side seemed to have an open clearing of some sort. There was a hard-packed, unpaved driveway that came off the road and led into a level place where cars could park or turn around; then the driveway disappeared into a cave of trees. Up beyond this, the open area became a small, irregular field of stones and low shrubs at the foot of a hill. Then, as I walked up the sidewalk, I came to a ring of tall palm trees close to the roadside. In fact, they were right next to the sidewalk. Bushes had been planted here and there on the small ring's perimeter and fine gravel scattered within in an apparently abandoned effort to landscape the empty roadside parcel.

I was tired, and I was ignorant of the island's topography. For all I knew I could spend the entire night in an erratic, unsuccessful search for a place to sleep. So I slipped through the ragged wall of bushes, quietly smoothed the gravel underfoot,

/39

and carefully pitched my tent in the closing darkness. As I lay inside my tent, just across the street from a large expanse of fashionable dwellings that reached down toward the sea, I became aware of that main troubling characteristic of nights in Hawaii that was to contribute greatly to my inability to live there. First, it must be understood that Hawaii is an isolated speck of human propagation in the midst of a vast, unpeopled sea. Perhaps there is no other outpost of humanity in the world that is farther removed from the vitiating lights of neighborhood populations. So the nights are very dark—no, they are black. On a moonless night they are a deeper shade of blackness than might be confronted in even the remotest of continental wildernesses. The stars, of course, assume a corresponding brightness of aspect. I am not lying when I say that the more brilliant stars in the Hawaiian firmament require that the night observer shade his eyes when letting his gaze rove in the near vicinity of their startling luminescence. But of course the glare of the starlight is hardly sufficient reason to depart from an otherwise enchanted and charming outpost.

As I lay in my tent that first night I quickly became aware that geographical isolation is the father of another disturbing nighttime feature: complete, pristine silence. As I lay motionless in my tent, and as I squinted up through the transparent mesh ceiling to the harsh sparkle of a particularly bright star, the surrounding silence became almost deafening in its intensity. Occasionally the words of a low conversation or the clink of glasses could be heard distinctly from somewhere within the tract of luxury homes. But this was almost a relief. In the interludes between those gentle clashings of dinnerware or the swells of distant laughter, I strained my ears to detect some tiny break in the uniform absence of sound. And when I did hear something, it was as if that noise, no matter how minute, radiated through the night air for the whole world's appreciation or scorn. The wind had subsided earlier so that the palms and the bushes and the forest down the road were utterly still. The birds had stopped singing, too, after sunset, but this did not prevent them from betraying their whereabouts; their presence was the only way I could account for those slight rustlings of foliage or tickings in the treetops nearby that could be heard as clearly as the chiming of small bells. Of course, when a car rolled down the roadway toward the bay it might as well have been the advance contingent of a cavalry raid or an escaped herd of stampeding cattle.

Now this strange and solemn quietude would not normally have provided me with any reason for vexation or dissatisfaction. Actually the silence engrossed me; the air had cooled to a level that allowed me to lie naked in perfect comfort; and the stark brilliance of the immense night sky seemed to clasp me in a rapture of wondering observation. But pretty soon I grew tired and I pondered sleep. I thought I might be in the last stages of mesmerized wakefulness when a car wheeled down the roadway, slowed, and with a conspicuous crunch of gravel turned into a driveway across the street, just off to the left of my tent. An automatic garage door opened with a piercing rattle, and the car pulled into the stall. Two car doors opened and slammed shut, and, as the garage door jostled downward, two sets of shoes clapped along the concrete. The garage door shut tight and the muffled sounds of jingling keys and a door thumping shut lingered in the quiet aftermath. I parted the front flap of my tent, and through the bushes I saw a light go on in an upstairs room of the condominium right across the street. Slowly I reclined back to my bedding and tried to relax.

The tension was slowly draining from my limbs when a knob turned and a door opened on the balcony across the street, just twenty-five or thirty feet from where I lay. After the door clicked shut, two sets of feet—now clad only in stockings, apparently— thudded softly across the balcony floor and a jarring scrape like a piece of furniture being moved lofted into the night.

I heard a creak, like a spring or a frame being strained. Then, such was the pure silence of the night, I could hear very clearly what could only have been—judging from the occasional creak of the furniture, the wet sound of separating lips, and the sometimes audible breathing—a long, passionate, kissing embrace. Meanwhile my torso and limbs were frozen into a pose of absolute stillness. I dared not so much as drag a finger across the plastic floor of my tent. The passage of each breath seemed to almost resound inside my little nylon hovel. For many minutes I listened in petrified attention as the sibilance of kisses or the creak of the furniture floated into the night. At times the two bodies would become utterly quiet, and I hoped that they were about to quit the balcony and go finish the job in a more appropriate location. But the minutes wore on with the lovers perfectly content to practice their art in the sweet ether of the tropical Hawaiian night.

Presently I began to itch. I had forgotten, I realized now, to rub myself with the ointment I had received from the clinic at the University of Minnesota just one month earlier. As usual, that prescription turned out to be more palliative than curative. Every four hours or so, if I didn't apply the salve, the red lesions that now covered perhaps a fourth of my upper body would degenerate into a turmoil of aggravation. For a couple of minutes I waited in a motionless state, listening to my measured respiration, while trying to withstand the increasing irritation of the rash. But finally I could bear it no longer. Slowly I lifted my right hand to my left elbow and scratched. I gritted my teeth as my fingernails plowed raspingly across a small patch of unhealthy skin. So far so good, but now the itching on my back began to intensify. I brought my right arm back to my side and, using that elbow for support, I tried to slowly do a kind of twisting sit-up. My body shook as I carefully raised it above the ground. The plastic floor crinkled, and the gravel grated below my elbow. Even that small exertion caused my breath to come harder as I attained a half-upright position. I stopped and listened to the total silence. For a minute or more my breath came in tremulous flows, and my heart pounded almost audibly. Then, at last, a relaxed, husky exhalation drifted across the darkness from the balcony, and my torso slumped with relief. Slowly I hoisted myself to a full sitting position. I scratched the red welts on my upper back, and my skin warmed with the relief. But then the itching on my left shoulder became most noticeable and I scratched that. I scratched the back of my neck and then my chest and then the area just underneath my left jawbone. Then the spot on my left elbow that I had scratched originally began to itch again, and I scratched that. I looked at my large cloth luggage bag and wondered about getting out the ointment. I had already opened the bag's zipper to get out the tent, but all my belongings in the luggage were inside loosely packed white plastic grocery bags. In the darkness I could only see what looked like a grotesque fresco of wrinkles and mounds. I did not even know which plastic bag my toiletries were in.

I concentrated again on the silent night, and the creaking of the furniture seemed to imply the obliviousness of my neighbors. Slowly I moved my right hand over to the left side of the tent to a position over the bag. Then, picking the cloth sack's nearest extremity, I pushed my straightened fingers into the tangle of plastic ridges and creases. I clenched my teeth as the sound of brittle, crumpling plastic filled the space inside my tent. I groped among the folds and crevices for the smallest sign of a toiletry, grimacing with tension whenever the sacks responded with maraca-like sensitivity. At last, my fingernail nudged something hard and solid. I pinched the object between my fingers and found it to be the cap of a shampoo bottle. Gently I moved my fingers along the plastic and found the top of the enclosing bag. Then I smoothly plunged my fist into the sack's mouth and began to finger the top layer of familiar objects. There was the toothpaste, an old aftershave bottle, a new bar of soap. The ointment was probably buried under the whole assemblage. I shoveled out a small hole in the surface of the collection and began to rummage through the deeper layers. I winced as the plastic rattled and the tubes and bottles clattered. The shroud of plastic seemed to roar as I delved my fingers among the articles and shuffled them from one side of the sack to the other.

A loud noise from the balcony stopped my fingers in place. I froze as once again the piece of furniture was scraped jarringly across the balcony floor. The thump of two pairs of feet retraced the pathway to the door, the knob clacked, the door opened, the footsteps receded to the interior, and the door was pulled shut. I swallowed hard and vented a large lungful of air. It was too late now to wonder if they had heard me. I searched hurriedly through the contents of the plastic sack and withdrew the tube of ointment. For the next few minutes my skin basked in the cooling ingredients. I put the tube away and thought to myself that perhaps I should leave this place. I took out a bottle of Canadian whiskey and pondered the question over a few slugs and some shots of water as chasers. Could they actually have heard what in reality must have been only the minute rattle of plastic and the soft clatter of toiletries muffled by a cloth bag and a tent? My head grew drowsier with the liquor and I began to rationalize my disinclination to move: they could have thought it was a mongoose, for example, which are as plentiful on Hawaii as squirrels are on the mainland. Or maybe they possessed the magnanimity to allow a destitute and innocuous homeless man the benefit of one insignificant night within the radius of their psychological territory.

The soliloquy did not last long. Within ten minutes I heard a car rolling slowly down the street. Through the orange tent I saw the glare of a bright searchlight. My heart thumped as the erratically shifting beam migrated toward me. Finally the harsh glare caught my tent and fixed itself on its translucent walls. The car turned slightly and pulled up to the curb to face me at an angle as it parked. In a panic I fidgeted on a pair of pants, shielded my eyes, and stepped out of the tent. I squinted around the intense beam and saw the blue police light on top of a blue Camaro. Inside the car a young, bespectacled Oriental man put a microphone to his mouth, and a loudspeaker broadcast his clipped entreaty. "Will you please move on, sir?" he said. "Yes," I gushed, almost gratefully. "Yes," I said, "thank you very much. Thank you." I would not be surprised if I actually bowed down to him as he turned his car around and drove slowly back up the hill. It's not important, really, where I ended up spending the remainder of that first night on the island of Hawaii. However, that first night should have acted as a prefiguration for me of those obstacles I would encounter later on the island. That first night encapsulated the essence of my difficulties there, which I will now be able to describe very economically in a future entry.

FRIDAY FEBRUARY 8, 1991   After that first adventuresome night on the Big Island, I undertook the excursion to South Point already described. The waters around that point, by the way, must qualify as some of the roughest in the world. The wind accelerates as it slides around the island's southeastern shore and beats up a sea of huge swells that forbid negotiation by any vessel that does not fit under the classification of "ship." After returning from that trip, I was able to rent a room fairly promptly in Kailua-Kona. Within a couple of weeks I obtained a job as a dishwasher in a Mexican restaurant "in town," on the main street that lines the broad, peaceful bay. The job was miserable but tolerable enough for six dollars an hour. The heat intrinsic to tropical latitudes and the clouds of steam flowing from the dishwashing machine combined to keep me drenched in perspiration throughout each shift. I was popping salt tablets like candy and driving off the more dryly attired waitresses and busboys in paroxysms of disgust as I hustled out to the service area to grab another tubful of dirty dishes or sweatily returned a rack of clean glasses and a welter of hot silverware to the shelves. I was a damn good worker, but I always looked as if I had just emerged from a swim in the bay. On those rare occasions when I had to cross through the dining room to use the restroom, customers would look with concern at the silverware or china resting on their linen tablecloths. Any piece of dinnerware graced by a waterspot would elicit furtive glances, hands would slide the offending articles, wrapped in napkins, below tabletop, and a sudden flurry of clandestine buffing would proceed to vibrate the tables and chairs in the dining room.

After a month or so of that job, my left elbow became very sore. The morning after each work shift, I could not even straighten that arm to a rectilinear position. Another infirmity I contracted from washing dishes was a severe numbness in my right hand. The spray gun that I utilized to hose off the dishes with hot water was in a continuously leaky condition. As I squeezed my hand around the activating lever and the nozzle itself, a stream of liquid ran down the connecting hose from above and immersed my tensed-up right hand in a perpetual bath of steaming H_2O. The parts to fix the leak had to be shipped from the mainland so my hand grew gradually stiffer, more numb, and less capable of limber movement as the weeks wore on. Near the end, it was difficult if not impossible to even so much as write my signature to make a withdrawal from the bank.

Now, that these afflictions developed on the job and ultimately induced me to quit is not so astonishing, given my catastrophe-riddled employment history. But here is what was strange about this particular job-related malady. After I quit and spent my days typing in my rented room, the soreness in my elbow and the numbness in my hand slowly subsided. But then, whenever I returned to the vicinity of the restaurant, those conditions would reappear in those same bodily locations, not so severely, but very definitely nevertheless. Actually, the symptoms would reemerge whenever I got close to the town of Kailua. For a while I thought that my bicycle was to blame. The operation of the brakes required the same kind of clamping hand motion as the dishwashing sprayer, and it was possible that the three-mile ride from my room into town somehow induced a slight fatigue or irregularity in my arm muscles that would account for the renewed soreness in my elbow as well. But when I walked into town a couple of times, the same two weird and sickening symptoms came on again. Of course, since Kailua was the main place to buy groceries, liquor, and other supplies along the northern Kona coast, this reaction was extremely inconvenient and annoying. I suppose doctors would classify a condition like that as psychosomatic. But its principal irritating quality is not the token pain or the numbness per se, but the sense of powerlessness it brings. No link can be discovered between the sensations induced and a causative agent, and this absence makes it seem as if the world has turned topsy-turvy and we are all floating in an atmosphere without rules or logic to moor us to a secure frame of reference. Well, after a couple of weeks of this eerie phenomenon, my psychological apparatus apparently returned to normal. I could walk right into the heart of Kailua without so much as an inkling of those former bodily burdens. So I was normal again. Come to think of it, I *was* drinking to excess in my rented room during that strange period, which might have anesthetized the elbow and revitalized the hand, except during those periods when a trip to town meant a temporary elimination of the necessary medicine from my body.

Saturday February 9, 1991   Hawaii's benign climate, combined with the forbidding cost of real estate, makes it attractive to build houses that are little more than the shells of more substantial structures. The walls, ceilings, and floors might be there, although sometimes even these are supplanted by screens or skylights, and they might be there in a very modern and appealing style, but they are little more than dividers to keep one room's occupants out of sight of the other. A builder constructing a houseful of rooms intended to be rented at the lower scale of prevailing market price, which on the Kona coast is usually around four or five hundred dollars a month, has little choice but to tack together a dwelling that satisfies only the most basic of shelter and partitioning requirements while still presenting a sleek, modern face to the marketplace. The prohibitive cost of the land upon which he erects the structure necessitates a style of construction that is cheap enough to maintain his expected return on investment. Thus, the weather and the real estate market on Hawaii have converged to bring into existence a large number of very thinly walled rental units.

I stayed in two of these rooms while living on the Kona coast—one for a month and the other for two. It is probably wise not to divulge the addresses of these abodes, since their owners are still living in them, but I can say that they are both located in subdivisions. The Big Island does not have neighborhoods, it has subdivisions. One can look up from the seashore at the edge of a scrubby, rock-punctuated desert just north of downtown Kailua and gaze at the vast forested slope that towers above the town like a broad green wedge thrust up from the sea. The summit is miles and miles away. Interspersed among the extensive fields of foliage, a scattering of roofs are detectable here and there, next to tiny projecting telephone poles, perhaps, and recognizable as a subdivision by the thin line of a main road that scores the adjacent mountainside from its base. The subdivision is actually much larger than it appears from the edge of the sea and up close is not distinguishable from a suburban neighborhood elsewhere in the country, except that the houses, like those in California, are somewhat crowded together. In Hawaii, though, the subdivision will likely be surrounded by an enormous expanse of wild, unoccupied land. Why this incongruity exists is explainable by reference to a combination of things.

A lot of these old lands, many of which are still crisscrossed by stone walls built centuries ago and marked by stone fire pits and other relics of ancient civilization, are owned by the government. Still more of the lands are owned by private trusts that for one reason or another decline to offer their holdings for development. A lot of the terrain, whether controlled by public or private interests, is so steep or rocky that development is precluded altogether. So whether it is a result of policy or a consequence only of an accidental convergence of circumstances, much of the affordable housing on Hawaii finds itself situated in a crowded cluster of similar buildings sequestered in the midst of an immense wilderness. Viewed from one perspective, this scheme appears prudent. If all of the people living on Hawaii today had been able to acquire their own twenty-acre estate, the whole island might be developed by now. But from another perspective—that of the person who rents a room in the subdivision—the scheme is nothing short of calamitous.

The subdivisions are not confined to the mountainsides, of course, and one of the rooms I rented was in a development just a few blocks from the ocean. But in both cases I would return home from work in the dead still of night to a room where the smallest sound penetrated the walls and expanded out to herald my arrival with trumpet blasts and thunder from on high. I usually did not get home until after the landlords of my dwelling, who invariably inhabited the quarters right next to mine, were asleep. If another tenant, perhaps renting the room two doors down the main hallway, was snoring that night, I felt relieved. The sound of his regular, chafing breaths would pervade the house and impart a low hum to the underpinnings of the whole establishment, so that I could at least undress and mix a drink without convulsing the household into wakefulness. But on those nights when that other tenant knew only quiet repose, a night after work was one of the most stressed and trying intervals of relaxation I have ever known.

I would close the door and gently tiptoe toward the lamp. Through the screened window, the lower stars seemed to be like white flames frozen in place and glowing out from glass enclosures fixed for eternity in the emptiness of remotest space. The air just outside the window was like an unresisting medium through which the very essence of the black night could press in and engulf the psyche with its spirit of silence and its patient, hollow inertia. I would click the light on, undress, and make a cocktail only with the greatest of care and delicacy. Sitting down on my bed, I would unfold a large paper bag as if it contained a heap of the world's most fragile Christmas tree balls. Slowly I would withdraw the groceries and place them on the night stand. My finger would work its way around the edge of the sour cream container and lift off the top as if I were removing the key-activating device in a ticking bomb. In slow motion I would grab the bag of flavored potato chips and pull apart the top two edges with the tenderness of one who is pulling off a bandage from a baby. Placing the dip-laden chip in my mouth, I would clamp together my molars and almost cringe as the crisp morsel began to crack inside my mouth. I would bring the full force of my teeth to bear on the french-fried wafer, and a crackling explosion would shatter the motionless air and reverberate into the night.

Later, after relieving myself in the commode, an operation requiring an expert sense of ballistics to avoid sending intimations of the rather private flow rippling through the proximate environment, I would flush the toilet and the whole building would resonate as if a small bomb had just been detonated in the plumbing. At this point it will be understandable to the reader why eventually I started to take my after-work showers at the facilities at the foot of the Kailua Bay pier rather than provoke the whole neighborhood into wakefulness by performing that thunderous duty within the echoing chamber of my gauze-walled bathroom. It will be understandable too, I hope, why I finally decided that I could not live on the Kona coast. To procure living quarters there with the privacy I desired would require paying a rental charge of perhaps eight hundred or a thousand dollars per month. So I knew I had to go.

WEDNESDAY AND THURSDAY FEBRUARY 13 TO FEBRUARY 14, 1991 Among the shops and restaurants that one finds in the little malls that bracket the bayside road in Kailua are a number of booths with attendants who furnish free information about tours, activities, and the like to inquisitive visitors. There is one question, though, that I am better qualified to answer. If a vacationer in Hawaii were to approach the booth I was in and ask for a list of minimal equipment requirements for camping on the Big Island, I would hand him a piece of paper with this enumeration: "1. One sheet." I would then explain that the sheet could be twin or full size, white or a floral print, or of any proportion of cotton or polyester materials that he thought most appropriate under the anticipated outdoor conditions. I would point out to him that the sheet, perhaps in combination with a long-sleeved shirt and a pair of trousers, would provide sufficient warmth and protection during even the most severe of Hawaiian cold snaps, at least if he camps in the lower altitudes and the sky restrains its inclination to rain. I would inform him also that the sheet might require a foundation of cardboard, laid over a stretch of level sand or a smooth stone by the beach, but that this is the only accessory he need acquire to experience a bugless and delightful lapse of slumber in the intoxicating night air of Hawaii.

If, in a flight of skepticism, he demanded to know my credentials, I would tell him that after moving out of the last room I was to rent in Kailua-Kona, on Christmas Day of 1990, I biked with some of my equipment to the south of town and set up a tent on a little patch of sand on top of a high cliff that fell to the sea, a location that was on private land, I was told by a passing bow fisherman, and where, he said, I could stay indefinitely without worrying that someone might tamper with my belongings. The next morning, I left my campsite and bicycled to a gas station about a mile and a half distant to buy coffee and donuts and, upon returning to my newly installed encampment, found that my tent had been dismantled and taken away, the sleeping bag stolen, and my clothes and utensils rummaged through to filch whatever other small article or device might be of use to an apparently very indigent and opportunistic thief. I would proceed to enlighten my client by describing the next week of my outdoor experiences, which would testify very well to the worthiness of a sheet as the sole piece of equipment necessary to sleep outside on the Big Island of Hawaii. After that, if he cared to listen further, I would narrate the remainder of my experiences on the Big Island in the following way.

I decided to give island living one more chance before leaving. I rented a storage closet in Kailua and took a bus to Hilo, where the rents were cheaper, according to the ads in the paper. The road to the island's eastern side traverses a bleak plateau of rock and gnarled trees until the town of Waimea, where suddenly the landscape blossoms into a living tapestry of meadows, forests, and fields. The highway swings down through cane fields to the sea, and jackknifes back and forth around enormous gorges where streams and cataracts pump life into palm trees and bamboo, banana trees and huge vines, so that the traveler believes he has arrived in paradise at last. The town of Hilo is a welcome transition for the wayfarer who might have submerged himself too long in the harsher hustle of the Kona coast. The town is old. Many of the sidewalks are engraved with the initials WPA, and at least one older bridge displays a plaque relating that its source of financing was the Federal Emergency Agency, way back before Pearl Harbor was bombed or statehood was an accomplished fact. The houses are almost universally roofed with corrugated metal and sided with vertical panels of wood. They spread out from downtown along the flat coastal lands or rise up on contoured roads toward the snow-capped mountaintop, so that the tourist might fancy that an Oriental giant has placed them there, actually, as decorative terrace markers in his lush tropical garden by the sea. In fact, the Oriental character of the place is not an illusion. A white man in Hilo is not unheard of, but a walk along the downtown streets or a stroll through a suburban-style grocery store will quickly gain him the experience necessary to lay claim to minority status. Many of the citizens are of Japanese ancestry, many are native Hawaiians, and many are probably such a complicated mixture of Oriental, Polynesian, Portuguese, and other European strains that it is hardly worth keeping track anymore. Why they all came to Hilo, making it the island's largest town, must be attributable to the diverse local agriculture, for it rains enough in that town to put the weatherman out of business. Any average citizen could achieve professional meteorological status by simply opening his eyes upon awakening each morning and stating, uncategorically, that today in Hilo, it will rain. It is not an unpleasant rain, however, and a person could spend long months, or years even, content to sit out the watery spells by a window, listening to the soft pelting drops on the metal roof, while watching a more intense storm showering the gray, shimmering sea in the distance. I did this on a few occasions in the motel room I rented there for a couple of weeks, a residency I had hoped would result in more permanent quarters. Unfortunately, the ads in the paper turned out to be illusory. Sure, there were reasonable places to rent in Hilo—a three-bedroom house for six or seven hundred a month or, more rarely, a studio apartment for three hundred and fifty. But almost all of the ads that I was concerned with were placed by agencies. The rental housing for individuals in Hilo turned out to be controlled for the most part by large companies who managed a great number of units and maintained long waiting lists of applicants willing to be patient for the privilege of becoming a tenant. I remember calling up one agency about a studio in a tower by the sea, going for four hundred and seventy-five a month. When the girl asked me how soon I needed the apartment, I ventured an apprehensive, "Well, maybe a week or two." She laughed in my face.

After a week and a half of vain searching, I finally gave up the idea of living on Hawaii. So now I am inhabiting a tiny little apartment in Las Vegas, on a busy commercial street and about an equal distance from both downtown and the Strip. I am the first tenant to live here since the place was refurbished after a fire, and I feel good about using the brand-new stove and sink and shower, and I am sure that I will be here for six months or maybe even a year.

It's been almost a year since I started the diary, and although I have not escaped the habit that prompted its inauguration into the realm of the world's greatest literature, still, I have a home now, at least for a while, which is something I could only dream about on this date one calendar year ago. So maybe this is a good juncture at which to end my story. I have journeyed from homelessness to more legitimate, and sheltered, status, a simple voyage that is not as dramatic as an ancient tragedy or a modern war but good enough for me. Of course, someday I will return to that magnificent "fleet of islands" in the Pacific. But next time I will not rely so heavily on the vagaries of the local real estate market. First I'll get a boat.

Part Four

THURSDAY JUNE 20, 1991   I have decided to reopen the diary in a postscript form. I suppose I could write a short story or an essay that would focus on more wholesome themes than drunkenness, but it seems more suited to a continuation of my writing that the subject be an activity that I have pursued with such uninterrupted dedication. I *am* an alcoholic. It is a condition that I am not averse to acknowledging. There are people, of course, who will attend AA meetings year after year, week after week, admitting that they are alcoholics. But then when they fall off the wagon and go into a bar for some drinks, you find that they have suddenly elevated themselves to the status of "social drinkers." Now I suppose their denial is understandable when viewed from a certain sympathetic perspective. But it does seem to me that they have turned the situation around—that in reality a person is an alcoholic only when he's drinking; that when he has finally accumulated a certain number of months or years of healthful sobriety he no longer should be classed under that somewhat derogatory heading. As an illustration, would a person who has succeeded in becoming slim and trim through Overeaters Anonymous introduce himself at his next meeting by saying, "I am John and I'm severely overweight"? Why shouldn't this scenario seem just as ludicrous when the problem is alcohol rather than food? I mean, what do I have to look forward to if I quit drinking for twenty years and I *still* have to call myself an alcoholic? By the same logic, I am still in need of a cure for the measles, I am still afflicted with the mumps and the chicken pox, and my appendix is in want of removal seventeen years after the operation.

Well, it's easy to have fun with the subject of alcohol, but that perspective ignores the painful aftereffects and the sheer physical devastation that follows in the wake of excess. For me, the main aftereffect, or hangover, is mostly emotional, or at least an aberrant physical state that contains within it a strange, even ghastly, emotional condition. You wake up after having drunk during all your waking hours the previous day, perhaps having consumed a full liter of hard liquor by the time you hit the sack. You open your eyes and find yourself shaking throughout—not just your hands and limbs, but your whole body shuddering and on edge as if you had fallen to sleep in a snowbank rather than a bed. Your next reaction to consciousness is hard to verbalize. At AA meetings I have attended I have heard it called fear, but that's not quite right. It's more like an overwhelming terror at the fact of existence itself. To get up and put the coffee on is a chore of such daunting proportions that you close your eyes and shiver and sweat and hope for death rather than even contemplate the difficulty of sitting up, putting your feet on the floor, standing, putting one foot in front of the other, and walking over to the stove. Then when you finally do it, the pain is even worse than you anticipated. Because combined now with the ache in your heart and the nervous chill in your veins is the realization that ever more complex tasks await you as the day progresses. Shaving, taking a shower, and getting dressed loom like basic training would to a new recruit. And if you finally succeed in concluding those chores, you sit down, sip some more lukewarm coffee, and practically slip into paralysis at the prospect of going outside, emerging from the shade, and cringing at the sparkle of the naked Nevada sun, and then proceeding to actually undertake some worthwhile or productive activity.

Saturday June 22, 1991   The first phase of an alcoholic's morning entails mulling the fork in the day's prospective agenda. Either he will start drinking almost immediately after waking or he will postpone intoxication until the sun has traversed at least some significant stretch of arc in the firmament. He must contend in either case and to one degree or another, however, with the supreme consternation that accompanies his hangover. If he can get cleaned up and dressed, perhaps clean his room and drink some coffee, he has achieved the equivalent of half a day's work. He bristles at each small task as if its performance were going to unleash a torrent of lizards and foul vapors into his immediate surroundings. To exert the effort to read a book—to actually allow his perceptions to be temporarily swallowed by the mindset of another person—takes on the horror of being lunged into the maw of a Tyrannosaurus rex. Even food—that sustainer of life and cheer—is transmogrified, by its capacity to check the river of welcome alcoholic effect, into a black and repugnant agent. So by now the alcoholic has decided. He sits at his table as the sun slowly ascends from the horizon, pours himself another strong brandy on the rocks, meditates on his gradual retreat from the scarred and smoky soulscape that greeted his awakening, and slowly sinks into a numbing alcoholic stupor.

   Usually I am not so unfortunate that I cannot get cleaned up and dressed before confronting what will be the day's agenda. I remember when I was homeless. Then, performing the basic functions of life—dressing, cleaning, eating—usually required so much time for packing and unpacking, and for traveling from one mission or agency to another that by the end of the day I felt a real sense of accomplishment—I could drink a quart of beer or a half-pint of whiskey while watching the sun set and feel justly rewarded for having so successfully navigated the redoubtable maze of charitable institutions. It is not like that today. Because I have been caught up in liquor's insidious cycle, I have accomplished very little over the last two or three months. In fact, this latter interval might someday be honored by me in a christening ceremony as "the most wasted period of my life." I have not exerted much in the way of personal effort to improve the situation, either. In fact, some of the things I've done in the last two or three weeks have only served to aggravate the hangover effect already discussed and caused me to congeal even more solidly into a posture of inactivity and sloth. But I find the contemplation of those misadventures so depressing that I better save their description until the next entry.

MONDAY TO SATURDAY JUNE 24 TO JUNE 29, 1991 My grandmother, who was from Ireland, used to say that in America your pocketbook is your friend. If that is true, then it is especially the case in Las Vegas. And as long as you have that one friend, bristling with cash, this whole town opens up to become one of your most sympathetic companions. Your faults and habits, your deficiencies in appearance or virtue, your quirks and peculiarities, your lack of refinement or grace, all wither into insignificance here when your social standing is vouchsafed by a wallet bloated with large, government-backed bills. The treatment given to high rollers in this town would almost make one believe that if the dead were to rise, they would be welcome *here,* at least, as long as they had a jingle in their pockets and a willingness to expend their resources on a long string of *extremely* risky investments.

For those of us not so fortunate to have either the prerogatives of the rich or the influence of the dead, Las Vegas can still provide one of the most wonder-filled experiences to be had perhaps anywhere in the world. It is permitted to drink alcoholic beverages as you walk along the sidewalk here, and so a number of times I have equipped myself with a small bottle, placed in a pocket or a bag, and set out to walk the three miles or so from my apartment to the Strip. Along the way I stop at a convenience store for a large cupful of ice and mix, and then time my drinking so that as the straw is just slurping up the last drops of the cocktail, I have arrived at another liquor store. In this way I might end up drinking close to a fifth (750 ml.) by the time I walk the eight or ten miles from my apartment to the south end of the Strip.

It is a very enjoyable walk. The thermometer might read 98 or 100 degrees, but it is a dry "Pacific slope" sort of heat, and

the breeze is usually sweeping down strongly from the surrounding mountains, so that I feel as if I am being bathed in a
warm, amiable fluid both inside and out. The palm trees flutter
and stream in the wind against a backdrop of immaculate blue
sky, the sidewalks are animated by a steady flow of people for
miles and miles between the two walls of huge gambling halls
and hotels, the sound of a player piano or a lounge band wafts
out with the refrigerated air from the wide doorway of a casino,
and, as I detour to wind my way through the labyrinth of "the
Sands" or "the Mirage," everywhere there is the knock of dice
against felt-covered tables, the glitter and toll of endless lines of
slots, the comforting click of poker chips and the clangor of
coins, and the impression, conveyed from all around, of a
peaceful, well-ordered colony, a structured world of the fantas-
tic that survives on and exudes the dignity appropriate to—an
enormous influx of cold, hard cash.

The problem is that by the time I get to the end of the Strip,
I am drunk. And in that state I do things that upon later reflec-
tion when sober seem deeply mysterious and nearly unfathom-
able in motivation. And what I have done on four occasions
now after traversing the Strip is gone to see a show, where I
have abandoned civility and become—a heckler. My career in
celebrity harassment so far comprises four different shows:
Redd Foxx and friends at the Hacienda, Sam Kinison at the
Dunes, the Highwaymen at the Mirage, and George Carlin at
Bally's.

Foxx was playing in a rather intimate theater with a stage
surrounded by tiers of linen-covered tables, and I ended up getting a seat about fifty feet off to the right of center. By the time
Foxx was five minutes into his routine, I had howled out a couple of abusive remarks that had brought an usher swooping
down quickly to admonish me into more decorous conduct. On
his second visit, after my third outburst, that attendant reproved
me rather severely, with intimations of a possible forced removal, so I was able to suppress my enthusiasm for the next half
hour or so. But then Foxx made a joke, whose first part I cannot
recall, which culminated in the punchline, "and two brothers
went through the green light." I shouted out, "and five went
through the red!" Foxx looked over at me and said, "What's
that?" I said, "and five went through the red!" Foxx repeated
that line on stage to the absolute dead silence of the whole the-

ater. You see, by "brothers" he meant fellow black men. Not wanting to seem racist, I then shouted out a joke I had made up a few months earlier that was meant to make *me* look stupid. "Hey Redd," I shouted, "why do people like me follow boxing?" "Why do people like you follow boxing?" he asked through the microphone. "Because we only have to keep track of two players!" I bellowed, but once again the joke, when repeated by Foxx on stage, was greeted by a strange, deathly silence. Not wanting to lose face completely, I started in on telling him another joke about how the more I drink, the stupider I get, but it's not all bad, because the stupider I get, the more I like this town. But before I could get five words into that one, Foxx shook his clenched fist at me, momentarily slipping into his "Sanford" role, and shouted, "If you don't shut up, I'm gonna put five right through your red light!" Of course, this brought an explosion of laughter from the audience, and I was forced to sit down in utter humiliation, though at least soothed somewhat by the knowledge that my raucous intrusion resulted in a laugh after all for the star.

With Kinison and the Highwaymen my outbreaks of tactlessness were confined to taunts at certain sensitive junctures in the respective programs. When Kinison started to discuss his problems with protests by homosexuals in other cities, I shouted out, "Not in this town!" two or three times as he proceeded with the monologue, each outburst bellowed with increasing urgency and volume, until I was perplexed into silence, for a time, by his utterly professional impassivity in the face of my gibes. With the Highwaymen I was similarly offensive. At one point, I waited until silence had descended on the audience in the short pause just after Willie Nelson had announced he would sing one of his somber ballads, when suddenly I roared out, "Do Big River by Johnny Cash!"

George Carlin's show was punctuated as well by general obstreperousness on my part, but the jeer that capped my career in heckling, and caused me to sink into abject mortification the next morning, came at the very end of Carlin's show, when, as he was bowing and acknowledging the audience's applause, I thundered out, "Put it in your ass!" two or three times so loudly I'm sure that my words sailed out over the waves of handclapping approval and made port in every ear in the place. Why do I do such stupid things? I mean, it's not as though Carlin didn't deserve the warmest of praise. In fact, I was surprised by how good he was after all these years. He has removed every last trace of reference to drugs from his routine, and utilizing some of the most commonplace experiences and occurrences as his subject matter, he manages to come across as one of the wittiest and most thoughtful comedians I have ever seen. So why did I demand so vociferously that he put it in his ass?

Part of my motivation for becoming a heckler must stem from my knowing that a great number of our celebrities have traditionally overindulged in drugs and/or alcohol. Liquor was probably the chief agent of debauchery in older days (although there were exceptions like Somerset Maugham and Oscar Wilde, who both took opium), but today many authors, comedians, and musicians seem to have adopted society's more advanced attitude toward recreational dissipation and prodigality in general. So it must be that I heckle because I am jealous of those on the stage. I don't have any illusions of possessing the talent to be a celebrity, but I know that otherwise I have all the qualifications.

Actually, though, I find it difficult if not impossible to pinpoint any valid motive for my misbehavior at the shows. When I look back on those nights, it's as if my memory at the time was suspended at my side, acting as a dim witness to a person different from myself. The alcohol had so saturated my being that I had become an organism operating independently of any natural impulse or authentic emotion. From a sober perspective, it almost seems as though I had become a puppet—a blob of pliable consciousness being manipulated by some demon uncorked by inordinate recourse in the bottle. Or as though my volition drew its fuel from some dark recess of the soul not normally visible to the mind's eye.

So I will close out the postscript on that note. Our nature as human beings is complex and inscrutable. One of the effects of marijuana that scared me so much and led me to quit was the sense that it was changing *who I was*. It no longer simply changed the way I felt, or altered my perceptions, or acted to open the doorway to different ways of thinking. It modified the kind of person I was or was to become. And now alcohol, at least in those deeper stages of intoxication, is doing something similar, causing me to act in ways that are utterly incomprehensible to me when sober. I have reached the point where, when very drunk, it's "the liquor talking," and not me, and that scares me, because I don't know who or what "the liquor" is.

In afterthought: Writing a book about alcohol and its effects is a two-edged sword. The intake of that substance provides the author with subject matter in the form of strange experiences and unusual perspectives at the same time that it undermines his ability to write about them.

Part Five

THURSDAY JANUARY 30, 1992   This journal will essentially be a continuation of the foregoing diary. I have decided to call it a journal, though, because of my frequently voiced intentions in the earlier narrative to quit the diary, without actually doing so. I imagine if I were to open up the "diary" anew, a reader might believe he would never reach the end. On an envelope I find this observation, written in what must have been one of my drunken fugues a few weeks ago: "I have been looking down at the bottoms of a lot of empty liquor bottles lately, and it's depressing. Not because I know I've drunk too many of them, but because I realize I can't afford another one." Nevertheless, I am hopeful that the change in name will steer me away from the intoxication motif; at least I am hopeful that the lesser penetration of that theme into the writing might indicate a general slowing in the rate of my decline into total ruin.

Somewhere I have read that Norman Mailer has said that alcohol is a good thing for breaking the obsession. Well, I agree with him that it is a good thing for that, at least if you are obsessed with raising yourself into a normal existence, if your outlook is riveted by hopes of improved health, or if you dwell excessively on raising the money to shelter yourself against the biting winter winds. He has also proclaimed that drinking has an automatic shutoff, but he has neglected to inform us that for a serious alcoholic it resides exclusively in the pocketbook. Well, actually things aren't so bad. I've been living outside now since the end of last August, and I have not been able to afford the debauchery of better days. I remember when I first moved out of my apartment here in Las Vegas. After a yearlong interlude of travel and lavish indoor living, I thought that never again would I be able to transcend the indignity of sleeping on the cold, vermin-riddled ground, never again be able to inure myself to the stares and innuendos of the public as I walked down the street or through a grocery store with luggage and bedroll in hand, never again be able to enjoy the simple pleasure provided by a single quart of beer and a sunset over the mountains, and I was right: it's infinitely worse after you have tasted of the amenities furnished by a conventional existence. But I also learned an important lesson during the period when I was squandering my inheritance.

I slowly came to realize that the previous years of homelessness had formed in me the idea that the simple efforts required to live a clean, healthy life—things like shaving, taking a shower, getting dressed, shopping for and preparing food, cleaning one's room, and the like—were supposed to be such arduous activities that no time should be left for anything else. Protracted homelessness had inculcated in me the notion that the minimum activities necessary to survive were enough. And if they didn't seem quite difficult enough, once I was living inside, to eclipse all other activity, then I made them that way by drinking to the point where I could hardly move without thinking that I had just dumbfounded the world with accomplishment. I remember watching myself go through the motions of making breakfast after a night of particularly crippling inebriation and being amazed that most people perform these tasks with so little consternation, so few grimaces, and such negligible heartache and grief. These people, I thought to myself, must breeze right through these things! I was astonished. So the lesson of my squandered inheritance is this: First, it can happen. Just because you receive money through death's conduit does not mean that it is some kind of divinely sponsored endowment that can't be wasted or abused. Second, that if it ever happens again, I better kick myself in the ass and get a job. Now, in reality, the first half of my year of wealthier circumstances was put to fairly good use, I think, first, by the dishwashing job in Hawaii and second, by typing, writing, and attempting in vain to sell this diary. But I pretty much gave up during the second half here in Las Vegas, and for that I deserve a big boot in the ass, which I have gotten, in nature's own way, by being forced into homelessness once again. I really actually remember, by the way, writing down that joke about the empty bottles.

FRIDAY JANUARY 31, 1992   Sinking into destitution after rising to the heights of twentieth-century consumption provides one with more than just the opportunity to indulge in severe dejection and remorse. It confronts one also with the challenge of struggling out of the quagmire and back into a loftier, more cash-rich position. It faces a man with both the folly of his past and the difficulty of his future. It leaves no middle ground for arranging one's tomorrows or devising a plan. It shifts one directly from the blind excess of affluence into the raw hardship of deficiency and want. It slides one from the prodigality of plenty to the asceticism of scarcity without any layover at the fulcrum of moderation and cautionary delay. It mocks you for arriving where you are at the same time it gloats over your failure to leave. It pinions you in the trough of degradation and need, forcing you to regret the fiascos of the past, at the same time that it taunts you with the unattainability of success in the future. It confounds the jewel that is dangling in front of your eyes with its mirror image that is hanging behind your head. It drives you up into spheres of euphoria and delight at the same time that it is preparing your descent into the canyons of perdition and despair. It. . . . It. . . . It. . . . Well, you get the idea.

SUNDAY FEBRUARY 9, 1992   For the last few months I have been working on a more thorough analysis of the food stamp proposal that I originated in this journal. It's amazing how involved the concept of PIK can get! I think I was very cavalier, if not arrogant, in believing that the superficial description of PIK in the journal was sufficient. A deeper probe of the subject a year ago would have betrayed my ignorance and allowed me to work and study under less trying conditions.

I have been living in Henderson, Nevada, for a month or so now; it is a working-class town on the eastern edge of Las Vegas, about fifteen miles from the Strip. Some rain here lately has compelled me to search out some unusual sleeping sites. On Thursday and Friday nights I unrolled my blankets underneath an old vacant house that is up on I-beams and blocks in an empty desert lot behind a shopping center here. On Friday I finished a week of construction work through the daily labor agency here, and on Saturday I spent too much money on half-pints of vodka and tall cans of Coors bought from a Circle K store on the main highway coming through town. The binge wore me out so bad that I gave up on the walk to the vacant house and spread out my bedding in a concrete culvert pipe lying by the side of the road, apparently in readiness for installation into a nearby ditch. The pipe was only about two feet in diameter, so it was somewhat difficult to worm my way in and out to relieve myself during the night. I woke up about eight, well past daybreak, so it's possible that some attentive motorist might have wondered at seeing the cylinder plugged up with rumpled bedding and stockinged feet. The question I am asking myself now is this: Am I insane, or is it possible for a man living in this rough-and-tumble way to write a proposal that will someday be enacted into law by the Congress and President of the United States?

SUNDAY FEBRUARY 16, 1992   Today I plan to go to the library and start describing the method a wholesaler or a final processor would use to account for any PIK wage payments received from an "antecedent" processor (that is, a processor sending a PIK wage shipment of either finished goods or ingredients to the wholesaler or the final processor). I thought it would be interesting to set down in this journal how I came to think of this particular aspect of PIK at this time. I had already worked out how a wholesaler would handle a PIK wage shipment of finished goods from an antecedent processor. But I had not yet contemplated undertaking a similar analysis for a final processor receiving a PIK wage shipment of ingredients from an antecedent processor until something unusual happened the other morning.

To explain what happened, I have to go back to 1987. In January of that year I had been working for two or three months for a gas station in Oceanside, California. I showed up for work one morning, outfitted in my uniform—dark blue pants and light blue shirt—and stationed myself next to the outside cash box in readiness for the next customer. For a moment, I must have gazed out in wonderment at the lucid display of blue up above, at the slopes of yellowed grasses rising steeply from level floors of cornstalks and orange trees, at the plateaus above, defined sharply by lines of luxury homes gleaming in the sun, and felt the whole scene being caressed by the gentle breezes of the Pacific from just a few miles down the road. I must have been marveling at my good fortune at having landed a job in a paradise such as this when suddenly the owner walked out of the station, came over to me, and told me I was fired for stealing from the till. I was so flabbergasted that I could only stutter a few weak protestations before the owner waved me off and walked back into his office. The allegation was so unfounded and the dismissal so sudden that I could only stand there for a moment in stupefaction before shuffling away in confused resentment.

I had to give up my rented room after that, and eventually I was forced to take my meals from a local charity kitchen. I heard someone there discussing the great number of job openings in Bakersfield, California, so I hitchhiked the 180 or so miles to that rural community and stayed for a night or two at their mission. The town did not seem to be a hotbed of opportunity for a newcomer, so I got back on the highway and began to hitchhike toward San Diego. One of the people who picked me up was a tall young man of Spanish ancestry who knew a lot about agriculture. He had been in Saudi Arabia acting as an adviser to the new desert farmers over there. Presently he was in the process of starting up a company in Bakersfield that converted the local produce into fillings for pastries and other baked goods. His company took the locally grown peaches, strawberries, grapes, oranges, and lemons and converted them into the jams and jellies that would ultimately make their way into pies, rolls, and other pastries. He was a very kind man. He told me that the county in which Bakersfield was located generated more agricultural revenues than most *states* in the country. He drove me around through vast orchards of nut trees owned by huge corporate ranches, through fields being planted in asparagus or broccoli by platoons of stooping Mexican workers, and through vineyards recently pruned for the upcoming growing season. He took me on a dirt road through rolling pastures dotted with cattle; he pointed out local landmarks where the rich locals gathered to celebrate their success. All in all he provided me with a fairly comprehensive tour of the area before dropping me off back on the main highway, where he wished me luck, handed me a five-dollar bill, and went on his way.

The other morning (coming back to the present time now) I was sleeping under the abandoned house out in the desert, to avoid the rain, when I awoke from a dream. I can no longer remember what the dream was about, but in my head, upon waking, was the idea of the memory of the experience I have just related. That memory, for me, is associated very strongly with the image of a five-gallon plastic pail filled with strawberry or peach pie-filling. How can you describe what a memory is? It did not *feel* like a memory or a thought that I would conjure up by a natural process of reasoning or wondering. It felt like a thought that was planted or jammed into my head by an outside force, as if the preceding dream were a living agent with a will and a purpose all its own. So from there, of course, I began to think about how an "antecedent" processor like a pie-filling manufacturer might fit into the communal scheme I have been writing about. It turns out, of course, that this is the perfect juncture in the sequence of my reasoning to think about the antecedent processor, since the economic treatment of his PIK wage output is exactly analogous to that of a final processor (which I had just written about). Would I have ultimately thought about the antecedent processor on my own? I believe so. I had intended, eventually, to get around to analyzing how a packager—a manufacturer of polyethylene bottles to hold orange juice, for example—might fit into the communal scheme, and it turns out now that the economic analysis of the packager's PIK wage shipment is basically the same as that of the antecedent processor's PIK wage shipment. So maybe all this "dreamthought" did was advance my thinking to coincide better with my writing.

MARCH ? 1992   Hunger is an interesting subject. It is intriguing to me at this point in time for reasons I would prefer not to discuss. I will venture the opinion, however, that hunger itself is not feared by people so much as the circumstances that facilitate its arrival. Why, when concepts like love and beauty, evil and good, virtue and depravity, liberty and tyranny, and the like are routinely accorded exalted treatment in the literature of the ages, is hunger so regularly shunned? What condition of man could be more important than that which drives him to the most excruciating of toils to circumvent its coming? Just because we do all in our power to avoid it, does hunger therefore deserve less scrutiny as an idea than, say, the concept of truth? Why should not hunger be raised into the pantheon of worthy conceptions and examined in every facet as if it were the most brilliant jewel in the firmament of human speculation? I would assert, for example, that hunger is the chief precursor of the work ethic. The threat of hunger's continual advent was very likely the first motivation for a man to establish the conviction that a regular schedule of work was anything other than a bore, a burden, and a general pain in the back. Hunger's looming potential thus precipitated that noble cast of mind and those admired habits that today bring us such worthy products as frozen waffles, cellular telephones, breakfast burritos, and video poker machines. Who could possibly argue, in the face of this formidable evidence, that hunger is therefore not a meatier subject upon which to ruminate than the loftiest conceptions concerned with truth, beauty, or the principles of democratic federalism?

I have been thinking lately of examining hunger in depth by once again entering into a fast to the death. The problem is that the long-term denouement of hunger is so easily thwarted by its short-term extinguishment. Oops! Got rid of it once again! And all your plans for a prolonged, dramatic suicide go down the drain in one moment of temporal weakness. But if I were capable of killing myself, fasting would be my method of choice. At least in its early stages, it is not so painful as arsenic or as repugnant as sending big chunks of your brain on a sudden ballistic journey. And besides, you get a lot more time to determine if your decision was correct.

I am drawn to the idea of a fast now because alcohol continues to ruin my life. People regard me as such a contemptible bum these days that is impossible to elicit a loan, even from people who ought to know that I would never ask them for money unless my situation was truly desperate. A few months ago, down in Las Vegas, I was sleeping on a walkway at the side of a new office building that had yet to be occupied. I woke up about two in the morning and, thinking it safe to leave for a few minutes—because of the deserted streets and the darkened businesses nearby—I walked to an all-night grocery store a couple of blocks away and bought some food for the morning. Upon my return, everything I owned was gone, as absent as if it all had vanished into thin air. Groundcloth, sleeping bag, cloth suitcase from Hawaii, clothes, toiletries had all been thought worthy of appropriation by the thief. Only one thing remained, flopping in the breeze over the adjacent parking lot—a cardboard sign with Laughlin printed on one side and Las Vegas on the other, which I had used on a recent hitchhiking trip to that gambling town on the Colorado River. The next day I called up a relative and asked for a $50 loan to tide me over until I got a check from working a part-time job at a local newspaper. That relative's refusal meant a week without brushing my teeth and with only one change of underwear and socks. It meant begging blankets from the local mission and eating at a charity kitchen. It meant . . . it meant a large pain in the posterior that I will not soon forget.

More recently alcohol has led me to run completely out of money once again. I don't know if I will be able to pay the $10 due on my storage closet next Friday. I was underneath the vacant house in the desert lot the other day, escaping the rain with innumerable quarts of beer, when a group of vicious school boys came along and taunted me with hurled rocks and epithets. I ran after a couple of them and probably would have killed them if exhaustion and better sense had not overtaken me. That night I called up my mother, who suffered a stroke last fall, and listened in anguish for the first time as she attempted to talk through her paralysis but succeeded only in the most child-like and pitiful way. The next day I suffered from the alcoholic horrors of a kind that I did not think was possible from beer alone. A call to an "old friend" resulted in his declining to help me with a $100 loan. My father has been dead now for almost two years from a disease that seemed more a malicious avatar of murder than a natural affliction, one whose onset coincided roughly with the burning of those writings that represented ten years' creative effort out of my life; I still cannot get anyone to help me with my music, and although I hold out hope of purveying the aforementioned food stamp proposal, the fact is that when I'm not working at some dirty, tedious construction job for $4.25 an hour, I am drinking to the point of unconsciousness and spending my money in ways that I can't even remember half the time. I might as well be paralyzed myself. So don't you think I might have an argument for starving myself to death?

SATURDAY APRIL 4, 1992   I'd better make this the very last entry in any kind of diary or journal dealing with alcoholism. That condition has become so serious for me the last couple of months that any humor I could possibly wring out of it would belie the malignancy of the problem. For a while I thought that I had discovered a new approach to healthy drinking by allowing my higher power to help me moderate my drinking rather than quit altogether. And it worked for awhile; every time I found myself drinking too much, it made me black out. I went for whole stretches of days where my only activities were working, sleeping, drinking, and blacking out. And the blacking out was much different than in the past, when I might have blacked out on occasion only to wake up in bed the following morning and wonder what I had done in the last couple of hours of the night before. Now I was blacking out for whole segments of a day, afternoon or evening, only to "wake up" and find myself walking down a highway without my bedroll and bag, for example, and finding them later a mile back on the highway's shoulder, where I apparently just sloughed them off as insouciantly as a snake would his withered skin. Now I was blacking out while leaving a laundromat and waking up later to find myself walking away from a casino with the remnants of a steak dinner in my teeth and my wallet lighter by twenty precious dollars. And the like. It's happened so frequently in the last few months that I can't even remember how many times or the circumstances surrounding each occasion. So at least my higher power was trying. But I think I'd like to rescind my for-

169

mer desire and allow my higher power to go tend to its own business. I no longer want a higher power, it is not *my* higher power anymore, I make no claims to it, take my higher power if you wish, and call it your own; walk away with it if you like, and never come back. I will moderate my drinking on my own, if it comes to that, or quit, or die, but I can no longer withstand the assistance of a higher power.

The consequences of excess go deeper than blacking out, of course. There is the acute remorse that stems from recalling, while sober, the offensive or inane things done while drunk. There is the authentically excruciating pain of withdrawing, over the span of a few days, from a prodigious binge. There is the bodily enervation. And the financial hardship. All of these have coalesced for me lately into a desire to commit suicide. Or, perhaps more accurately, into a desire to challenge my higher power, with a fast to the death if necessary, to leave me alone and allow me to quit drinking. Excuse me, I did not mean *my* higher power. I meant *the* higher power . . . well, not *the* higher power perhaps, since there must be particular ones, scattered here and there, that are not as omnipresent as the main one. So I will call the one I am referring to *this* higher power.

This higher power has had me under its dominion since the middle of February 1979, when the relentless torment that persists to this day commenced. It is the cause of my drinking; it is the cause of my ruination; it is the cause of every bad and painful thing in my life; it is the cause of circumstances that have spurred me to write, make music, and invent, and so I suppose it is the cause of my possibly making some money someday, too. But I can't stand it anymore and I've been contemplating an escape. The scene of these ruminations is rather incongruous. In Henderson and the Las Vegas Valley here they have had more rain in the last month than in any other corresponding time in recorded history, and this has caused the surrounding deserts to bloom into a riot of greenery and colorful wildflowers. There is a great expanse of desert east of town that sweeps up to the mountains which fringe the Lake Mead Recreation Area, and this vast stretch, normally barren except for the usual scattering of scraggly creosote and other impoverished shrubs, is now a veritable meadow bristling with color and life. There are large tracts of otherwise unadorned desert, sloping to the base of the mountains, that now look as green and rich as a huge landscaped lawn. And in the lower sweeps the bushes and plants already there are choked at their bases by gardenlike greenery and flowers in a kaleidoscope of colors and form. It is in this idyllic setting that I have unrolled my bedding of late and, contemplating the purity of the sky and the brilliant light all around, and watching the occasional butterfly or bee meander among the nearby blossoms, and smelling the freshness of the new shoots underneath, it is here, I say, in this wonderful new desert world that erupts into life only every seven years or so, that I have lain and planned out my death. Since fasting and recent alcoholic abuse do not combine well, it is here also that I have lain in the trembling turmoil of withdrawal, eating soda crackers in anticipation of the sixty-to-ninety-day ordeal. You see, I had made up my mind to do it. The circumstances were not the best, I knew. It grieved me unspeakably, for example, to think that I would not be able to visit and cheer my poor, paralyzed mother before meeting with my demise. Never would I know the pleasure of a wife, the delight of children, or the security of a steady, irrevocable income. Two months in the desert is a long time, even when you eat on a regular basis, so I knew I would need to find some shelter against the possible rains and a place where there is shade. I got up and walked into Henderson, along the wide highway that splits the town, where previously I had found a large sheet of plastic in a construction dumpster, from which I had cut a groundcloth. I thought that I would find a similar sheet there that would serve as a tent, but alas, when I arrived the dumpster was gone! For a moment my spirits brightened, and I thought that maybe, just maybe, fate had prepared me an alternative plan.

I walked uncertainly down the wide boulevard, where crews had recently planted saplings and palms, and, crossing a side street, walked along the edge of a smoothly raked dirt ditch and, looking down into the large trough, saw there a huge piece of thick clear plastic perhaps twenty feet by ten, and folded in half, with a cardboard tube nearby from which the magnificent expanse of plastic had apparently been very carelessly unrolled and discarded. I looked at the plastic and then up to the clear blue sky and thought about walking past. A flicker of hope rustled through my mind as I watched the patrons of a grocery store across the street, bustling and conversing, and thinking about dinner, and conducting their affairs with the breeziest lack of concern. Then I looked back at the plastic, envisioning its gleaming new surface stretched tautly over a centerline, so suited to my intentions, and I knew I could not walk past. No, destiny was calling me to the grave. I fetched up the plastic, toted it to my campsite, finding a very fine piece of black twine along the way to serve as a centerline, and that evening I consumed a final meal of raw brussels sprouts and soda crackers. I had prepared myself well in other ways, too. I had a stack of ten books at my side, because I knew I would reach a point, in ten or fifteen days, maybe, when I would be too weak and emaciated to travel to the library. The principal component of my preparation, though, was a device to keep my mind occupied that entailed studying and analyzing the concept I had praised so copiously in the previous entry of this journal: the concept of hunger. I thought that even if I didn't make it the whole way to expiration, I would acquire enough material on the various aspects and dimensions of hunger to be able to write a book subsequent to the ordeal.

The next morning I got under way pretty well, lying around, dipping into a book on occasion, and studying the adjacent flowers, but pretty soon I began to realize that the chief distraction I had planned to rely on was something I already knew quite a lot about. I had already starved for nine days and nights out in California back in 1986, and I've had fairly extensive engagements with less severe forms of the condition in the preceding and intervening years, and I thought that if there were anything of substance to learn on the subject, I very likely was already in possession of the facts. This notion was reinforced when, as each hour passed, I looked inward, trying to extract some kind of principle or axiom from the increasing intensity of my cravings, and found that the subject, unlike others, was one in which repetition does not facilitate the digestion of facts or the formulation of new experiments and hypothesis. I paced around as another hour passed without bearing any scholarly fruit, and finally, as one o'clock rolled around without a trace of inference or logical deduction to show for my efforts, I gave up the ghost. I walked a mile or two to a casino with a 99-cent breakfast special, dined there on fried eggs, bacon, pancakes, and a surfeit of coffee, and experienced not the slightest twinge of regret that my experiment had gone so awry.

MONDAY AUGUST 10, 1992   They say that an alcoholic drinks to "feel normal." But if feeling normal is as good as I usually feel after taking a few solid belts, I'm going to quit right away. But of course it's true that chronic alcoholism is largely a continual striving to dissipate the painful effects of prior drinking. For me those effects are like an icicle in the soul. I shudder on the inside and tremble on the outside as if my viscera had been stored overnight in a cold-storage locker. Days I feel that way are becoming more frequent, and those are the days I commence with the bottle almost immediately after waking and drink throughout the day. It's depressing—not least because one's self-image tends to plummet when one contemplates his accomplishments in this regard. Not that I accomplish nothing while drinking. Ironically, those days I wander around town in an excruciating bout with Mr. Barleycorn are the days I formulate many of the concepts that go into *A Proposal for Food Stamp Reform*. Perhaps drinking just supplies me with the patience to examine very meticulously some of the more frustrating ideas. But then it takes me so long to dry out sufficiently to stop the tremors that I end up wasting many days that I could have used to write down the ideas I thought about while drunk.* The whole process is very arduous. I cannot think of a more painful period in my life—except perhaps the first years of my adolescence when puberty and a Catholic, all-boys military academy combined to render me suppressed, guilt-ridden, distraught, and not in possession of a healthy aversion to suicide. In any event, I hope *this* part of my life will soon be over. If it has to last another year, I might just fling myself into a ditch somewhere and suffocate in the mud.

TUESDAY AUGUST 11, 1992   In his book entitled *Drink—A Self-help Book on Alcoholism* (1979, p. 103), Constantine Fitzgibbon raises an interesting question:

> Similarly, again, when we read and talk of environment we are talking about the world in the old ritualistic sense of "the world, the flesh and the devil." What, by the way, has

*Rereading this entry in February of 1995, and after having extensively revised the manuscript it mentions, I realize that many of the notions I "formulated" during these jags were mistaken. But at least I kept my mind on the problem.

happened to the devil? The scientists seem to have mislaid him, and the Christian churches have forgotten him. The poets have not, and perhaps his fingerprints are to be detected on Jung's shadow persona. Certainly he would appear to be very much in evidence in certain aspects of alcoholism.

Another excellent book on alcoholism is *Understanding the Alcoholic's Mind: The Nature of Craving and How to Control It* by Arnold M. Ludwig, M.D. (1988). I liked this book because it discusses in some depth methods people use to resist taking the first drink. The religious aspect of recovery is placed in the context of a more objective range of tools used to stay sober. The doctor states, for example (p. 89), that it is not his intention "to argue for or against the importance and necessity of a spiritual experience for the process of recovery, but rather to note that it is an authentic phenomenon that cannot be easily ignored."

Now, it seems to me that these two quotations point out the basic contradiction in the idea of a supportive higher power and the AA philosophy that promotes it. For if one admits that the sobriety-fostering higher power is a real supernatural entity, one must admit as well that a real supernatural entity can exist that encourages the development of alcoholism in the first place. If the "higher power" touted by AA is an actual supernatural agent, not just a state of mind, a set of rules, or an ethical outlook, or purely a higher region of normal human consciousness, then there is nothing in our experience as human beings or in the precepts of logic that can rule out the existence of a supernatural agent that causes an individual to become addicted to alcohol. By claiming that a supernatural force helps individuals to stop drinking, but at the same time denying that a supernatural force might occasion the habit to begin with, we impose on the spiritual realm a one-sidedness that is not warranted by our knowledge of those things that are outside of the material world. For me, this argument is not merely intellectual diversion. It is a logical exposition of something I know to be true.

MONDAY SEPTEMBER 28, 1992   It's 6:30 A.M. I am in a small landscaped park in Henderson, Nevada, and the cool, fresh desert air is slowly being illuminated by the dawn. I was just told at the labor office to be back there at 8:00 A.M. for a job that is to start at 9:00. About two and a half weeks ago I got lucky and was sent out to work at a gold mine about sixty miles south of here, out of Searchlight, Nevada. The mine is actually right across the California border, and the ride to and from the labor office took up about three hours of the day. We worked ten hours, so by the time I woke up in the desert each morning, cleaned up, shaved, packed up my bedroll, went to work, came "home," ate dinner, and shambled back to the desert, about four or five hours was left for sleep. I was one of only two of the original twelve workers to not miss a day up until last Wednesday, when I happened to be one of the six workers arbitrarily cut from the ticket. I thought I was one of the better workers, and my resulting evaluation of the competence of the mine's managers was not slow in coming. Anyway, I was able to save up about $350, of which I now have $240.

A gold mine is not what it used to be. The Castle Mountain Venture is located in a pristine wilderness of Joshua trees, steep foothills, rugged mountains, and a vast desert tableland that transmogrifies in the distance into a horizon of classic-looking buttes and serrated ridges. The mine itself is close to two other more traditional mines where actual nuggets were extracted in the late 1800s and the 1930s. But today the gold is obtained more in the manner of iron or copper, by processing huge amounts of ore taken from the ground. There is a vast, excavated pit hidden within the perimeter of Castle Mountain, an odd, almost circular formation of spires, domes, and crenelated ridges that seem to give the interior an almost sanctuary-like quietude and solemnity. The ore is trucked up from the floor of the enormous hole and delivered to a mill where it is crushed to the consistency of driveway gravel mixed with dirt. At this point the ore does not look much different from crushed lime-stone except for a more yellow or gold-tinted hue. The ore is now transported by truck or conveyor belt to a large leach pad. The base of this pad is nothing more than a very smoothly graded expanse of slightly inclined land upon which a layer of felt-like "geo-tech" and an immense piece of thick plastic have been laid. One of our jobs was to pick up stones on the bare table of land and toss sand on the rougher areas to make sure the felt and plastic were not pierced once they were laid down and the ore piled on top.

Once the ore is finally deposited, the great mounds are lev-eled off by bulldozers to a height of forty feet, and the resulting pad is covered with a network of drip lines that feed a solution of water and cyanide down into the ore. One of our other jobs was laying this network of plastic tubing, capping it off, and testing it for leaks. Despite our being warned of the liquid's deadly potential, the regular workers there did not seem concerned about getting sprayed or immersing their hands in a gushing leak for a little washup. It must be a pretty weak solution. At any rate, once the cyanide starts percolating through the ore, it combines on a molecular scale with proportionately minute quantities of gold. The metal drains down through the ore in solution form, clear as water, runs along the plastic and through buried diversion tubes, finally flows out from underneath the great heap of earth, and is pulled by gravity through troughs and pipes to a processing plant nearby. The pad we were working on must have been ten football fields in area. Although they just started leaching at the mine eight or nine months ago, they expect to mine about 100,000 ounces a year of nearly pure gold in the near future. As a comparison, one of the regular employees of the mine told me he used to work at a mine in northern Nevada that extracted more than a million ounces a year. All of which makes me think—about what I will write in the next entry.

SUNDAY OCTOBER 11, 1992   Speculation in precious metals probably serves a legitimate function. Since the metal's scarcity determines whether it is precious, and therefore whether it is the object of speculation, the hoarding of that metal becomes the equivalent of stockpiling it for future emergency use or for the day when its extraction becomes economically unattractive. In 1990, the total production of new gold in the world was 5,000 tons. Undoubtedly, part of each year's output is applied to industrial uses. Some part goes into the fabrication of jewelry. But, although I don't have the statistic at hand, it is almost certain that a large proportion of all newly mined gold goes directly into the vaults of the speculators. Even the purchase of gold jewelry is motivated in part by investment considerations. One has to wonder, in this day of the worldwide fiat currency, how much of the demand for gold—its price is currently around $340 per ounce—is prompted by its historic role as the most valuable of those metals that constituted money. One wonders, in other words, what the price of gold would be if all of its historical associations with money were suddenly extinguished and the memory of man contained only a conception of that metal as it has been used for artistic or industrial purposes. If we were to ever return to the gold standard or to a gold currency itself, this collective amnesia would act only to render the world's gold stocks less than perhaps would be convenient when the abandonment of the fiat currency took place. If the fiat currency lasts, though, will the idea of gold as money gradually loosen its grip on the minds of the investors and cause a decline in the metal's price?

These are the things I know I would think about if I were to work permanently at the gold mine out of Searchlight. The setting there was in contrast to the work performed. While we wandered for hours on end over the hard-packed soil, picking up rocks or shoveling sand under the hot sun, the vast wilderness of Joshua trees and the desert all around seemed to gleam in the still aridity, and the blue skies shone and sparkled with more brilliance than any metallic artifact ever fashioned by man. What a waste, I would think to myself, to come to a place like this only to make sure that the world's safes contain a few thousand more pounds of gold.

I know that I must seem like a spoilsport. And I know that the superfluous products of capitalism are something like froth on the stein: byproducts whose regulation or suppression would impinge on the very process that supplies us so efficiently with the things that really are necessary to our survival. But at the same time, I would be profoundly troubled if I had to devote a /77 lifetime of toil to produce something whose chief appeal lay in its ability to facilitate the art of the speculator.

SATURDAY OCTOBER 17, 1992   The food stamp manuscript is now in finished form and ready to be typed.

MONDAY DECEMBER 7, 1992   My relatives have balked at sending me some money to rent a room in order to type the food stamp manuscript, and it is now gathering dust in a storage closet.

WEDNESDAY DECEMBER 16, 1992   I am still gaining a subsistence by working through the daily labor agency in Henderson. You sweat during the day, at the construction sites, but shiver as soon as you stop working. When the sun is out it is brilliant, and the outward folds and ridges in the surrounding mountains glow in dry relief. There is snow on many of the peaks to the west and north. This winter is starting out colder than the last one here in Las Vegas. I hope a trend is not a justified inference. The evenings, on days I can get work, are horribly empty and cold. Whatever faint warmth reached your back during the day now recedes suddenly as the sun sinks behind the mountains. A gray winter twilight penetrates the valley just as you get off work and ride back to the office for your check. Then, walking down the street with your paycheck in pocket, there is an ache in your bones and an indescribable void in your heart. It comes from . . . well, from what? From living outside now for over fifteen months? From a couple of weeklong interludes of sulking and drinking in the desert? From disappointment over my relatives' declining to help? Or am I just getting older?

SUNDAY DECEMBER 20, 1992   The nights are very cold now, and comfortable sleep is a challenge. This holiday season my salvation has come from a remodeling job. While digging up the ground to enlarge a Smith's grocery store here, the construction crews were forced to excavate seven or eight large corrugated metal pipes, about four feet in diameter and twenty or twenty-five feet long. Apparently they were buried originally to channel some kind of underground flowage. They are somewhat squashed—ovalized—from years of compaction by the overhead soil; but their interiors are clean, except for a shallow bed of gravel on their floors, and with their ends capped off with a piece of cardboard or an old rug, they make adequate shelters against the sharp winds and freezing rains of the night. They are lined up presently in a vacant stretch of desert behind the grocery store, and I hope they are not moved too soon. They make the night tolerable, not really pleasant, and waking up in the morning is still a chore—no, it's an ordeal.

At 3:30 A.M. I emerge directly from the warm cocoon of my bedding to the frigid desert air and actually get nauseous from the contrast. I double over with the dry heaves as I fumble around to put on my shoes and get on the jacket I had used as a pillow. The reaction lingers as I leave the tube, drag out my possessions, and go through the excruciating routine of folding and rolling up my bedding in the icy darkness. I shoulder my bags and bedroll and hustle over to a nearby Texaco convenience store, where I thaw out at a table with a cup of hot coffee and a book. In a few minutes I step into the restroom and there take advantage of a high gooseneck faucet to fill up a gallon plastic jug with hot water. I leave the gas station then and march to a vacant lot about a block away that is enclosed on three sides by a brick wall. In a dark corner of the lot I reach the flattened cardboard box that serves as my shower floor. Here I shave and, if it's not *too* cold, strip naked and dump the remaining hot water over my head and body. Drying off and dressing are not accomplished at a languorous pace. Then I walk over to the daily labor office and the whole thing starts again.

SATURDAY DECEMBER 26, 1992   I am changing my strategy. Originally I rejected the possibility of typing the *Proposal* in the Henderson library because, although they have two word processors there that can be used for free, there is a per-patron limit of two hours a day. However, it has already been more than two and a half months since I finished writing the manuscript. By now I could have had most of it typed. So if I do a little bit each day for the next few months, I might actually have a marketable product on hand by the time the first hundred-degree day hits Las Vegas.

THURSDAY FEBRUARY 11, 1993   Stress over money is a common affliction. But if those who so suffer would just follow my example, they would have nothing to worry about. If they followed my lead, the source of their anxiety would dry up as fast as a rain puddle in the desert, and the vapors would trail away with mysterious swiftness and dispatch. Like me, they would be broke. Like me, they would own not even a single penny to cause torment and sleepless nights. This morning, when I finally surrendered my last token of wealth—a free drink ticket from a casino that I gave to a fellow daily laborer in exchange for a cup of coffee he had brewed on his Coleman stove—I felt a sudden surge of elation. "Free at last! Free at last! Free at last!" I rejoiced. A profound sense of liberation seemed to rise up in me as I thought back on the days of grief and despondency leading up to my final release. Always agonizing, always fretting, always scheming, always lunging towards this expedient or the next in order to escape the dreaded day when the evacuation of my wallet would finally occur.

Of course, the broken resolutions and the three-day binges didn't help. There is nothing more effective in focusing the mind on one's dwindling supply of money than the need for another bottle to appease the inner monster of withdrawal. When a slow spell hit the labor office earlier in the week I was finally forced to recognize the inevitable, and a certain calm resignation overtook me. I went down to Pastor Gary at the Giving Life Ministry and got some food there for the first time in nine months. Last spring, Gary had signed me up for three nights of employment cleaning up the Silver Bowl after the Grateful Dead concerts, and instead of working I got drunk and used my admission pass to gain entrance to the last half of the first night's concert. I didn't *plan* not to show up for any of the three nights of work, but that's the way it happened. So since then, due to my embarrassment, my emergency provisions have been carrots, bread, and cupcakes from the local Salvation Army. But on Tuesday Gary gave me an ample bag of food and said I could come back on Friday if I signed up again for food stamps, which I did this morning, after seven months without them. So a certain tranquillity grew within me as I slowly became aware of my impending penury. Then this morning, when that last little certificate of exchange took flight from my wallet, I heaved a great sigh of relief, took a sip of coffee, and marched down the street in gratitude and exultation, for the cause of all my troubles had finally, and completely, disappeared.

SATURDAY MARCH 20, 1993   Why is God tormenting me? Why is He punishing me so severely? Oh sure, St. Patrick's Day was a real convivial occasion. I woke up in a ditch by the side of Boulder Highway reeking from five days of almost nonstop intoxication. My clothes were soiled and saturated with old sweat, and my breath smelled like offal. I lay on my back with my head on the sand of the dirty, littered wash while my kidneys ached in supplication. My hands trembled and my torso quaked as I reached for the bottle and slugged down part of the remaining liquid. But what was left was all I had, and I was almost out of money. So now, as the situation became clear, the anguish of withdrawal was intensified by the dread of destitu-

180

tion—of not getting work that week through the labor agency, of walking around in filthy clothes with a bagful of the same, of not having enough for coffee and its wake-up incentive and so oversleeping a job I might be assigned, and on and on. I am not saying that God is the cause of all this. But His willingness to continue tormenting me in the face of this degrading agony is terrifying. I do not know if I have "the fear of God" in me. But the realization that He would persist in this cycle of torment and intoxication until I died is enough to scare the hell out of me. Maybe not scared so much by death itself—and final release—as by an awareness of the chief agent in its execution.

My father used to say that everything has a purpose. But what reason could there be for this protracted ordeal of my own? Well, in my limited wisdom it seems to me that if God is going to be angry over something it is going to be over a particular kind of blasphemy. And that is the kind of blasphemy where you put words in His mouth through some kind of artistic vehicle. Of course, this would make Jesus and Moses two of the most sacrilegious figures in history. But in myself I am talking about a different kind of man, a difference that would surely make this sin of greater consequence for me than when it is committed by a historical divinity. At any rate, my sin is embodied in a dialogue that I wrote as part of a story called "Dooligan's Lament." In that dialogue, the Devil in the form of a kangaroo with horns converses with a Wizard in the form of a man. This Wizard has the powers of creation and whether you call it a Wizard or a Blizzard, if it has the powers of creation, you are putting words into the mouth of something whose real-life counterpart can get amply enraged.

The problem with all this is that the dialogue in "Dooligan's Lament" is part of all those writings that I burned up in 1989 and which I no longer have. So where resides the complaint? Something that happened to me on the day *before* Saint Patrick's Day might provide a clue.

Before sunrise on that day I woke up in the same condition I would wake up in the next day except that I was farther up the highway, ensconced between a couple of shrubs at the base of a large billboard. And I realized after groping around in the dark that my partially filled bottle of vodka was no longer conveniently lodged in the shrub to my left. In a panic I got up and pressed my foot around the shoots and wildflowers that once again, after an exceptionally rainy winter, thronged amidst the stalks of the surrounding shrubs. In the dark I could not find the bottle. In the dim light of dawn I could not find the bottle. And in the harsher light of morning I couldn't find it either. This is a sin! I thought to myself, for I was completely broke. Whoever stole that bottle is now inflicting as much pain on me as if he had injected me with some kind of spasm-inducing poison.

I was just about to give up searching when I remembered something that had happened to me about a year and a half earlier at the main Las Vegas library on Flamingo Road. They used to have open, rolling areas of grass around that library, and one sunny afternoon in late fall I was reclining with a book on the lawn when a man of medium build, wearing jeans and with a large scruffy beard, walked by and blurted out his intention to look for a bottle of whiskey he had hidden here the day before. He said he wasn't sure he could remember where he had left it. But off he strode and in twenty minutes or half an hour he returned, seemingly somewhat flushed, and announced that he had found the bottle, finally, after a desperate but determined search around the perimeter of the building.

I remembered that incident on the morning of the sixteenth, when I was frantically searching for my own bottle, and I thought, well, maybe it wouldn't hurt to look for a few more minutes. I looked down toward the ground, at the base of a shrub, and the first place I looked, the very first spot I set my eyes on, I thought I saw a small green rectangle of paper that looked like a dollar bill. But no, it couldn't be, I thought, it was much too small for a bill and seemed a lighter green, like a cheap bill from a game. I picked it up though and excitedly discovered that it had been folded three ways. I spread open the paper and trembled in amazement as a sun-faded but very genuine ten-dollar bill crystallized before my eyes. "Holy balls," I said to myself, "this is almost like some kind of miracle!" But there was no time for philosophizing now. The booze was on the shelves only half a mile away, and I quickly rolled up my bedding, gathered up my belongings, and started moving aggressively through the desert. But in a wash just a few yards away I was stopped in my tracks. There, standing upright in the sand, not far from a collection of empty beer cans, was an apparently unopened can of Coca-Cola with a picture of Santa

Claus holding up a can of Coke. I grabbed the can, shook it, and found that it had indeed been left unopened. "Perfect for my morning cocktail!" I shouted and lunged off again through the desert. So this is how it came to pass that I was able to have at least a few drinks on the morning of the next day.

Sunday April 11, 1993 (Easter Sunday) Of course, I don't normally have an affinity for filthy clothes and an unkempt appearance. It is one of the elements of excess that make the condition so degrading.

This beautiful sunny morning, as I was rummaging through the produce dumpster at the side of a Lucky's grocery store, a car pulled up, and a portly woman with a bright, round face got out and walked toward me. At first I thought she might be wanting to delve into the refuse herself, and I felt uneasy over the possible competition. Instead, she approached, held out her hand and gave me a brand-new twenty-dollar bill. As I beamed and stammered out my gratitude, she explained that she and her male companion, now waiting in the car, had seen me rolling up by bedroll in the vacant sector of desert adjacent to the store. Across that patch of desert there is a grassy burial ground and a crematory where some Easter Sunday services had just been held. The couple had spotted me while they joined with the rest of the congregants and a brass ensemble in launching some hymns into the cool morning air.

It had seemed a little inconsistent to me earlier, as I lay in my bedding listening to the stately music, that a holiday with at least some intimation of a general resurrection should be celebrated at a place where many of the departed have been reduced to ash. Was it cruelty that motivated those early morning supplicants to so ardently announce the bodily resurrection of Jesus in the presence of so many unsuitably disposed-of souls? Or were they just privy to some aspect of the hereafter not comprehended by the general population? In any event, I was quick to tell the charitable lady about my habit of working through the daily labor hall and my attempt to type up a book in the library—I felt as though twenty bucks' worth of generosity deserved some justification greater than a holy day of obligation.

I have to admit that the people of Henderson have been extraordinarily kind and giving. Nowhere else in the country have people approached me with such frequency to offer food, clothes, and even money. This might have something to do with the fact that there are not *too* many homeless here. A surplus of that kind will turn people sour after a while. This seems to me to be a general precept of human behavior that is ignored by the homeless population at their own peril. Why do they concentrate themselves into specific areas, provoking the contempt of the local population, and depriving themselves of the goodwill and benevolence that can be evoked only when they are seen on a less frequent basis?

The typing is going slow—the word processors were down recently for a couple of weeks due to a computer virus—but I am advancing nevertheless and will probably finish sometime before the end of the century. I have to admit that the lack of support from my relatives was probably a good thing in the long run. I have already added one whole new section to the book that clarifies some previously muddled areas, and I am now working on a second section that will illuminate some of the accounting aspects of PIK.*

THURSDAY MAY 13, 1993   The late Eric Hoffer's book, *Before the Sabbath* (Harper and Row, 1979), is a diary that is less a chronicle of his personal experiences than a running exposition of his thoughts on many intellectual questions. I remember reading a couple of his books a number of years ago, after hearing he was both a longshoreman and an author known for his profound ideas. My ignorance of the other authors he cites and his knowledge of history put me to shame, but one entry in his diary, for April 3, 1975, contains a couple of succinct references to an idea I have addressed more extensively in this very document. "Take efficiency," writes Hoffer. "Capitalist production is the most efficient the world has seen. It takes fewer workers to do a job in a capitalist society than anywhere else. But by using as few workers as possible, capitalist society is without the wide diffusion of a sense of usefulness essential for social stability." Later, he writes that "most capitalist societies are being swamped with educated people who disdain the triviality and hustle of the marketplace and pray for a new social order

---

*I eventually scrapped this second section without having completed it. When the project got complicated, I realized that this was one facet of PIK whose explanation ought to be relegated to the accountants.

that will enable them to live meaningful, weighty lives." From what I have so far read of the rest of the book, Hoffer's style inclines toward the aphoristic. But the certainty that seems to ring out of his pronouncements is tempered by his acknowledgment that his is an exploratory journey and by his apparent willingness to be uniformly dogmatic across the whole range of issues.

What prompts me to mention Hoffer here is another theme woven through his writing that happens to coincide with a personal observation of my own. Hoffer, who tramped around the West for many years, was an older man in his seventies before he wrote *Before the Sabbath*, and many of his comments seem conditioned by what he viewed as the excess of the sixties. In the same entry for April 3, for example, Hoffer states, "We were not prepared for the disintegration of values and the weakening of social discipline caused by the elimination of scarcity." And, in his entry for February 23, 1975, he announces, "The legacy of the 1960s: a revulsion from work; a horde of educated nobodies who want to be somebodies and end up being busybodies; a half-submerged counterculture of drugs and drift still able to swallow juveniles (of every age) who cannot adjust to a humdrum existence."

Hoffer's censure of laziness struck me, because a couple of weeks ago I was rereading through the last year or so of this journal, and the impression I have conveyed of my own character in this respect is not gratifying. But what I did afterwards was review, in my mind, my accomplishments for the year 1992. That year, although I was homeless, I worked the equivalent of every weekday of the year, about half-time, according to my W-2. (If you add some so far unrelated "experience" I acquired during the summer months, it would be even more.) In addition, I wrote the major part of a very complicated book about payment in kind. That I could do all this and still indulge in those extended, squalid binges that scar my memory of this period is almost unbelievable—but I guess it all happened. At any rate, let's say it did not happen—that I did not work and create as I did but just laid low and exerted only that minimal effort necessary for survival. Now, if I had done this, which is not extremely distant from the truth, then Hoffer would have us believe that I did it for some very abstract reasons. I did not do it, for example, because I was a lazy tramp, but because I had a great appreciation of the lack of a "wide diffusion of a sense of usefulness essential for social stability." I did not do it because I was a dissolute vagrant, but because I was an educated person who "disdain[s] the triviality and hustle of the marketplace." I did not do it because I was an indolent lush, but because I was a human manifestation of "the weakening of social discipline caused by the elimination of scarcity." And of course I did not do it because the Devil had been hounding me to distraction for the previous thirteen years, but because I was praying "for a new social order that will enable me to live a meaningful, weighty" life and because I could not "adjust to a humdrum existence." Some of this might be true, but it seems to me that the generalizing intrinsic to the didactic style necessarily blankets over parts of the truth.

SATURDAY JUNE 5, 1993   This last week I worked four days for a landscaper, picking and trenching the hard ground around a large house owned by a doctor. We planted a lot of shrubs and trees and wheelbarrowed a lot of rock. It's the kind of strenuous work that usually leaves me feeling purged of alcohol's harmful residues, but today my kidneys still ache from drinking a lot of vodka and beer over the duration of the job (at night, that is). It must be a bad sign when vigorous exercise does not rectify the damage wrought by liquor.

Now I have to keep working next week (I hope) to make a monthly payment of $67 on an old student loan, which up to now I had delayed a number of times with forbearances and deferments. The food stamp proposal is going slow. I had to stop typing for a month or so to rethink and rewrite a whole complex chapter. But once I finalize this part, I look forward to smooth sailing.

MONDAY JULY 19, 1993   I have just come back from the doctor, where some "burns" on my feet were reexamined and new bandages applied. Last Tuesday I was working at a coal-fired power plant about fifty miles south of Las Vegas when, shoveling hot sand and coal dust in a room called the combuster, I noticed some blisters on my feet. Because I had just acquired the tennis shoes I was wearing (used), I thought the blisters were the result of chafing. But from the start, the large, unopened ulcers contained a yellow-green substance that caused me to think they were infected.

So on Friday, after two more twelve-hour days in that hellhole of a plant, I went to the labor agency's doctor and was told that the "blisters" were really third-degree burns that had hardened into leathery "eschars," which were now in need of excision. The doctor was surprised to find that the burned tissue extended the whole depth of the skin, right down to the muscle and fat. He thought this especially "weird" (his word) in view of the fact that I did not actually feel the burns as they occurred. I felt like telling him that when you work in such a hot, miserable, dirty place as the power plant, someone could stick a pole up your ass and you might think it was just a recurring nuisance of the job. Still, it *does* seem strange that I could be so seriously "burned" without taking any sudden notice of the fact. The doctor was able to completely sew up two of the cavities that resulted from the eschars' removal, but the third was too large for complete closure. After I rejected the option of a skin graft from the thigh, the doctor proceeded to reduce the size of the largest cavity by the use of "skin transfers." This is a technique borrowed from plastic surgery in which the skin on the margin of the wound is sliced at an angle to the wound's perimeter, the resulting tongue of skin is shifted over slightly, where its tip is sutured to the peripheral skin at the farther location, and this most recent incision sewn back up. In this way, after four or five such transfers, the oval was shrunk to a size more likely to heal.

It was something to watch the doctor insert a tool under my skin, loosen it from its former moorings, and then use a scalpel to slice away a thick triangle of integument for shifting, all while my foot was perfectly numbed by the local anesthetic. If a person is ever inclined to believe that there is something in our human sensibility that is spiritual in character, if he thinks, as I sometimes do, that the sum total of our sensations, emotions, perceptions, and thoughts might constitute a "soul" of sorts, then watching his own minor surgery like this will certainly cause him to entertain a more materialistic creed. If a small dose of xylocaine can so extinguish sensation that a person can observe the mangling of his own skin with the same concern he might feel when watching someone peel an orange; if, when the anesthetic's role is enlarged accordingly, the whole of the body's sensible components might be so numbed; and if, in combination with this physical annihilation, consciousness can be obliterated as well by alcohol or some other drug, then where resides the soul? The person so nullified might appear wakeful and even functional, yet for all he feels he might as well be dead. No, the soul cannot have any connection to our senses, if it exists at all.

TUESDAY JULY 20, 1993   The problem now is money. Or maybe I should say the problem *aggravated* now is money. I have about $150 in food stamps and cash to last the "several weeks" the doctor tells me it will take for my "burn" to heal. A week and a half ago I sent off a letter begging the student loan service back in Minnesota to grant me yet another forbearance on my $67.15 monthly payment, which I made last month for the first time in a year and a half. It's possible on this particular descent into extreme penury that I will have to give up my mailbox— $30 every three months due on August 11. I will have to pay the $10 monthly charge for my storage closet, though—I don't want to haul my writing around on my back. It's possible also that in the long run I'll get a small check from the State Industrial Insurance System for my temporary disability. But I have as much faith in the state's alacrity in this matter as I have that the desert will suddenly be forested with oaks.

THURSDAY JULY 22, 1993   I have not written much in this
journal ostensibly devoted to alcoholism in the last six months. Mostly, I think my experience with the intoxicant has been too hideous and personal to relate. Specifically, each time I engaged my nemesis for an extended bout, which was maybe a third or half the time for a long while, I would end up with a soreness in my lower back that I could tell originated in the internal organs. In my ignorance, and because the right side's pain seemed to predominate, I thought that my liver had finally succumbed. I worried about this for a long time, especially over the Independence Day holiday when the pain seemed to linger despite my tapering back to a quart of beer a day. Then I picked up an anatomy book in the library and found out the liver is actually in the upper right part of the abdomen, close to the heart. I also happened to spot a sentence in one of the health-related books that stated that exercise might reduce fat in the liver and so

possibly preclude a disorder. I have gotten plenty of exercise over the last year and a half and feel very strong—sometimes shoveling gravel it seems as if I am tossing sugar pops from an enlarged spoon—so perhaps my liver is safe. But that means the pain I do feel must come from the right kidney or ureter and that something there has perhaps become infected. But if this is true, the antibiotic I am presently taking for my "burns" might very well take care of the problem—if I continue to moderate my intake of the poisonous instigator.

Yesterday I finished typing a chapter I wrote originally last summer but which I rewrote entirely over the last few months. About half of what I now have typed wasn't even in the original manuscript. Now, I hope, I can finally start typing in earnest and get away from the frustrations and euphoria, the tedium and the stormy anguish that always seem to accompany my attempts to produce the written word.

TUESDAY JULY 27, 1993   I have just returned from a "pre-trial conference" with the Deputy City Attorney of Henderson. One hot afternoon last May, I ducked behind a bush next to a grocery store in town here and committed an act of urination. I thought I was hidden, but the bush was apparently not so leafy near its base as near its top, and my private parts must have been more public than I had intended. A cop car happened to turn around the corner of the building at just the right time, and I was given a ticket for "lewd and dissolute conduct." The conscientious officer accosted three boys who happened to be walking by and who, much to my surprise, clearly witnessed my villainy. Their names, addresses, and testimony were all duly inscribed by the officer, and I was allowed to leave. Then, at the arraignment last June 29, I pleaded not guilty, mainly because the dictionary defines lewd as "showing or intended to excite lust or sexual desire, especially in a vulgar or offensive way." I really do believe that Henderson lacks a more accurately worded ordinance for urinating in public. Another time, more than a year ago, a Henderson cop car roared up to me behind a 7–11 store as I relieved myself. The cop lunged toward me as I finished my business, flipped impatiently through his violations book, and finally told me to go out in the desert next time and wasn't I lucky he couldn't find the correct law.

Today, I was able to plead "nolo contendere" (no contest),

and the charge will be dismissed if I complete twenty hours of public service work by October 27. I could have continued my not guilty plea and requested a jury trial, but I thought the twenty hours of public service work was an acceptable hedge against the possibility that a Henderson jury might think that pissing in front of a few mischievous eleven-year-old boys was meant to excite me or them into a frenzy of sexual desire.

SUNDAY DECEMBER 5, 1993   I have been working at the gold mine for the past few weeks and I have managed to save $300 (they have raised the hourly wage to $7.50). Yesterday I went to the doctor and was diagnosed as having a kidney infection. They provided me with some free antibiotic pills that they had received as samples. In combination with ten days of abstinence, the medicine ought to effect a cure. Actually, I knew three or four months ago that I was suffering from some kind of internal inflammation or infection which, if not directly caused by alcohol, was certainly aggravated by it. If I drank too much, a specific area toward my right lower back would twinge with intermittent pain. When I worked a job that required lifting or bending, pain would spread through my whole lower back. I let it go for so long because I didn't have the money to pay a doctor, and I didn't want to endure the humiliation of applying for assistance through the Clark County welfare office. But the condition has had the salutary effect of making me cut back on my drinking and even go for days at a time without touching a drop. In principle, my newfound temperance is not such a radical departure from my former immersion in true alcoholism. I can still blame it on a disease.

WEDNESDAY DECEMBER 22, 1993   Well, the twinging pain I felt in my right back turned out not to be a kidney infection after all. Another doctor I went to see said he did not know what the problem was. But my continued state of ignorance with respect to the exact nature of my ailment is not especially troublesome. I have now attained the same level of knowledge as the two physicians who charged me $50 apiece for their hard-learned opinions.

I am presently enjoying the fifth evening of a seven-day, work-free stay in a motel room in Boulder City (a town built originally to serve the laborers building Hoover Dam in the

1930s but now more of a bedroom community serving metropolitan Las Vegas). On the day we were laid off from the mine (last Friday), by coincidence I caught a bad cold/flu bug of some sort that just knocked the hell out of me and persuaded me to rent this room and lay low for a while. Up until today I spent most of the time in bed. But this afternoon I started rewriting what will probably be the last chapter of the food stamp proposal that will have to be rewritten. Actually, I was "rewriting" it more than two or three months ago by thinking and using a small calculator to fill up a legal tablet with problems and exercises. At this point, I am so sick of the whole subject that bringing myself to do a simple high-school-level problem requires about three days of meditation, severe physical trials, two months of hard labor, a few hundred dollars gambled away on slot machines or expert medical advice, and a bottle or two thrown in for good measure. Now I can hardly say that I feel much better, and on Christmas Day it will be back into the freezing nights for me, with only a bedroll for comfort. I saw on TV tonight that Santa Claus was removed from some giant mall in Denver because of death threats against him. "What a blessing," I thought to myself, "if that were to happen to every Santa in the nation. All parents would immediately rejoice at the prospect of less demanding toy lists. People like me would be relieved at the lesser intensity of an extraneous celebration. And all the Santas of America would be provided with a greatly deserved holiday vacation."

THURSDAY JANUARY 6, 1994   An article in the latest edition of *Audubon* magazine tells of the egregious environmental sins now being committed by the gold-mining industry in northern Nevada. These include disfiguring otherwise pristine landscapes with huge open pits, roads, and piles of scrap rock and tailings; murdering swarms of waterfowl by the negligent omission of protective covers over surfaces of cyanide-impregnated waters; destroying aquifers and streams by cyanide and acid wastes that are allowed to drain through significant parts of the region; and using enough electricity to power a good portion of New York City.

I have never been to the gold mines in northern Nevada, so I must accept these infractions as fact. I do have two objections to the article, however. First, the writer reflexively proposes federal regulation to solve the problem. Possibly this reaction is one that liberals now deem a prerequisite to an "environmental" stance on an issue. But the writer backs up his argument with evidence that the needed environmental control will never be carried out by the state of Nevada because of the wonderful economic growth that gold mining brings to a region. He did not mention that right across the state line, in the "golden state" of California, state regulation is much more severe and correspondingly more successful in protecting the environment.

At the Castle Mountain Mine where I worked, all aggregations of cyanide-laced water are either enclosed in tanks or pipes or shielded with netting against the incursion of thirsty birds. Laborers spend a lot of time repairing or replacing any damaged netting. All around the mine, one hears the sporadic explosions of propane guns that simulate gunfire to further discourage the encroachment of birds or other wildlife. During my last one-month foray at the mine, the company was busy placing open water tanks around the far perimeter of the claim to divert even more birds to safety. It is true that the leach pad itself, perpetually moist with cyanide water, is left unprotected and that birds die there. But will an imaginative solution to this facet of the problem be likely to originate in Washington any more than in Sacramento?

As for the other problems mentioned by the *Audubon* author, they are being addressed in a similarly stringent way at the Castle Mountain Mine. The thick plastic lining underneath the leach pad traps any harmful residues and routes them to the processing plant for treatment. Any leaks detected are uncovered at great expense and sealed up with as much speed as the situation allows. I was present at the mine once, about nine or ten months ago, when a massive pit in the leach pad was being excavated for this very purpose. And why shouldn't the mining company be preoccupied with sealing such a leak, even in the absence of regulation, when the surrounding area will be saturated not only with poisons but with a high concentration of expensive gold as well? The Castle Mountain Mine is also required to restore much of the area with native flora after completion of the mining, and a large greenhouse is operated there by a professional botanist for just this purpose. According to a recent annual report, all of these measures combined have earned the Castle Mountain Mine the reputation of being a "showcase" of environmentally conscious gold mining. So on the environmental issue my argument is not that there should be no protection but that federally mandated protection is not necessarily the best answer. Does the author of the *Audubon* article believe that the state of California, teeming now with 30 million people and able at times to pay its state employees only with chits and IOUs, is so rich that it can better afford to reject the economic uplift of large-scale gold mining than the state of Nevada? Why didn't this author take the time to study some of the environmental safeguards instituted by the local government right next door, rather than sail so assuredly into the haven of federal control?

My second objection to the *Audubon* article might furnish the motive I have requested. In the last paragraph, the author states, "Other minerals, such as iron, copper, and lead—which are also covered by the 1872 law—are necessary for the manufacture of machine parts, electronics, and plumbing fixtures, and are thus vital to preserving the vigor of American industry. Yet it's difficult to see how the gold boom now pocking the West relates to national security or even to need. Uses of gold such as the manufacture of electronics could easily be satisfied with stocks hoarded in vaults and central banks. And virtually all the gold now mined in the world is used for jewelry."

These last words indicate to me that this article is yet another instance of an environmental argument disguising a more profound economic contention. Like the unemployed lumbermen in the Northwest, who to this day blame the increased productivity in the logging industry on the spotted owl, the author here seems to be using the environmental question as a vehicle to approach a more fundamental and frightening economic reality, namely, that capitalism by its nature exploits resources for frivolous products. It is hard to confront this question directly because one of the obvious solutions would entail a severe abridgment of freedom. So people come at it in a roundabout way, asserting that centralized control is necessary to preserve the environment rather than to better the human economic condition. To state baldly that the authority of the federal government ought to be invoked to steer productive activities away from the manufacture of jewelry is simply not acceptable. I happen to agree that the federal government's resources are more appropriately directed toward other concerns. However, open discussion of the problem might foster more imaginative solutions than pretending that the environment is the only issue.

SUNDAY JANUARY 16, 1994   Earlier in this journal I described the vast stretch of empty desert that lay between Henderson and the mountains girdling the Lake Mead Recreation Area. This was to be the site of my glorious departure from this life by way of self-imposed starvation. I refer to this land in the past tense because it is now crossed by paved roads and filling rapidly with housing developments, bingo parlors, and retailers. The sandy wash where I used to build fires from dried creosote branches to cook chicken and pork chops is now underneath the wooden floor of a recently framed two-story house. I suppose if I had persevered in my fast, and if its duration had been on the outer extremities of the range for that ordeal—eight or nine months—I would have spent my last days emaciating across the street from a newly opened supermarket or fast-food restaurant.

It could be that after two years my employment for Labor Finders of Henderson, Nevada, has finally come to an end. On the thirteenth of January, I walked to that office and picked up a check for $55 that was my daily, after-tax pay for the work I did at the gold mine on the thirteenth of *December*. They had lost my check, or it was stolen, and they had to "wait for a bank statement" before they could pay me. This rankled me no end. Did they think I was actually holding the original check and was planning to cash it after I had wrangled a replacement from them? I don't know of any other person working through that office who has my seniority. Yet they would not trust their longest working employee enough to simply stop payment on the original check and issue him a new one.

In the latter part of December, I sent a letter to the president of the company demanding payment and warning him that if it was not forthcoming I would file a claim against his company in the Henderson small claims court. I had let slip to the company's accountant, on one occasion when attempting to obtain my check, that I might send such a letter. Apparently that gentleman is the one who receives the president's mail, because the certified letter was refused upon delivery. Maybe the accountant did not know that such a refusal is tantamount under the law to a signed acceptance. In any event, I was now free to file suit. I bided my time, however, because I did not have the $50 necessary to file the suit (which would have been reimbursed to me upon winning) and because I had filed a claim for unemployment compensation. This claim might have been justified and found valid, in case of an appeal, on the basis of this absent compensation for eight hours of work. As I have related, I was finally paid the $55 one month after I earned it, which obviated the lawsuit and precluded the appeal to the unemployment office. Nonetheless, I am still waiting on an initial decision on the unemployment claim, which would pay me the magnificent sum of $49 per week. I am getting food stamps again now, for the first time in six or eight months, which helps.

All of these matters, so inconsequential or routine in the larger world of business and day-to-day enterprise, are magnified to crisis proportions when you are living outside and have no cash income. About three months ago, my bag of clothes and toiletries was stolen from a hiding place in an evergreen bush close to the casino I was patronizing at the time. At that time I could go back to work and replace those belongings; now, without money or employment, such a loss would escalate to calamitous dimensions. Does the reader believe that the historic hurricane in Florida in 1992 involved disruption and deprivation? I ask you, were those Florida victims required to go without toothpaste and razors for weeks after the tragedy? Were they forced to walk around without underwear and socks for a month after the blow? The wind may confiscate your roof or topple the walls from around your bedstead. But until the atmosphere gets roiled and violent enough to scatter every piece of extra clothing, every razor and fragment of soap, every sock and comb you have to the four corners of the earth, leaving you with only the clothes on your back and a headful of frazzled hair, I will not pity you in the least.

FRIDAY JANUARY 28, 1994   I have not had a drink for five days. I have had many such intervals over the last four or five months, prompted by the crazy symptoms that otherwise proceed from a binge. Not only does my kidney ache, but my eyeballs seem to sink into their sockets, my head seems to swim around unanchored to physical reality, my ears buzz, my pulse races, and my heart hurts. This morning I went through my regular routine. I got up before sunrise and made up my bedroll in the cold desert air. I loathe making up my bedroll in the cold desert air. If I could have excised that one task from my life over the last two years, my happiness would have ascended to unequaled heights, because on that one task I have concentrated all of the resentment, rancor, and scorn that can be extracted from a miserable existence.

After the ordeal, I walked down the highway a mile or so to one of my regular haunts, a Carl's Jr. restaurant where I have taken my morning coffee for perhaps half of the days over the last two years. I hunkered down in my usual booth, placing my bedroll and bags under the table, and commenced writing down a few pages' worth of highly sophisticated mathematical techniques for determining payrolls under a system of PIK. I left after an hour or two and walked to a lone building in the midst of a large parking lot nearby. I sat myself against a wall facing the sun, in the lee of the chilly breeze, and ate sausage and tortilla chips for breakfast. And I thought about death. Not about volunteering for it this time, but about how fragile or contingent life is and how the arrival of death is prevented by a very intricate web of chemical reactions, physiological functions, and environmental inputs, any one of which could go haywire at any moment. It seemed to me that my life just then was hanging by a very thin biological thread, and I became scared.

But what is there to fear? I asked myself. If I die, I answered, I will not be able to finish my complicated book about PIK. All of the work I have done will go down the drain, and I will never feel the huge sense of accomplishment that will undoubtedly accrue to me upon completing the book. Yes, I rejoined, that is the essential fear—that some future happening will be prevented by my death. Therefore, I concluded, I can only dissipate this fear by focusing more on the present moment. Eureka! I exclaimed. Therein lies the answer! I must now steer my mind away from concentrating so fully on the future and live more in the present day.

I felt an immediate sense of relief and started at once to look around me, observe the present reality, feel the present sensations, and think about the present condition. It was then that a deep pang of sorrow touched my heart, for I realized, looking at my bedroll and bag, the expanse of empty, sun-faded blacktop, and the sun glistening coldly in the stark blue sky, that in the present there was nothing to live for. At least, I thought, if I looked to the future, there would be something worth living for in the present. Tentatively, I shifted my outlook partially back to what yet lay ahead. Not too far ahead, however, because I had to keep in mind the likely possibility of dying in the present. I then thought about how I really did enjoy the writing and the thinking, activities pleasurable in the present partly because of their hoped-for ramifications in the future. I adjusted back to the present a degree or two, listing toward port, and attained a kind of satisfactory commingling of present-day enjoyments with future anticipations, all blended in with the governing realization that it could all end with a heart attack or a stroke at any moment. With that compromise under my belt, I packed up my sausage and chips, shouldered my bedroll and bags, and headed over to the library for more excursions into uncharted excogitative terrain.

Friday February 18, 1994   I do not feel too badly about my situation at this moment. During the last year, I made over $5,000 through the daily labor hall. Most of the work was for $4.25 per hour, and a lot of that was pick-and-shovel jobs on hard caliche ground sites. "Caliche," according to *Webster's New World Dictionary*, is "crusted calcium carbonate formed on certain soils in dry regions by evaporation of rising solutions." To the construction worker or landscaper, caliche is alternatively defined as "a thick, malignant layer of earth, hard as concrete, always situated precisely where one is about to dig." A hot summer day spent with a pick over a caliche site will make you forget a lot of your troubles. I recommend it as therapy for anyone who is anxious about the performance of his carburetor, who fears sliding to a C+ in math, or who has nightmares about depletion of the ozone layer. After a day with caliche you will not object if the whole earth suddenly vaporizes into ozone, nor will you regret the extinction of your own life in the process. Anyway, I can feel good about contributing something to the local economy for the last two years, actually, even though it is growing too fast and is fueled by an inordinate influx of fools and ignoramuses.

I also feel good about the progress I am currently making in rewriting a chapter called "The Communal Office." This particular rewrite has been a long time a-brewing. I started rewriting it last fall sometime, believing that only minor alterations were necessary. When I discovered that some fundamental changes were in order, that *a lot* of rewriting was in store, I stopped, stunned into immobility so to speak, and took a month or two just to get used to the idea. This kind of paralysis has struck me twice on this book, the first time when my mother declined to help me with money to type the first draft, and the second with the present chapter. I don't know why this happens. Maybe I am just the kind of person who has to be thoroughly prepared for an activity before I start. I think college might inculcate some of this attitude. I know it is not so prevalent among blue-collar workers.

Sometimes in my life, when looking for blue-collar work, I have been offered jobs on the spot—"Go home, change your clothes, and come back ready to roll." I have declined most of these jobs, immediately after applying, just because they have transpired so abruptly. "Well, you see," I explain to the boss, "I just can't do it so soon." "Why not?" he says. "You're not doing anything this afternoon, are you?" "Well, no," I say, "but I just . . . I just have to be more psychologically prepared for the job." The boss looks at me, then looks over at the job site, where a worker is doing the same thing I would be doing if I accepted the job—loading bags of flour onto a truck or screwing wire onto one metal plate after another. "You have to get psychologically prepared for *that?*" says the boss. "Yes," I say. "I'm sorry, I just can't work for you on such short notice." I then turn around and walk away from the boss, who stands there with my application in his hand. Anyway, I am now progressing nicely on "The Communal Office" chapter, which makes me feel good.

I also feel good now because I have been collecting a $49 unemployment check for each of the last few weeks, and it looks as if they might continue coming for the next four or five months. Eighty-eight dollars a month in food stamps allows me to slip by *relatively* comfortably. I still have to bathe and shave occasionally with a gallon of cold water in the frigid winter air, but a vehement round of weather-bashing is usually enough to dissipate the unpleasantness. In this regard, I am thinking about starting a new religion with pagan gods like those invented by the ancients. Except this would be a modernized version with the three gods being (1) Space, (2) Time, and (3) Matter. My motivation is purely selfish: I just think I would feel a lot safer if I could always direct my cursing at observable phenomena, rather than take the chance that I might address the more ethereal deity promulgated by conventional religions.

SUNDAY FEBRUARY 20, 1994 Of course, I would have to include myself among the fools and ignoramuses mentioned in the last entry, because I am part of the influx that is now causing Las Vegas to grow faster than any other city in America. I describe the newcomers so negatively because it seems that all of the lessons this country has absorbed in the last few decades are forgotten the instant an opportunity arises to put them into practice. This city is expanding the same way Los Angeles or Phoenix must have done in former years. The same sprawl, congestion, pollution, and crime that would have emerged if this city had been built forty years ago have emerged today. One senses that if a new continent were suddenly made available to the people of the earth, the same extermination of wildlife, the same careless exploitation of resources, and the same degradation of the environment that characterized the settlement of North America would occur all over again.

The issue is not one on which I can easily take a position because . . . well, because living in a boomtown is not a wholly melancholy experience, even for a person who doesn't belong there in the first place. It's good to know that if I really wanted one, I could go out and get a job tomorrow, or this afternoon. It's exciting to live in a place where people are bustling and achieving, where projects are underway, where money is flowing, where people are talking and planning—all in an atmosphere of dynamic optimism. And if it weren't for the spark of incentive supplied by capitalism, this city never would have expanded as it has or maybe even started. I can just imagine a contingent of sedate government planners descending on the Las Vegas Valley to map out and establish a city. Maybe by now they would have something similar to Boulder City, which is an attractive, clean, well-ordered little place. But it is only that—a small town of a few thousand people—and their restaurants charge over three dollars for an order of pancakes and eggs.

I suppose I am of two minds with regard to Las Vegas's growth. From the elevated parts of Henderson, one can peer down at the Las Vegas Valley and on many days see only a pall of caramel-colored smoke hanging over the city. At the same time, boomtowns like this provide people with an outlet for their ambitions and a place to exercise a kind of maverick mentality. I don't know the answer to the basic dilemma, but I haven't moved yet.

MONDAY AUGUST 29, 1994 I have not been diligent in writing the journal, so I will summarize the last six months. When I started collecting unemployment compensation last January, I thought I was through writing *A Proposal for Food Stamp Reform* and needed only to type up some remaining pages. In accordance with the book's history, my belief was mistaken. The "nonlocal" payroll determinations in "The Communal Office" chapter of the book required much, much more thought and elucidation, and I eventually added more than a hundred typewritten pages to the text. This addition, in combination with the expansion of some other chapters, will bring the *typewritten* manuscript to about 475 pages, a multifold increase over the handwritten manuscript I had "completed" just about two years ago. At present I have only to type up about thirty pages and make some minor corrections and the project will be done.

My financial condition has recently improved. I stopped filing unemployment claims last May, a few weeks earlier than if I were to have exhausted all of the benefits, because they called me into a meeting for which I was not prepared. The next couple of months were arduous. I had to go back to work for another daily labor place here in Henderson, a line of activity I thought I had forever left, since I believed last January that I would sell the food stamp proposal before running out of unemployment compensation. Eventually I went to work directly for a landscaper for whom I had worked intermittently over the last two years. I made $6.25 per hour during a month of torrid toil before I quit to spend more time on the book.

At the time I took the job, working on the book was not an option. On July 2, I was in a car that was pulled over for DUI (Driving Under the Influence). The driver and I were both put in jail, but I was released after eight hours of "protective custody" (that is, no charge). That's when my trouble started. In order to obtain my belongings, including the handwritten version of the nonlocal payroll determinations, out of the arrested driver's impounded car, I had to get a notarized statement from him permitting me to enter his car. I looked all over this city, calling up every jail and prison, going through the court files in the Clerk of District Court's office, and questioning anyone who might know where the driver of the car had been transferred to, but I could not locate him. Finally, after a couple of weeks of frantic frustration (without much in the way of clothing or bedding), I was informed that the car had been released to the driver's girlfriend. A few more telephone calls got me her name and address, and I was able to contact her and retrieve my writing at last.

If I had lost those complicated nonlocal problems before having had time to reread and fully absorb the concepts, I think I would have committed suicide. At any rate, I said my finances have improved: I deposited a $1,700 check in a local bank last Thursday and am now just waiting for the check to clear. The money came from a concerned relative, and the way the transaction was explained to me I am not sure if it is actually a gift, a loan, or my rightful portion of someone's estate. Whatever its status, the money is the most welcome income I have ever received. I have been homeless now for three years, and if I have to work one more sweaty day out of a minimum wage labor hall, go "home" one more night to a bedroll in the desert, or take another "shower" in a concrete drainage ditch, I believe I will self-destruct. A change is in order.

SATURDAY NOVEMBER 5, 1994   Some change has occurred, but it is not in the general pattern that has governed my financial situation for so long. After a little over two months, the $1,700 I received from my family is depleted. I used some of it to stay in motel rooms. I worked for a couple of weeks, too, helping to set up the fixtures in a new T.J. Maxx store. I finished typing *A Proposal for Food Stamp Reform* and sent samples to five publishers. Three rejected the book, but with encouragement, while the fourth asked for a copy of the manuscript, which I sent a week and a half ago and which now ought to be the object of their evaluation. A few days ago I completed an eight-page article entitled "A PIKfare Proposal" that explains how a state agency could set up a workfare program using a simple version of the payment in kind mechanism. I'd like to incorporate the article into the book, so I'll wait before trying to sell it to the magazines. Meanwhile, I guess it's back to the daily labor hall for me on Monday morning.

FRIDAY DECEMBER 2, 1994 November was abnormally cold, and the nights have been painful. About ten days ago, I was lucky enough to find a large cardboard box not far from a vacant desert lot here in Henderson, and I have been sleeping in that most nights since. In the morning I flatten it out, and at night I raise it back up by rearranging the flaps. So far none of the neighborhood kids who cross the lot on foot have wrecked the box, which, like the weather, is abnormal. Another night, in a newer and wealthier part of Henderson called Green Valley, I chanced upon an unoccupied freezer locker, newly installed into a partly constructed restaurant, and I was able to sleep and drink comfortably there for the night (sleep and drink are not transposed here, since I executed the latter on waking in the morning).

This week I worked three days through the daily labor agency. It would have been four, but I declined the repeat ticket because this guy I worked with was extremely irritating. Although he was just a fellow daily laborer, he spent most of the day walking around the job site—a nearly completed factory— giving orders to the other daily laborers. Occasionally he would go out to the car for a beer, and on the afternoon of my last day I found him sprawled out in the back seat taking a two-hour nap. Finally, near the end of that day, when he had returned to bark out more orders at the other workers and myself, I looked at him and told him to go to hell. He looked somewhat disconcerted and said, "Oh come on, Tim, you just misunderstood me." I said, "I didn't misunderstand anything. You've been walking around here giving orders all day long and you're not a boss, you're just a fellow laborer. If you want somebody to find a shovel or clean up this hallway, just do it your fuckin' self." He started to protest, but I cut him short. "Listen," I said, "I don't want to hear anything more about it," and I walked away. During the ride home, we were subdued and after a while we even spoke some conciliatory words. But I knew that guy would go right back to his old ways the next day, so I told the office supervisor to take me off the ticket. Instead, today, I am in Green Valley again, where my mailbox is, but I still have not heard any word from the publishers.

SUNDAY DECEMBER 11, 1994 It is early morning in Green Valley, where I am drinking coffee in a recently built Chevron gas station/mini mart. Outside, the spacious lot and new pumps are brightly illuminated against the surrounding darkness. Just a block away, I awoke an hour ago on a ledge that borders a very deep and very steep wash that meanders through the fine neighborhoods of Green Valley. Water always flows through this wash, though sluggishly at times, and in those stretches that have not been converted to concrete canals, I have seen ducks and minnows, and, in the air, kingfishers, hawks, and other predators on the wing. There are many streams like this one in the Las Vegas Valley, or at least there are many miles of the few that do flow through here on their way down to the Colorado River (that is, Lake Mead). Many segments of those streams still in their natural state are choked by a protective bower of sprawling trees, shrubs, and weeds, and during the summer, if you can penetrate this prickly veil, the air becomes as cool as the blast from a just-opened refrigerator. It seems too bad that all of the valley's streams were not as well preserved as the few remaining stretches. But flood control and the desire to develop to the maximum required that the washes be contained. And I suppose a network of wild concourses would invite coyotes down from the mountains and promote the propagation of snakes, spiders, and other hostile vermin.

In all the times I have lived and slept in the deserts of the Southwest, I have encountered two scorpions, two tarantulas, and two harmless snakes. One night, a number of years ago, down by Phoenix, a coyote started howling a few yards from my tent, which was a galvanizing awakening to be sure, but my terrified roar, abrupt emergence from the tent, and a few wildly hurled rocks drove him off pronto. The worst experience was with a scorpion right here in the peaceful confines of Green Valley. Half a mile from where I sit, there is an open flat area of one or two square miles that used to be farmland. The sandy, rock-free soil is still soft, but many patches are now overgrown with towering copses of tumbleweed-like plants and smaller shrubs. It is in the interstices of these overgrown tumbleweeds that I hide sometimes and take a shower with a gallon of hot water stolen from a nearby Carl's Jr. restaurant. One time, I was standing naked and barefoot on a small piece of plastic, dousing myself and watching as the water drained off the plastic and coursed directly into a small hole a few inches from my toes. It seemed like a curiously capacious hole, and I was amused that some impudent prairie dog's domicile was now being so effectively flooded out. Then a three-inch-long scorpion crawled out of the hole and positioned himself about six inches from my right foot. Never in my life have I focused so unwaveringly on an object while performing an unrelated task with my hands and body. Watching the scorpion for the tiniest movement of its legs or pincers, I carefully toweled myself off, put on socks and shoes, and backed away with my belongings in tow to a safer piece of ground. I continued to eye my disturbed little friend as I finished dressing and then vowed, as I departed, to never again take a shower on anything but solid ground.